Studies in Education and Culture
David M. Fetterman, General Editor

1. Re-visioning Educational Leadership: A
   Phenomenological Approach
   by John G. Mitchell

2. Schooling, Jobs, and Cultural Identity:
   Educational Reform in Quebec
   by Linda Kahn

3. Cross-cultural Literacy: Ethnographies in
   Multiethnic Classrooms
   by Marietta Saravia-Shore and Steven F.
   Arvizu

4. Puerto Rican Children on the Mainland:
   Interdisciplinary Perspectives
   by Alba N. Amber, and María D. Alvarez

PUERTO RICAN CHILDREN ON THE MAINLAND
Interdisciplinary Perspectives

Alba N. Ambert
María D. Alvarez

GARLAND PUBLISHING, INC. • NEW YORK & LONDON
1992

Library of Congress Cataloging-in-Publication Data

Puerto R· an children on the mainland : interdisciplinary perspectives
Alba N. Ambert, María D. Alvarez
    p. cm. — (Garland reference library of social science ; vol..
636. Studies in education and culture ; vol. 4)
    ISBN 0–8240–4499–1 (alk. paper)
    1. Puerto Ricans—Education (Elementary)—United States.
2. Puerto Ricans—Education (Elementary)—Canada. 3. Puerto Ricans—
United States—Social conditions. 4. Puerto Ricans—United States—
Cultural assimilation. I. Ambert, Alba N., 1946–
II. Alvarez, María D. III. Series: Garland reference library of
social science ; v. 636. IV. Series: Garland reference library of
social science. Studies in education and culture ; vol. 4.
LC2693.3.P84 1992
305.23'089687295073—dc20   91–14209
                                      CIP

Printed on acid-free, 250-year-life paper
Manufactured in the United States of America

To Puerto Rican children, whose exemplary courage, resilience, and good nature have helped us become better human beings.

SERIES EDITOR'S FOREWORD

This series of scholarly texts, monographs, and reference works is designed to illuminate and expand our understanding of education. The educational activity each volume examines may be formal or informal. It may function in an exotic and distant culture or right here in our own backyard. In each book, education is at once a reflection and a creator of culture.

One of the most important motifs sounding through the series is the authors' efforts to shed light on educational systems from the insider's viewpoint. The various works are typically grounded in a phenomenological conceptual framework. However, they will vary in their manifestation of this common bond. Some authors explicitly adopt anthropological methods and a cultural interpretation of events and circumstances observed in the field. Others adopt a more generic qualitative approach—mixing methods and methodologies. A few adhere to a traditional phenomenological philosophical orientation.

These books are windows into other lives and other cultures. As we view another culture, we see ourselves more clearly. As we view ourselves, we make the familiar strange and see our own distorted images all the more clearly. We hope this immersion and self-reflection will enhance compassion and understanding at home and abroad. An expression of a common human spirit, this series celebrates our diversity.

David M. Fetterman
Stanford University and Sierra Nevada College

CONTENTS

THE EDITORS

María D. Alvarez is currently an Adjunct Associate Professor at the Center for Latin American Studies, University of Florida, Gainesville, Florida. She received her Ph.D. in School Psychology from New York University in 1983 and was awarded First Place in the 1984 Outstanding Dissertation in Bilingual Education Competition. Dr. Alvarez has been a practicing school psychologist, teacher trainer, and consultant for school districts in Massachusetts, Connecticut, Florida, and New York. She has also been a Senior Research Associate at Teacher's College Columbia University's Institute for Urban and Minority Education, a psychologist and program evaluator for the Puerto Rican Family Institute in New York City, and a visiting faculty member of the Graduate Program in Bilingual Special Education at Regis College, Weston, Massachusetts.

Fluent in four languages, Dr. Alvarez specializes in the non-biased assessment of language minority groups, in the design of educational planning for bilingual children with special learning needs, and in bilingual schooling. To this effect she has done extensive work with Hispanic and Haitian migrant children. Her doctoral research, conducted in Spanish Harlem, was a study of the personal, domestic, and school variables that promote or hinder academic achievement among Puerto Rican students. Using anthropological methods, she has conducted ethnographic research in different cultures, especially in Haiti, where she has studied child socialization, health-seeking behaviors among rural families, and child feeding beliefs and practices.

Alba N. Ambert is Senior Research Scholar at Athens College, Athens, Greece, where she conducts psycholinguistic and educational research and offers inservice teacher training. Previously, she was Visiting

Scientist at the Department of Linguistics and Philosophy, Massachusetts Institute of Technology. As a National Research Council Postdoctoral Fellow, Dr. Ambert performed research on the language development and language disorders of Puerto Rican children living in the United States. She was Assistant Professor and Director of the Bilingual Special Education Teacher Training Program at the University of Hartford, in Connecticut. Dr. Ambert has written numerous articles and several books on bilingualism, bilingual special education, and the language disorders in Spanish-speaking children, including the co-authored book *Bilingual Education: A Sourcebook*. The *Ambert Reading Test (ART)*, developed by Dr. Ambert to diagnose reading problems in Spanish-speaking children, grades K–6, is currently used by school districts in the Northeast. She has presented her research findings at national and international conferences. She received her B.A. from Universidad de Puerto Rico and her M.Ed. and Ed.D. degrees from Harvard University. Dr. Ambert has recently been awarded the Literature Award of the Institute of Puerto Rican Literature for her novel *Porque Hay Silencio*. She has published two volumes of poetry. Her poetry and short stories have been published in literary journals in the United States and Puerto Rico.

CONTRIBUTING AUTHORS

Sandra Estepa received her B.A. in Social Work from the Universidad Católica de Puerto Rico and her M.S. in Social Work from Columbia University. She has over ten years experience in health and mental health care planning and administration, with particular emphasis on services for Latino communities. Ms. Estepa is co-founder and Executive Director of the Latino Commission on AIDS, a coalition of prominent leaders and advocates striving to organize Latino communities and mobilize policymakers to combat the spread of AIDS. Prior to this, she was Program Officer for Health at the New York Community Trust, a private foundation in New York City.

Clare Figler holds a B.A. from Texas Women's University, an M.A. from Boston College, and an Ed.D. in School Psychology from the University of Massachusetts at Amherst. She is also a Certified Family Therapist, trained at the Boston Family Institute, in Brookline, Massachusetts. A licensed psychologist and Nationally Certified School Psychologist, Dr. Figler has been a teacher of special needs children and worked as a Bilingual School Psychologist in the Boston Public Schools for fifteen years, where she specialized on issues related to Puerto Rican families in transition to the mainland. Currently, she is Assistant Director at the School Psychological Services Unit of the Boston School Department, and an Adjunct Professor at the Lesley College Graduate School in Cambridge, Massachusetts. Dr. Figler is also engaged in private practice.

Peter J. Guarnaccia received his Ph.D. in Medical Anthropology from the University of Connecticut in 1984. He worked closely with the Hispanic Health Council, a research, action, and training institute focused on the health of the Puerto Rican community in Hartford, Connecticut. After receiving his Ph.D., Dr. Guarnaccia did a postdoctoral fellowship in Clinically Applied Medical Anthropology at Harvard Medical School. He became actively involved in a broad critique of cross-cultural psychiatric studies with an emphasis on the mental health of Puerto Ricans. Dr. Guarnaccia currently is an Assistant Professor in the Department of Human Ecology at Cook College, Rutgers University, and is a core faculty member of the Institute for Health, Health Care Policy and Aging Research. He received the First Award from the National Institute of Mental Health for a research project which will combine anthropological and epidemiological methods to study *ataques de nervios* in Puerto Rico.

Kathryn Hill has been affiliated with the bilingual program of the New Haven, Connecticut, Public Schools since 1972. She has been an English as a Second Language teacher, a resource specialist, a project coordinator, and is currently curriculum/staff developer. She received a B.A. in psychology from Yale University, an M.S. in elementary education from Southern Connecticut State University, and a Ph.D. in bilingual education, with a Title VII Fellowship, from the University of Connecticut. She is fluent in Spanish and Portuguese and has collected folkloric material in these languages and in English. In 1979 she made a Folkways Records album called *Who Goes First? ¿Quién va primero? Children's Counting-out Rhymes* in Spanish and English.

Carmen I. Mercado is Assistant Professor of Education in the Department of Curriculum and Teaching at Hunter College of the City University of New York. She received her Ph.D. in language and literacy from Fordham University. Formerly, Dr. Mercado served as Program Coordinator of the New York Multifunctional Resource Center (MRC) based at Hunter College. She was also an elementary school teacher for eight years in the second Spanish/English bilingual school in New York City. Her major research interest is in conducting ethnographic research with teachers and students in elementary and intermediate grades.

Susan Meswick, an applied anthropologist, is an Assistant Professor in the Department of Sociology, Anthropology, and Social Work at St. John's University in Jamaica, New York. She completed her doctorate in

Anthropology from the University of Connecticut in 1986. In 1987 she received a Masters in Public Health with a specific focus on health needs of children in school settings. Dr. Meswick has conducted research on the migration, health, education, and needs of the urban poor. Her dissertation research focused on the problems which migrant Puerto Ricans face on the mainland. She served as a consultant for numerous agencies, including the Hispanic Health Council in Hartford, Connecticut, Westchester Institute for Human Services, New York State Mental Health Association, and United Nations Nongovernmental Organizations.

Andrés Rodríguez, Jr., is Director of the Office of Fiscal and Programmatic Reviews, Division of Bilingual Education, New York City Public Schools. Formerly, he directed two demonstration projects in School District 3—New York City, and was a Bilingual Reading Clinician for several years. He has taught reading and English as a Second Language to youth and adults since 1972. He received an M.S. from City College of New York and a Ph.D. in Reading and Administration from Fordham University. Currently, he is a candidate for the Ed.D. degree in Educational Administration and Supervision at Fordham University.

María Rosa Tapia is an educational psychologist. She has an M.S. in Counseling Psychology from Long Island University and an M.A. and a Ph.D. in School Psychology from New York University. Dr. Tapia has conducted research and done clinical work with Puerto Rican children in the United States, including Puerto Rican children in special education programs. Related experience includes school consultation, school inservice training for teachers in cross-cultural psychology, and parents workshops. Dr. Tapia is currently Manager of Child and Adolescent Outpatient/ Inpatient Services, Department of Psychiatry, University of Florida Hospital in Jacksonville, Florida.

ACRONYMS

CVF	Children's verbal folklore
DPP	Dropout Prevention Program
ESL	English as a Second Language
L1	Native or first language; mother tongue
L2	Second language
LEP	Limited English proficiency
LM	Language minority
SES	Socioeconomic status
SPED	Special Education
B/SPED	Bilingual Special Education

PREFACE

Few groups have been as stigmatized and as misunderstood as Puerto Ricans on the U.S. mainland. While social, racial, linguistic, economic, and immigration issues have played a part in creating and perpetuating this state of affairs, the situation has undoubtedly been compounded by misinformation stemming from misguided research efforts.

The research studies gathered in this volume serve to debunk some of the myths that have circulated for many years concerning Puerto Rican children. These myths are built on a "deficit" model of the Puerto Rican child's development and focus largely on the "language deficiencies," "academic retardation," or "cultural deprivation" experienced by the children. The studies reported in this book, however, offer a balanced, culturally sensitive, and constructive view of Puerto Rican children on the mainland.

While acknowledging the dismal statistics, the problems, the stresses, and the vulnerable points, the chapters here presented aim at identifying the support systems that enable people to cope; the important and positive ways in which children are developing; the personal and cultural strengths that can be built upon; and viable solutions to at least some of the challenges confronting Puerto Rican children and their families today. In line with this interest, each article concludes with a series of recommendations and/or with an analysis of the practical implications that can be derived from the data presented and analyzed by each author.

Since the volume focuses on children, most of the chapters deal with education and schooling. In cases where chapters address other aspects of a child's development, findings and implications are analyzed so as to be of use to people working in school settings. The volume is thus oriented toward practitioners in school and/or clinical settings, but due to the methodological and scientific quality of the studies, it is also well-suited for academic purposes.

The book is divided into five major sections, plus an annotated bibliography. The first section, Current and Historical Perspectives, consists of two chapters. The first chapter, by Alvarez, provides current demographic data on Puerto Ricans on the United States mainland and an overview of research with Puerto Rican populations. The other chapter in this section, by Ambert and Figler, offers historical and cultural perspectives on Puerto Rican immigration and summarizes the major characteristics of Puerto Rican immigrants.

The second section of the book, Language and Culture, encompasses three field research studies. Ambert presents results of an investigation with Puerto Rican kindergarten children and concludes that rather than being "language deprived" the children in her sample are "language enriched," because, in addition to exhibiting normal development in their native language, they are simultaneously acquiring a second language. Hill's study reveals an untapped cultural and linguistic resource that Puerto Rican children bring with them to school and that has been largely overlooked up to now: a rich tradition of verbal folklore. She explores how children's verbal folklore can be used in the classroom and by other workers, to promote both cognitive and affective growth. In the third chapter in the Language and Culture section, Tapia looks into the motivational orientations of Puerto Rican schoolchildren and seeks answers to whether their orientations are cooperative, competitive, or independently motivated. She then explores the implications of these various learning and motivational styles for education and psychology.

Part III, Schools and Schooling, comprises three studies. Alvarez compares the impact of person, home, and school variables on the achievement of first grade Puerto Rican children and concludes that the major impact on achievement does not depend on personal attributes or on domestic variables, but on the schools attended by children. She argues for schools becoming more responsive learning environments. Indeed, a model of a responsive learning environment is presented by Mercado, in her fascinating account of a teacher-researcher-student collaborative model currently in progress at a New York City middle school. Mercado describes a process whereby seemingly unmotivated Puerto Rican students, with unimpressive achievement levels, can be motivated and trained to become investigators. The third paper in this section is a review of the literature on dropouts and dropout prevention. In this chapter Rodríguez provides numbers and general information, summarizes several recent studies, and discusses some of the most promising approaches to dropout prevention currently in use.

The chapters in Part IV deal with Health and Healing. Estepa offers general health statistics, but the major thrust of her chapter is the presentation of program models that are successfully delivering health care services to the Puerto Rican population in the areas they serve. Addressing a more specific topic, Guarnaccia focuses on asthma. He explores Puerto Rican families' health cultures and coping strategies for dealing with childhood asthma and illustrates this information with case studies representing various conceptions, treatments, and health-seeking behaviors.

Part V consists of two investigations on the effects of immigration on children and families. Meswick's study with Puerto Rican adolescents provides a close look into the various stages of immigration. By documenting the health, economic, behavioral, and social differences among children and families at five different immigration stages, it debunks the myth of treating Puerto Rican immigrants as if they were one large group. In another "close-up" view of Puerto Rican families, Figler compares families with and without handicapped children in terms of the stresses and support systems they exhibit; again it is instructive to see how different they are.

The last section is an Annotated Bibliography, contributed by all the authors, of publications spanning the decade from 1980 to 1990. The bibliography includes books, articles, doctoral dissertations, reports, and conference presentations. The topics largely correspond to the topics addressed in the five sections of the book, plus a section on psychological, behavioral, and emotional issues. The focus of the bibliography is on children, although other works have been incorporated when the topic was considered relevant to youth.

Grateful thanks to Marie Ellen Larcada for her encouragement and support and to Jeanne Weismantle for her helpful comments.

María D. Alvarez
Gainesville, Florida
February 1991

PART I

Current and Historical Perspectives on Puerto Rican Children on the Mainland

CHAPTER 1

Puerto Rican Children on the Mainland: Current Perspectives

María D. Alvarez

This chapter serves two major functions. First of all, it provides a statistical profile of the Puerto Rican population in the United States—especially on variables that relate to children and adolescents—and views Puerto Ricans in the context of other Hispanics and of the general U.S. population. Secondly, the chapter offers a perspective regarding research and information-gathering efforts on mainland-based Puerto Ricans over the last several decades.

A Demographic Profile of Puerto Ricans on the Mainland

Population size. According to 1989 Census Bureau data (cited in De La Rosa & Maw, 1990), Puerto Ricans are the second largest Hispanic group currently residing in the continental United States, comprising approximately 2.3 million people. This figure constitutes 11.6% of the total Hispanic population in the U.S., and well over one third of the total population of Puerto Ricans, since current estimates place the island population at 3.5 million. There are indications of continued growth in the mainland-based Puerto Rican population, given the 41% increase between 1970 and 1980 (U.S. Department of Commerce, 1985).

Puerto Ricans in the U.S. are a highly urbanized group, some 95% currently residing in urban areas (De La Rosa & Maw, 1990). Yet there have been substantial

3

population shifts in the last decades and an increasing movement away from large urban centers like New York City into smaller cities in neighboring states. For instance, according to U.S. Census figures (USDC, 1985), in 1970 some 64% of all Puerto Ricans on the mainland lived in New York State (mostly in New York City), but by 1980 the proportion had diminished to 49%. By contrast, during the same ten-year span, the Puerto Rican populations of New Jersey, Connecticut, Pennsylvania, Florida, and Massachusetts augmented, to the point that Puerto Ricans make up the largest Hispanic groups in the states of Connecticut, Pennsylvania, New York, and Massachusetts.

Despite the shifts, New York State still represents the largest concentration of Puerto Ricans in the United States. The 1980 Census placed this population at about 1 million, specifically at 986,389 (USDC, 1985). Rodríguez (1989) reports that Puerto Ricans make up 12.67% of the total population of New York City.

Age. Puerto Ricans are a young population, trailing closely behind Mexican-Americans, who appear to be the youngest of all Hispanic groups in the U.S. Median age for Puerto Ricans in 1988 was 24.9, with 40% of the population under 19 years of age. By contrast, median age for Hispanics in general was 25.5, and for the total U.S. population it was 32.2. Percentage under 19 was 38.7 for Hispanics and 29.3 for the total population (USDC, 1988).

Household composition and income. The disparity in the number of males vs. females among Puerto Ricans is the highest of any group in the nation. Census figures for 1988 (USDC, 1988) reported a breakdown of 46.7% males vs. 53.3% females. While the difference may result from census undercounts, differential immigration and migration patterns, increased risks for Puerto Rican males in U.S. urban environments, or life expectancy issues, it is certainly a noteworthy feature, which differs from current breakdowns for Hispanics (50.2% males vs. 49.8% females) and for the general population (48.6% males vs. 51.4% females).

Disparity is also noted between Puerto Ricans and other groups in family size and in family types. In terms of size, the Puerto Rican family average of 3.39 persons more closely resembles the average for the general population (3.17) than the Hispanic average of 3.79 (USDC, 1988). With respect to family types, variations are wider. Puerto Rican households include fewer married couples (51.6%), in contrast to 69.8% for other Hispanics, and 79.5% for the general U.S. population. There are also more Puerto Rican female-headed households (44%), compared to 23.4% for other Hispanics and 16.3% for the general population (USDC, 1988). As seen in Census figures (cited in Gurak, 1988), however common it may be for Puerto Rican women with children to live without a spouse (almost 50% do), the number of families with children headed by a man without a spouse is small for all Hispanics, including Puerto Ricans (3.3%).

Yet the major impact of one-parent homes is not demographic but economic. Female-headed households are associated with extreme poverty, especially for Puerto Rican families with children. Poverty affects 58.3% of households headed by women. Stated differently, one out of two Puerto Rican children under 18 years of age is currently living in poverty (De La Rosa & Maw, 1990). This surpasses poverty levels for whites (14.6%), for African-Americans (44.2%), and for other Hispanics (37.9%).

A possible impact of female-headed households is the prominent role of mothers in the daily functioning of families, a pattern that holds true even for two-parent families. In a study of 98 Puerto Rican families living in Spanish Harlem, Alvarez (1983) found mothers to be the major disciplinarians in most homes (76%). Mothers were the family member most apt to help children with school work (over 60% did); they also constituted the links between their families and the schools. While the dominant role of the Puerto Rican male is highlighted in the literature (c.f. Fitzpatrick, 1987; Vázquez-Nuttall & Romero-García, 1989), the preeminent role of females in the day-to-day workings of families and in imparting discipline to their young children has been documented both on the island (Halsted, 1966; Landy, 1959) and, increasingly so, on the mainland (Borrás, 1989, García-Preto, 1982). Given current household composition trends on the mainland, the female role is expected to expand.

Income and employment. Regarding income, 1989 figures reported by the National Council of La Raza (De La Rosa & Maw, 1990) place Puerto Rican median family income at $18,932, lower than any other group except African-Americans. Puerto Ricans have the highest percentage of families living below the poverty level (30.8%) and the highest percentage of families in the "Under $10,000" income category (29.1%). Puerto Rican males and females both have low labor force participation rates (69.6% for men vs. 41.7% for women). Men tend to hold service jobs and semi-skilled positions, while women work predominantly in clerical and semi-skilled jobs; both groups are poorly represented in managerial and professional areas.

Income and schooling. There are strong associations between schooling and income, with the major watershed being the high-school diploma. Thus, relatively small differences are found in the poverty rates of those Puerto Ricans reporting no school (39%), less than 8 years of school (32%), 8 years of school (30%), and 8–11 years of school (32%). But when it comes to a high school diploma, differences are pronounced. In contrast to the high poverty rates of non-graduates, the poverty rate for high school graduates is 16%, a substantial decrease (De La Rosa & Maw, 1990).

Education and schooling. Hispanics make up about 10% of the total U.S. school enrollment. However, this global figure masks a rather serious trend in the schooling of Hispanic children: the high numbers that leave school each year. Thus, while Hispanic enrollment in grades 1–4 is 11.8% and 10.3% in grades 9–10, it drops to 7.4% in grades 11–12 (De La Rosa & Maw, 1990). In just about every measure by which academic success is evaluated, Hispanics—especially Puerto Ricans and Mexican-Americans—fare poorly. Thus, there are high dropout rates in both high school and college; dramatic school suspension rates (especially among Mexican-Americans); a disproportionate number of students, especially males, enrolled below modal grade; large numbers of overage students; and high grade retention rates. At the same time, Hispanic students are less likely than whites, African-Americans, or Asians to be enrolled in programs for the gifted and talented (Cohen, 1988) and more likely to be overrepresented in special education categories such as learning disabilities and speech/language handicapped (Ortiz & Yates, 1983).

For Puerto Ricans in particular the current education situation is bleak. The 1988 National Education Longitudinal Study (cited in De La Rosa & Maw, 1990), which focuses on eighth grade student achievement nationwide, found the situation of Puerto Ricans seriously compromised in just about every subject category studied: reading, writing proficiency, mathematics, science, and computer competence. In addition, 34% of Puerto Rican eighth graders reported grades in the lowest quartile. Furthermore, many appeared disoriented as to their high school and future work plans. This disorientation is associated with low test scores, low grades, and low self-esteem. In other indirect measures Puerto Rican eighth graders also compare unfavorably: More time is reportedly spent watching TV (25.7 hrs/week) and less time engaged in homework (4.6 hrs/week) or outside reading (1.6 hrs/week) than is the case for the general population—for whom TV watching averages 21.4 hours, homework takes up 5.6 hours per week, and outside reading, 1.8 hours.

Figures for school attendance further reinforce this bleak picture. By March 1988 about 2.4% of adults in the U.S. had completed fewer than five years of school; of the Puerto Ricans on the U.S. mainland, 9.6% had completed fewer than five years. Nationally, the percentage of adults 25 years old and over who have completed high school is 76.2%; the percentage of Puerto Ricans on the mainland is 50.7% (USDC, 1988).

Traditionally, the personal or domestic factors linked with dropping out of school have received more attention than the systemic or school-based characteristics that induce students to drop out, which means that just by the way data are collected and analyzed learners and parents are more often found "at fault" than the schools that serve them (see Alvarez, in this volume). National surveys (cited in De La Rosa & Maw, 1990) have identified a number of domestic factors linked to dropping out of school: single-parent homes, low parental education, low family income, sibling dropout, limited English proficiency, and home alone more than three hours on weekdays. Puerto Ricans, together with African-Americans and Mexican-Americans, exhibit the largest number of risk factors, with 41% of Puerto Ricans exhibiting two or more of those factors and only 30% being risk-free. If one were to add school-based risks to the picture (e.g., teacher experience, teacher motivation, limited role models, curriculum offerings, school climate), the situation would look even more serious.

Language and bilinguistic competencies. Spanish continues to be the major language of communication among Puerto Ricans in the U.S., with some 91% of Puerto Ricans reporting they speak Spanish at home (Rodríguez, 1989). Part of the reason for such strong language maintenance patterns resides in the constant influx of newcomers from the island. A study in New York City (cited in Gurak, 1988) found that 48% of Puerto Ricans in that city were born on the island.

Yet Alvarez (1983) found increased use of English among second generation Puerto Rican children for whom parents had reported Spanish to be the first language (91%). While 76% of children interacted with their parents exclusively in Spanish, only 47% of them used Spanish exclusively when interacting with siblings at home. Most children used either both languages with their siblings (26%) or English exclusively (27%). Another indication of the transition experienced by children was found in their Lau categories, an indicator of relative proficiency in oral English and Spanish based on tests and teacher ratings. Only 57% of children were rated Spanish dominant, in contrast to a self-reported Spanish dominance of 81% among their mothers. The number of bilinguals among the children was also large (37%), in contrast to the maternal indication of 4%. Alvarez also found marked sex differences in language use among both adults and youth. For children, about 52% of boys were either bilingual or English dominant, in contrast with 31% of girls. For other household members (N=371) about 66% of males were either bilingual or English dominant, in contrast with 38% of females. Conversely, 62% of females vs. 44% of males were Spanish dominant. The trend thus appears to be toward language shift, and Puerto Rican males seem to be making a faster transition into English than Puerto Rican females. This pattern is also observed in analyses of large scale survey data (U.S. Commission on Civil Rights, 1976).

Evolving Perspectives on Research with Puerto Ricans

While there is a considerable amount of research regarding Puerto Rican populations, comparative or predictive research on this population has been limited. Whether correlational or experimental, research on Puerto Ricans has been plagued by ill-defined samples. Puerto Ricans are often mixed with other minority groups—usually African-Americans or other Hispanics—and the results are analyzed as if they referred to homogeneous rather than diverse groups (cf. Cohen, 1966; Prior, 1974). Problems are noted also in studies that have dealt exclusively with Puerto Ricans. It is not uncommon to find statements such as "subjects were low SES Puerto Rican children," with no further elaboration about immigration and migration experience, levels of acculturation to U.S. urban life, linguistic proficiency, education and employment status of parents, etc., despite the fact that the Puerto Rican population comprises a whole gamut of people ranging from new arrivals in the process of initial adaptation, to second or third generation people who may have never lived on the island. Research problems have also stemmed from the instruments used in measuring and defining the various constructs (cf. Oakland, 1977; Oakland & Phillips, 1973; Samuda, 1975).

Another source of difficulty has been the meaningful assessment of language, an important variable with bilingual children. A thorough analysis of a child's bilingualistic competencies would entail a complex process which would include measuring: (a) proficiency, i.e., the amount and quality of a child's language in four areas (listening, speaking, reading, writing); (b) linguistic domains (phonological, lexical, syntactic); and (c) sociolinguistic contexts (home, school, community). Proficiency, linguistic domains, and sociolinguistic variables need to be measured in each of the two languages (Alvarez, 1977, 1988; Ramirez, 1979, 1990; Silverman, Noa, & Russell, 1976). Investigators have frequently settled for less than an adequate assessment of language competency when carrying out their studies; in some cases they have failed to acknowledge language altogether.

In a critical review of research models in education of Puerto Ricans, Quintero-Alfaro (1979) regarded them as "too sporadic, quantitative, static, costly, and in many cases, irrelevant to the needs and priorities of the groups involved" (p. 24). Santiago-Santiago (1981) found that a disproportionate number of basic research studies focused on linguistics, whereas very few researchers had made educational experience, achievement, performance, and cognitive functioning their major focus of attention.

After reviewing many studies, four basic approaches to research with Puerto Rican populations may be identified: (a) the "disadvantaged" approach; (b) the "political" approach; (c) the "culturally syntonic" approach; and (d) the "empowerment" approach. While the *Zeitgeist*, or trend of the times, may steer investigators in one direction vs. another, these approaches are not necessarily localized in time. In the next paragraphs the four approaches are briefly described.

The "disadvantaged" or "culturally deprived" model. This approach focuses largely on deficits, on comparisons of one group vs. another, and on painstakingly pinpointing the weaknesses and deficiencies of Puerto Ricans— weaknesses that are often identified through the use of biased or culturally inappropriate instruments. How do the youngsters fare in terms of perceptual dysfunction? Linguistic interferences? The research questions themselves are set up to confirm already suspect traits. In the same vein, research that searches for achievement differentials in the characteristics of learners and homes, while ignoring the potential impact of learning environments, reflects a de facto alignment with the view that the major variations in achievement result from learner or domestic variables.

But evidence with other populations suggests not only that all three are important components, but that major behavioral and achievement differentials result from school effects (Madaus, Airasian, & Kellaghan, 1980; Rutter et al., 1982).

The "political" approach. The second model, the political approach, is best exemplified in those writings and/or investigations conducted with a heavy political emphasis and with such pressing search for social or programmatic relevance that all method is overpowered. Under this tradition the balance between rigor and relevance long alluded to in the literature (Bronfenbrenner, 1977; Gibbs, 1979; Ryan, 1971) is tilted in the direction of relevance and very little emphasis is placed on producing methodologically sound research or well-documented essays. While the message may be inspirational, the scientific and programmatic usefulness of this body of literature is limited.

The "culturally syntonic" approach. The third model, which characterizes the investigations presented in this volume, attempts to strike a balance between methodological requirements and programmatic usefulness. Some of the characteristics of this "culturally sensitive" or "culturally syntonic" approach to research are: (a) it seeks untapped areas of inquiry and new research topics; (b) it aims at generating new information by collecting fresh data from children and their families rather than rehashing existing data; (c) research bears direct relevance to the classroom or direct practical applications to the solution of pressing human problems; (d) studies are conducted or the literature reviewed with methodological rigor without losing sight of programmatic usefulness; and (e) while acknowledging weaknesses, investigators also seek to identify and build upon strengths.

The "empowerment" phase. A fourth phase is envisioned when young Puerto Rican youth from the lowest socioeconomic stratum of society themselves take control of their research agenda. As Mercado in this volume shows, when introduced to the general area of research, young Puerto Rican youngsters are not only able to understand the basic mechanics of research and to communicate this understanding to the scientific community, but they are, in addition, in the unique position of having a firsthand knowledge and a firsthand accessibility to individuals and situations, in a way that few researchers can.

Conclusion

This chapter provided a statistical profile of Puerto Ricans on the mainland regarding those variables that impact on the day-to-day lives of children and youth. By most measurable standards, the socioeconomic and educational situation of Puerto Ricans in the U.S. continues to be seriously compromised. One way of impacting on this situation is to analyze the factors that control and impede Puerto Ricans' access to better job opportunities, to more responsive schools, to more accessible health care, and to more culturally compatible programs, etc. Part of this process entails debunking the myths and the stereotypes that contribute to perpetuating the current state of affairs. This chapter has highlighted the importance of culturally sensitive research in opening up new avenues of inquiry, in documenting strengths, and in identifying culturally syntonic solutions, all within a cadre of social and programmatic usefulness. The answers obtained depend largely on the questions posed. Let us pose only relevant questions, for the problems are pressing.

REFERENCES

Alvarez, M.D. (1977). Practical considerations in the psychoeducational assessment of minority students: The case of bilingual Hispanics. In *Proceedings of a Multi-Cultural Colloquium on Non-Biased Pupil Assessment* (pp. 79–116). Albany, NY: State Education Department.

Current Perspectives   *13*

Alvarez, M.D. (1983). *Puerto Ricans and academic achievement:
    An exploratory study of person, home, and school variables
    among high-risk bilingual first graders.* Unpublished doctoral
    dissertation, New York University.
Alvarez, M.D. (1988). Psychoeducational assessment of bilingual
    students: Current trends and major issues. In A.N. Ambert
    (Ed.), *Bilingual education and English as a second language:
    A research handbook, 1987–1988.* (pp. 297–332). New York:
    Garland.
Borrás, V.A. (1989). Dual discipline role of the single Puerto
    Rican woman head of household. In C.T. García Coll &
    M.L. Mattei (Eds.), *The psychosocial development of Puerto
    Rican women* (pp. 200–213). New York: Praeger.
Bronfenbrenner, U. (1977). Toward an experimental ecology of
    human development. *American Psychologist, 32,* 513–531.
Cohen, A.S. (1966). Some learning disabilities of socially
    disadvantaged Puerto Rican and Negro children. *Academic
    Therapy Quarterly, 2*(1), 37–41; 52.
Cohen, L.M. (1988). Meeting the needs of gifted and talented
    minority language students: Issues and practices. *New
    Focus,* National Clearinghouse for Bilingual Education,
    Occasional Papers in Bilingual Education (8).
De La Rosa, D., & Maw, C.E. (1990). *Hispanic education: A
    statistical portrait 1990.* Washington, DC: National Council
    of La Raza.
Fitzpatrick, J.P. (1987). *Puerto Rican Americans: The meaning of
    migration to the mainland* (2nd ed.). Englewood Cliffs, NJ:
    Prentice-Hall.
García-Preto, N. (1982). Puerto Rican families. In M. McGoldrick,
    J.K. Pearce, & J. Giordano (Eds.), *Ethnicity and family
    therapy* (pp. 164–186). New York: Guilford.
Gibbs, J.C. (1979). The meaning of ecologically oriented inquiry
    in contemporary psychology. *American Psychologist, 34,*
    127–140.
Gurak, D.T. (1988). New York Hispanics: A demographic overview.
    In E. Acosta-Belén & B. Sjostrum (Eds.), *The Hispanic
    experience in the United States: Contemporary issues and
    perspectives* (pp. 57–78). New York: Praeger.
Halsted, D.W. (1966). *An initial survey of the attitudinal differences
    between the mothers of over-achieving and under-achieving
    eleventh grade Puerto Rican students.* Unpublished doctoral
    dissertation, Michigan State University.
Landy, D. (1959). *Tropical childhood.* New York: Harper & Row.

Madaus, G.F., Airasian, P.W., & Kellaghan, T. (1980). *School effectiveness: A reassessment of the evidence*. New York: McGraw-Hill.

Oakland, T. (1977). *Psychological and educational assessment of minority children*. New York: Brunner/Mazel.

Oakland, T., & Phillips, B.N. (Eds.) (1973). *Assessing minority group children: A special issue of the Journal of School Psychology*. New York: Behavioral Publications.

Ortiz, A.A., & Yates, J.R. (1983). Characteristics of limited English proficient students served in programs for the learning disabled: Implications for manpower planning. *NABE Journal*, 7, 41–54.

Prior, D.R. (1974). Inner city elementary pupil mobility, reading achievement, and environmental process variables. Unpublished doctoral dissertation, Fordham University.

Quintero-Alfaro, A.G. (1979). In the search of alternatives: Notes on socialization and education. *Metas*, *1*(1), 3–30.

Ramírez, A.G. (1979). Language dominance in pedagogical considerations. In National Multilingual Multicultural Materials Development Center (Ed.), *Language development in a bilingual setting* (pp. 156–170). Los Angeles: National Dissemination and Assessment Center.

Ramírez, A.G. (1990). Perspectives on language proficiency assessment. In A. Barona & E.E. García (Eds.), *Children at risk: Poverty, minority status, and other issues in educational equity* (pp. 297–304). Washington, DC: National Association of School Psychologists.

Rodríguez, C. (1989). *Puerto Ricans born in the U.S.A.* Winchester, MA: Unwin Hyman.

Rutter, M., Maughan, B., Mortimore, P., Ouston, J., & Smith, A. (1982). *Fifteen thousand hours: Secondary schools and their effects on children*. Cambridge, MA: Harvard University Press.

Ryan, W. (1971). *Blaming the victim*. New York: Pantheon.

Samuda, R.J. (1975). *Psychological testing and American minorities: Issues and consequences*. New York: Dodd, Mead.

Santiago-Santiago, J. (1981). The Puerto Rican in the classroom: A conceptual framework for future research. *Metas*, 2, 52–82.

Silverman, R.J., Noa, J.K., & Russell, R.H. (1976). *Oral language tests for bilingual students: An evaluation of language dominance and proficiency instruments*. Portland, OR: Northwest Regional Educational Laboratory.

U.S. Commission on Civil Rights (1976). *Puerto Ricans in the continental United States: An uncertain future*. Washington, DC: Author.

U.S. Department of Commerce (1985). *We . . . the Mexican-Americans, the Puerto Ricans, the Cubans, and the Hispanos from other countries in the Caribbean, Central and South America, and from Spain.* Washington, DC: Author.

U.S. Department of Commerce (1988). *The Hispanic population in the United States: March 1988* (Advance Report). Current Population Reports, Population Characteristics Series P-20, No. 431. Washington, DC: Author.

Vázquez-Nuttall, E., & Romero-Garcia, I. (1989). From home to school: Puerto Rican girls learn to be students in the United States. In C.T. Garcia Coll & M.L. Mattei (Eds.), *The psychosocial development of Puerto Rican women* (pp. 60–83). New York: Praeger.

CHAPTER 2

Puerto Ricans: Historical and Cultural Perspectives

Alba N. Ambert and Clare S. Figler

Introduction

Puerto Rico has experienced a long history of colonial limitations imposed by outside forces, and systematic attempts to undermine the cultural and linguistic characteristics of its people. Although the island's history is complex, the social and political issues of predominant concern are related to the extent and intensity of change which has occurred and continues to occur throughout the entire fabric of Puerto Rican society (Fitzpatrick, 1987; López, 1973; López & Petras, 1974; Mintz, 1975). To understand the constantly changing social, political, and economic status of Puerto Ricans, these changes must be seen in the context of colonial domination and the resultant economic exploitation of the island and its inhabitants by the dominant society. The historical and political developments that have shaped the Puerto Rican of today and the cultural characteristics which define Puerto Ricans will be the topics of this chapter.

A Historical and Economic Overview

The *Taínos* were the indigenous people of Puerto Rico, who lived in a peaceful society built around the hereditary authority of the *cacique*. When the Spanish colonizers arrived in 1492, the *Tainos* were ill-prepared for the Spaniard's ruthless quest for riches which would place them in a position of subjugation and untimely death (Wagenheim, 1970). After annihilating the *Taino* population and thus eliminating the slaves they exploited, the Spaniards imported African slaves to work the sugar cane (Mintz, 1985). The elements of what would become the Puerto Rican people were present in the melding of the three racial groups that intermingled in Puerto Rico at the time of Spanish colonization: *Tainos*, white Europeans, and black African slaves. By the 18th century, Puerto Ricans had acquired the cultural characteristics of a distinct people and no longer thought of themselves as Spaniards (Figueroa, 1971).

During the centuries of Spanish domination, Puerto Rico was a strategically located, well-fortified, military installation, poised against Dutch, British, and other European incursions. It was also an important source of income for the Spanish Crown, with its production of sugar, sugar-related products, coffee, and tobacco. The gradual erosion of Spanish dominance in the world culminated in the Spanish-American War. Spain lost the war, and as a result of the Treaty of Paris in 1898, Puerto Rico was ceded to the United States. The U.S. imposed military rule in Puerto Rico, and the island passed from the autocratic rule of Spain to the autocratic rule of the United States. Puerto Ricans had no constitution, no citizenship, no suffrage, and no representation. Thus, the island became a colony of the United States (Hauberg, 1974).

In 1917, just before U.S. involvement in World War I, U.S. citizenship was granted to Puerto Ricans through a process in which Puerto Ricans were not consulted. Despite U.S. citizenship, Puerto Ricans still had no representation in Congress, nor did island residents have the right to vote in U.S. elections. This state of events survives to this day. U. S. citizenship is a technical rather than an emotional status for some Puerto Ricans, particularly those who reside on the island. This is not surprising, considering that islanders are barred from participation in the U.S. political process, a process which affects Puerto Ricans directly in all aspects of life. Many

Puerto Ricans seem to be only tangentially aware of their United States citizenship (López, 1973; Wagenheim, 1975). On the other hand, Puerto Ricans appear to accept the status quo. This acceptance has led to the opinion that Puerto Rico's lengthy subservience to both Spain and the United States has discouraged, if not totally hindered, its people's desire for political independence (López, 1973). Five centuries of colonial domination amply explain this phenomenon.

Prior to the 1940's, Puerto Rico maintained a cash-based economy heavily dependent on sugar. By the 1920's North American absentee landowners controlled almost all the sugar, coffee, and tobacco production on the island, reaping immense profits at a time when the worldwide demand for these crops was very high and farm workers were paid six cents an hour. The need for agricultural laborers was so great that women entered the workforce in large numbers. Furthermore, as a result of U.S. participation in World War II, Puerto Rico became increasingly important militarily and Puerto Rican men continued to be inducted into the armed forces.

However, agriculture suffered serious reversals after the war (López, 1987; Wagenheim, 1973; Wagenheim & Jiménez de Wagenheim, 1988). Between 1950 and 1965 "Operation Bootstrap" took place. This long-range planned economic development program, subsidized by U.S. investments, extensively and permanently industrialized Puerto Rico in 15 years with little attention paid to the ailing agricultural sector.

Farm workers migrated to the cities to earn their livelihoods as low-cost laborers in the emerging U.S.-owned industries, but the massive industrialization of the island could not absorb all of the available work force. As a solution to this problem, the Puerto Rican government concocted a plan through the Industrial Development Company and the Development Bank to export laborers to the United States. For this purpose, the Bureau of Employment and Migration was established, with funds provided by the U.S. government (Nieves Falcón, 1975). The immigration of Puerto Rican laborers to farms in the United States was strongly promoted by the government to alleviate the crushing rise of unemployment caused by the sudden industrialization of the island with its consequent surplus of agricultural workers who had no experience in industrial jobs. In addition, the U.S. industries established in Puerto Rico were capital-intensive with few employment opportunities for Puerto Ricans (Rodríguez, 1989). To deal with the growing surplus of labor, the government of Puerto Rico entered into contractual agreements directly with farm owners in the United States to provide inexpensive agricultural laborers. Although Puerto Rican immigration to the United States dates back to the 1900's, it was between 1946 and 1964 that the "great migration" occurred (Rodríguez, 1989).

Thus, the mass migration of Puerto Rican workers began and with it the cycle of migration back and forth between the island and the mainland according to seasonal work availability. The birth and perpetuation of large scale migration to the mainland is, in large part, a direct result of an economic plan based on the rapid industrialization of Puerto Rico (López, 1973).

Since its industrialization, Puerto Rico has presented a facade of material prosperity, while underlying endemic poverty is widespread (Nieves Falcón, 1975). Therefore, Puerto Ricans continued to immigrate to the mainland in search of work, not only in agriculture, but in industrial, service, and professional areas as well. Many have stayed. Although New York was the principal target of Puerto Rican migration, many Puerto Ricans migrated to Connecticut, Illinois, Massachusetts, New Jersey, and other areas (Nieves Falcón, 1975). Unemployment, worsened quality of life, and discontinuities between the cultural values held by Puerto Ricans and those in the U.S. were sources of stress on the mainland. When the stresses became too intense, when family values overpowered economic ones, Puerto Ricans returned to the island and the unique feature of Puerto Ricans' migration experience continued: return migration (Hernández, 1976; Rodríguez, 1989). On the other hand, it is important to point out that many Puerto Ricans never returned. Third and fourth generation Puerto Ricans live in cities like New York, Philadelphia, and Chicago and consider themselves natives of their cities as well as Puerto Rican.

In summary, the broad historical and econ‹ perspectives which characterize the people of Puerto 1 as a distinct group include: the subjugation of the island by Spain and its subsequent occupation by the United States through negotiations which excluded Puerto Ricans and perpetuated their subjugation; the permanent industrialization of the island in an unheralded, quick swoop from 1950 to 1965; the extent of change in the social and economic climate of Puerto Rican society as a result of this speedy and enforced industrialization; and the ongoing immigration to and from the island and the mainland.

A Cultural Overview

The values upon which people base their daily lives are difficult to delineate specifically. In this respect, Puerto Ricans are in the same situation as a majority of the world's people whose lives are challenged by rapid, external changes in their social environment. However, the situation of Puerto Ricans differs from other immigrants in the unique colonial situation and the ambiguous status they occupy in its relationship with the United States. The swift transformation of Puerto Rico from an agricultural to an industrialized society necessitated many adjustments in the hierarchy of values of Puerto Ricans. Value modification was necessary for survival on both the island and the mainland.

 Puerto Ricans bring with them many strengths and cultural values which reinforce these strengths. Among the greatest sources of strength for Puerto Ricans is family life.

Family Life

Membership in a family is basic for Puerto Ricans; they function within this framework. That both the mother's and the father's names are components of Puerto Ricans' names is an indicator of the importance which membership in a family brings to bear on their sense of identity. Family building is considered a most important cultural goal; it is not a tangential by-product of unions among members. For Puerto Ricans, childbearing and the establishment of families are major goals. Furthermore, one of the Puerto Ricans' greatest responsibilities in life is to the family. Within the family structure, children are expected to show *respeto* to their parents and other adults. Life is a shared process in which the participants are the *primary* social group members (Fitzpatrick, 1987; Rogler, 1965), that is, the members of the nuclear and extended family.

The nuclear family is a basic model of family structure in the world community. So it is for Puerto Ricans, although extensions and modifications of the basic nuclear mother-father-child unit exist. Fitzpatrick's (1987, p. 74) four-fold typology of the Puerto Rican family makes this model clearer.

The nuclear family. This is the traditional unit of parents and children living together. The increase in the island's and the mainland's social and economic mobility has tended to increase the strength and relevance of the nuclear family at the expense of the extended family. In order to take advantage of employment opportunities in new areas, the nuclear family must often leave familiar home and surroundings. Tightly knit bonds with extended family members are often severed because of distance. Thus, the nuclear family must rely on itself for most of its needs without the support of relatives.

The extended family. In this system, strong bonds are maintained with natural or ritual kin. Several generations may live in the same household or in separate households in the immediate neighborhood. Frequent visits between relatives are typical, and strong supportive exchanges are maintained. In Puerto Rico, the extent of interchange among extended family members is great, thereby minimizing the isolation and privacy of the nuclear family. However, contrary to popular stereotypes, only one-fifth of extended Puerto Rican families in the U.S. live under the same roof. Alvarez (1983) found that 16% of the Puerto Rican children in her East Harlem sample lived in extended households. Among Puerto Rican families living in the South Bronx, Garrison (1972) found that 20% lived in extended households.

The extended nuclear family. This modification is composed of a father, a mother, their children, and the children of another mate's previous unions. A typical response from children during exchanges about family members is one akin to, "He is my brother on my mother's side."

The mother-based family. In this structure, the mother and children of one or more men reside in the home without the presence of a permanent husband/*compañero*. This type of family is becoming increasingly common. It is currently estimated that 44% of Puerto Rican families are headed by females. Yet, data on Puerto Rican families below the poverty level further reveal that the figure can reach 77.4% (U.S. Bureau of the Census, 1985). This situation has serious implications for traditional male-female family roles and for child rearing (Borrás, 1989).

With Puerto Rican women increasingly becoming heads of households on the mainland, they must assume the dual role of father and mother, which affects the adaptive abilities of the family (Borrás, 1989; Pelto, Román, & Liriano, 1982). According to Borrás (1989), the socialization process of Puerto Rican women does not prepare them for the role of child disciplinarian. A mother is expected to provide love and affection, not punishment. As a result, mothers tend to be inconsistent in their disciplinary patterns. In addition, Puerto Rican female heads of households must deal with overwhelming environmental pressures, such as devastating housing conditions, serious financial difficulties, and aggravated health problems due to the conditions of poverty in which they live, as well as linguistic and cultural dissonance. Faced with problems of this magnitude, that these women report a high incidence of stress is no surprise (Pelto, Román, & Liriano, 1982).

Family Values and Evolving Sex Roles

Culturally sanctioned values which directly affect the Puerto Rican family include: (a) the machismo/marianismo complex, or the pervasive model of expected gender-related behavior which mandates that the male be demonstratively brave, potently exuberant, and dominant over women and wife and that women be submissive, passive, selfless, and home-centered; and (b) the sexual double standard which provides, among other things, for greater independence and freedom for boys than for girls.

The sexual double standard creates what might appear to be an impossible dilemma in Puerto Rican families. The many facets of this dilemma have been documented by numerous investigators both in Puerto Rico and among Puerto Ricans on the U.S. mainland (Borrás, 1989; Comas-Díaz, 1989; Margarida-Juliá, 1989; Mintz, 1975; Vázquez-Nuttall & Romero-García, 1989). On the one hand, girls are trained and expected to be quiet, submissive, and obedient. They are to devote their lives to the maintenance of a good home and family. Boys are trained to be respectful and submissive to adults during childhood years, but are expected to be active, restless, daring, and parents are more likely to ignore their acts of disobedience (Borrás, 1989). They are then expected to become independently aggressive with their emergence into adulthood. When girls reach adulthood, however, they are supposed to become the backbone, the anchor of the family because this is the woman's expected role. Women are more responsible and more secure, but have less social freedom than men. Nevertheless, men are expected to be the authoritarian heads of the household. The ideal underlying the roles in the Puerto Rican family is for the woman to maintain a home and children with a serious, stable man. The man provides for a home which his wife and the mother of his children cleans, orders, and runs. At the same time, the man seeks unlimited freedom for socialization with friends.

Spousal system. The spousal system of the low-income Puerto Rican family has frequently been described as "strained" because of the different expectations imposed by the culture on men and women (Figler, 1979; Mintz, 1975; Stycos, 1955). The climate of the marital system is one of unchallenged authority of the husband over the wife and children, with a physical or symbolic maintenance of this authority, whether or not the husband is present in the household (Fitzpatrick, 1987).

As is generally observed in patriarchal-authoritarian families, few activities are shared between spouses. As a result, the need for overt communication between husband and wife is minimal. When family decisions are made, the husband dictates and the wife adheres (Rogler, 1965). Although the predominantly male-dominated spousal system of the Puerto Rican family seems a bit inflexible in comparison to the more egalitarian Anglo family, it is nevertheless more predictable. The relationship between spouses may be less intimate and more rigid, but it is more stable (Nuttall, Nuttall, & Pedalino, 1978).

The dynamics of the spousal system in the traditional Puerto Rican family reflect cultural expectations which center on the different sexual role expectations. The wife is dutifully bound to the home and to the bearing and rearing of children, while the husband's greater social and sexual freedom is accepted. There is little overt sharing of activities between the spouses, therefore, there is little communication. The authority lies primarily with the man, with the expectation that this authority be demonstrated publicly.

Parental system. The Puerto Rican parenting system adheres to and responds to the values of the culture. Children are universally loved and cherished—especially the younger children. Loving and caring for children is often extended to the point of overprotection. As the children grow and develop, the critical expectation is that of unequivocal respect for parents, coparents, adults and others. Parents exert much effort in order to align children's behavior with the traditional patterns of obedience and *respeto*.

Many Puerto Rican parents consider American children—who are taught to be self-reliant, aggressive, competitive, and verbally inquisitive—disrespectful. Ideally, in bringing up Puerto Rican children, independence is curtailed while adherence to parental and family demands is encouraged (Figler, 1979).

Table 1 summarizes the salient features of Puerto Rican life. Although condensed and oversimplified, the areas provide a generalized overview. (For a more detailed discussion, see Figler, 1979.)

Table 1
Generalized and Composite Features
of Puerto Rican Life

Historical	Indigenous *Taínos*. Colonized by Spain. Introduction of African slave culture. Genetic and cultural fusion. Acquired by U.S. Swift change from agricultural to industrialized society. Emergence of a middle class.
Values	Sense of personal dignity. Respect critical and supersedes love. Seek personal friendships based on confidence. Belief in ordered supernatural. Family values and obligations foremost. Support derived through personal relationships.
Family	Traditional family ideals. Differential treatment of children. System based on sex. Machismo ideals expected of sons and husbands. Marianismo ideals expected of wives and daughters. Sense of strong family responsibility. Family is strong support system.
Social Dynamics	Need for personal interaction. Privacy minimally valued. Opinions of social community critically important. Strong sense of personal community. Social support networks from families and neighbors expected and cherished.
Language	Spanish. English is taught as a second language in Puerto Rican schools. Different levels of bilingualism in the U.S.
Religion	Predominantly Catholic with more personalistic Pentecostal traditions becoming increasingly popular, especially on the U.S. mainland. *Santería*, which syncretizes African and Western religious traditions, is also popular.
Ethnicity	Gentle intermingling of color-based differences. On island softer boundaries and wide range of color lines coexist. Exclusion and inclusion based on color not as intense and emotional an issue.
Societal Features	Class-structured society, more traditional and less mobile than mainland society. Overt expression and declaration of feeling socially acceptable and expected. Ethnicity permeates all class lines. Strong national-ethnic identification.

| Migration and Acculturation | Migration and return migration involves one third of the island population. Migration internal and external. Return an on-going process and a family endeavor. Migrants usually younger adults seeking betterment for family. Migrants better educated than average island Puerto Ricans, but less so than average for mainland. Mainland Puerto Ricans are dwellers. Accessibility of return migration differentiates Puerto Rican migration patterns. Acculturation difficult, since new migrants are continuously establishing themselves. Value differences, discrimination, and racism cause of great conflict and stress. |

The Mainland Experience

The concept of migration is commonly understood to involve the uprooting of groups of people from one place to another. It is a traditional response of people to the intrusions of a social system into such important areas as religion, political integrity, economic viability, or family status. People usually move toward "betterment," or at least that is the intention (Fitzpatrick, 1987; López, 1973).

Migration is the first step of the more complex process of acculturation. Migration and acculturation are two dynamically different phenomena, although typically fused in the literature of migration patterns. Figler (1979; 1980) conceptualized a model which delineates the differences between migration and acculturation. Table 2 reproduces the theoretical and historical implications of the two phenomena —migration and acculturation—in an effort to scrutinize more clearly the two as part of the Puerto Rican experience.

Table 2

Comparative Overview of Migration and Acculturation

Migration	Acculturation
♦ Observable, distinct action taking place at a specific time.	♦ Subtle, long-range, on-going dynamic—a continuum beginning with the migration and culminating with intermarriage and total identity with the new culture. Occurs in different stages and at different times for each individual and in each family. Indirectly inferred, not observed. Reflected by language, diet, customs, ecology, psychological motivations.
♦ Motivated by impingement or infraction of an important life system in the primary society. Impetus is one of betterment, improvement of life.	♦ Process based on hope for future.
♦ Can be repeated or reversed in the process of return migration	♦ Cannot be easily reversed, if at all.
♦ A group, rather than a typical individual phenomenon	♦ An individual process which may not necessarily be paralleled by a group.
♦ Can occur internally within the same culture	♦ Cannot occur internally, by definition.
♦ A process involving physical separation from a familiar place and people.	♦ Intellectual/emotional cultural adjustment to meanings and new ways to negotiate these meanings. Capacity to accept new meanings affects degree of acculturation.
♦ Achieves immediate results.	♦ Achieved in later stages or subsequent generations.

Migration of Puerto Ricans

Migration from Puerto Rico is usually a family migration. Either the nuclear family transplants itself intact or, if its migration is staggered, a speedy reunion of the family unit on the mainland is anticipated. In a typical pattern of the migration flow, which the authors have often observed, the father leaves first, then sends for the rest of the family. When the family reunites on the mainland, there are wide differences in the degree of acculturation between the father and the rest of the family, including English proficiency. A parallel pattern of movement involves a woman with children who is separated from her husband.

A great part of the Puerto Rican migration to the mainland in the last 30 years consisted of a search for economic opportunity. Information about the availability of the opportunity filtered through the family intelligence network (Senior, 1972). Once the trend was established —the door opened, so to speak—other factors may have caused certain Puerto Ricans to try their luck on the mainland: a poor marriage, overbearing parents, a sense of adventure, and the availability of better schools, hospitals, and social services (Hernández, 1976; López, 1973). However desired migration may be, families experience the stress of separation and uprooting. Mobility and stress, therefore, are common occurrences in Puerto Rican society, where so many of its members are constantly on the move. In addition, the Puerto Rican family on the mainland is often isolated, ignored, discriminated against, and vulnerable, a situation which generates additional psychological, physical, economic, and social stress (Canino, Earley, & Rogler, 1980; Figler, 1979; 1980; López, 1973).

A composite summary of the central themes which have been observed in the lives of mainland Puerto Ricans is presented in Table 3. The categorization of the areas is based on a model by Figler (1979). The data are divided into the following areas: (a) statistical information; (b) family; (c) education and employment; (d) community and housing; (e) language, politics, economics, and stresses; and (f) values and religion.

Table 3
The Puerto Rican on the Mainland

Statistical Profile	◆ Second largest Hispanic group in the U.S. ◆ Significantly younger than national average, predominantly involves school-age children. ◆ One third of all Puerto Ricans live on the mainland; not the same third because of cyclical move of different people. ◆ Close to 2.5 million Puerto Ricans on mainland.
Family	◆ Size of family generally larger than average U.S. family. ◆ Scattering of extended family members in various sections of the city. ◆ Pervasive overcontrol of children in response to actual and perceived danger of the neighborhood. ◆ Weakened family supportive networks because of dispersion of extended family.
Education and Employment	◆ More educated than island standards, but less educated than mainland standards. ◆ Less educated than other Hispanic groups. ◆ Underrepresented in high schools and colleges. ◆ School drop-out rate very high. ◆ Typical employment as service workers, operatives, manual laborers. ◆ Underemployed. Victims of downward mobility; quality of employment decreases because better jobs not readily accessible to inner-city dwellers. ◆ More consistently unemployed than all whites and non-whites. ◆ Employment more subject to layoffs, seasonal status.

Community and Housing	<ul><li>Mainland community is heterogeneous, composed of established members and recent arrivals.</li><li>More recent arrivals prefer Puerto Rican neighborhoods.</li><li>Increased settlement in cities other than New York.</li><li>Those in smaller cities appear better adjusted and are treated as more of a novelty by mainstream society.</li><li>Prefer to live near schools, hospitals, stores, in areas that are safe from drug traffic and other crimes.</li><li>Paths of migration within urban city usually determined by lines of transportation and housing availability.</li><li>Dwellings typically rented.</li><li>More established Puerto Ricans venture out to neighborhoods not settled by other Puerto Ricans.</li><li>Ideal preference for two- or single-family homes rather than public housing.</li><li>Cold climate considered initially stressful.</li></ul>
Language, Politics, Economics, Stresses	<ul><li>Language difficulties almost universally felt to be most obvious problem.</li><li>Political underrepresentation. Lumped together with other minority groups in governmental representation.</li><li>Minimal overt political demonstration.</li><li>Poorer than mainland population, but not poorest of island population.</li><li>Below other Hispanic groups socioeconomically.</li><li>Suffer stresses of powerlessness related to poverty and discrimination.</li><li>Overrepresentation in crime and drug statistics.</li></ul>

	‣ Generally a disadvantaged group on the mainland.
Values and Religion	‣ Experience conflict between U.S. and Puerto Rican cultural values; personal values, expectation of respect from children and other adults, machismo/marianismo, double sexual standard and others.
	‣ Religion does not play a crucial role in acculturation.
	‣ Supportive religious experiences provided in Pentecostal, Spiritist, and in more traditional religions, such as Catholicism.
	‣ *Espiritismo* a common phenomenon interwoven with more traditional practice.

Return Migration

The cyclical quality of a constant wave of migration is a unique Puerto Rican phenomenon. One-third of all Puerto Ricans live on the mainland at any one time. It is not always the same third because of the constant pattern of in and out movement (Fitzpatrick, 1987; Hernández, 1976; López, 1987; Rodríguez, 1989). Further, Puerto Ricans generally return to the Island as a result of the economic and employment opportunities which exist in the mainland at a particular time. Several surveys and reports suggest that return migration has increased while migration to the mainland has decreased (Fitzpatrick, 1987). This could reflect an historically different trend. Previously, the number of migrations to the mainland has been greater than those back to the island. The demand for blue collar workers on the mainland in routine or repetitive jobs has decreased in recent years, as has the availability of affordable housing for low-income people. These factors have promoted increased return migration (Hernández, 1976; Rodríguez, 1989). Citing a Junta de Planificación 1986 study, Rodríguez (1989) states that the majority of Puerto Ricans left the island to work and the majority of Puerto Ricans who enter the island do so for the same reason.

Economic factors are decisively related to both the quantity and the quality of migration to and from the mainland. However, transplanted Puerto Ricans are sustained by their perceived expectation that the family will offer help when it is needed. The family contingent which has remained in Puerto Rico represents a backup, an emergency resource, which is to be used when needed in periods of crisis. Disillusionment with mainland life and its pervasive discrimination against Puerto Ricans (Fuentes, 1980; Hernández, 1976; U.S. Commission, 1976) is considered a crisis. In essence, a situation exists where, contrary to the waves of immigration which began at the turn of the century, a contingency plan is possible and readily available to Puerto Ricans.

Puerto Ricans, of whatever social class, who migrate to the mainland perceive that they can always go home again. Table 4, adapted from the work of Hernández (1976) and Figler (1979), summarizes the major variables related to Puerto Ricans' return migration.

Table 4

Aspects of Puerto Rican Return Migration

- Option to return readily available.
- United States citizenship of Puerto Ricans minimizes re-entry problems (passports, visas unnecessary).
- Disillusionment with mainland life promotes return to island.
- Commitment to mainland community and to acculturation to U.S. life weakened or interrupted.
- Children's educational process interrupted.
- Children's education scattered between the island and mainland; therefore, maintenance of primary language is relevant.
- History of maintenance of family ties with the island. Visits, vacations, telephone conversations frequent.
- "Typical" return migrant stays less than 10 years on mainland.
- Migration to mainland often seen as temporary.
- Non-Puerto Ricans perceive return migration as an expected pattern for Puerto Ricans.

- Migration to mainland part of a more general movement pattern on island away from rural areas.

- Marriage and family formation often coincide with migration.

- Difference in income between island and mainland a major incentive for migration, and deterrent to return.

- Negative aspects of island life tend to be minimized; negative aspects of mainland life tend to be maximized.

- Social networks perceived to be anchored in Puerto Rico. Island news and political/social developments continue to be relevant.

- Return migrants who are socially and educationally proficient serve as social changers and activists on island.

- The stronger the social and psychological ties to Puerto Rico, the more predisposed migrants are to return to Island, irrespective of financial factors.

What Now?

The situation of Puerto Ricans in the United States is not the same as that of other immigrants. Puerto Ricans have a unique colonial history and a unique set of circumstances that bring them to the mainland. Rather than the acceptance and ready assistance that other immigrant groups have received in the last fifty years, Puerto Ricans, despite their U.S. citizenship, have traditionally been denied access to employment, training programs, adequate housing, proper health care, and quality education. The impact of racism, a prevalent specter in U.S. society, has been particularly damaging to generations of Puerto Ricans who have ventured to the mainland in search of a better life. The continued, unjustifiable placement of Puerto Rican children in special education classes, the chronic and untreated health problems Puerto Ricans experience, and the marginal existence many live in the devastation of the slums attest not to any inherent "deficiency" in Puerto Ricans that prevents their rising above the circumstances. Rather, these are examples of the scandalous treatment this population has suffered. The unconscionable exploitation, the razing of personal values and self-esteem, the institutionalized and systematic suppression of a dominated people are in large measure responsible for the situation of Puerto Ricans in the United States. The situation need not remain as it is. As the chapters in this volume confirm, tangible efforts are possible, especially in education and health, to remedy the precarious situation of Puerto Ricans in the U.S. The remedies will require that society assume responsibility for its deplorable schools, its subhuman housing, its rundown public health system, and the violence that poverty breeds. The remedies will require an assault on institutionalized and individual racism and the negative stereotypes that it fosters. In short, we must borrow from their cultural values and treat Puerto Ricans with dignity and *respeto*.

REFERENCES

Alvarez, M.D. (1983). Puerto Ricans and academic achievement: An exploratory study of person, home, and school variables among high-risk bilingual first graders. Unpublished doctoral dissertation, New York University.

Borrás, V.A. (1989). Dual discipline role of the single Puerto Rican woman head of household. In C.T. Garcia-Coll & M.L. Mattei (Eds.), *The psychosocial development of Puerto Rican women* (pp. 200–213). New York: Praeger.

Canino, I., Earley, B., & Rogler, L. (1980). *The Puerto Rican child in New York City: Stress and mental health.* (Monograph No. 4.) New York: Fordham University, Hispanic Research Center.

Comás-Díaz, L. (1989). Puerto Rican women's cross-cultural transitions: Developmental and clinical implications. In C.T. Garcia-Coll & M.L. Mattei (Eds.), *The psychosocial development of Puerto Rican women* (pp. 166–199). New York: Praeger.

Figler, C.S. (1979). Puerto Rican families: Their migration and assimilation. Unpublished manuscript, University of Massachusetts, Amherst.

Figler, C.S. (1980). A comparative study of Puerto Rican families with and without handicapped children. Unpublished doctoral dissertation, University of Massachusetts, Amherst.

Figueroa, L. (1971) *Breve historia de Puerto Rico.* Río Piedras: Edil.

Fitzpatrick, J.P. (1987). *Puerto Rican Americans: The meaning of migration to the mainland* (2nd ed.). Englewood Cliffs, NJ: Prentice-Hall.

Fuentes, L. (1980). The struggle for local political support. In C.E. Rodríguez, V. Sánchez-Korrol, & J.O. Alers (Eds.), *The Puerto Rican struggle: Essays on survival in the U.S.* (pp. 111–120). New York: Puerto Rican Migration Research Consortium.

Garrison, V. (1972). Social networks, social change, and mental health among migrants in a New York City slum. Unpublished doctoral dissertation, Columbia University.

Hauberg, C.A. (1974). *Puerto Rico and the Puerto Ricans: A study of Puerto Rican history and immigration to the United States.* New York: Hippocrene Books.

Hernández, A.J. (1976). *Return migration to Puerto Rico.* Westport, CT: Greenwood.

López, A. (1973). *The Puerto Rican papers: Notes on the re-emergence of a nation.* Indianapolis: Bobbs-Merrill.

López, A. (1987). *Doña Licha's island: Modern colonialism in Puerto Rico.* Boston: South End Press.

López, A., & Petras, J. (Eds.) (1974). *Puerto Rico and Puerto Ricans: Studies in history and society.* New York: Wiley.

Margarida-Juliá, M.T. (1989). Developmental issues during adulthood: Redefining notions of self, care, and responsibility among a group of professional Puerto Rican women. In C.T. García-Coll & M.L. Mattei (Eds.), *The psychosocial development of Puerto Rican women* (pp. 115–140). New York: Praeger.

Mintz, S.W. (1975). Puerto Rico: An essay in the definition of a national culture. In F. Cordasco & E. Bucchioni (Eds.), *The Puerto Rican experience: A sociological sourcebook* (pp. 26–90). Totowa, NJ: Littlefield, Adams.

Mintz, S.W. (1985). *Sweetness and power: The place of sugar in modern history.* New York: Viking.

Nieves Falcón, L. (1975). *El emigrante puertorriqueño.* Río Piedras: Edil.

Nuttall, E.V., Nuttall, R., & Pedalino, M. (1978). *Coping with stress: An ecological analysis of Puerto Rican and Italian low income families.* Report to the National Institute of Mental Health.

Pelto, P., Román, M., & Liriano, N. (1982). Family structures in an urban Puerto Rican community. *Urban Anthropology, 11,* 39–58.

Rodríguez, C.E. (1989) *Puerto Ricans born in the U.S.A.* Boston: Unwin Hyman.

Rogler, L.H. (1965). *Trapped: Families and schizophrenia.* New York: Krieger.

Ruiz, R.A., & Padilla, A.M. (1977). Counseling Latinos. *The Personnel Guidance Journal.* March, 401–408.

Senior, C. (1972). Puerto Ricans on the mainland. In F. Cordasco & E. Bucchioni (Eds.), *The Puerto Rican community and its children on the mainland.* Metuchen, NJ: Scarecrow.

Steward, J.H. (Ed.) (1965). *The people of Puerto Rico: A study in social anthropology.* Urbana: University of Illinois.

Stycos, J.M. (1955). *Family and fertility in Puerto Rico: A study of the lower income group.* New York: Columbia University.

U.S. Bureau of the Census (1985). *Persons of Spanish origin in the United States: March 1985* (Advance Report). Washington, DC: U.S. Government Printing Office.

U.S. Commission on Civil Rights (1976). *Puerto Ricans in the continental United States: An uncertain future.* Washington, DC: Author.

Vázquez-Nuttall, E. & Romero-García, I. (1989). From home to school: Puerto Rican girls learn to be students in the United States. In C.T. García-Coll & M.L. Mattei (Eds.), *The psychosocial development of Puerto Rican women* (pp. 61–83). New York: Praeger.

Wagenheim, K. (1970). *Puerto Rico: A profile.* New York: Praeger.

Wagenheim, K. (1975). Puerto Rico: A profile. In F. Cordasco & E. Buccioni (Eds.), *The Puerto Rican experience: A sociological sourcebook* (pp. 91–113). Totowa, NJ: Littlefield, Adams.

Wagenheim, K., & Jiménez de Wagenheim, O. (1988). *The Puerto Ricans: A documentary history.* Maplewood, NJ: Waterfront Press.

PART II

Language and Culture

CHAPTER 3

The Enriched Language of Puerto Rican Children

Alba N. Ambert

Introduction

Language is a source of pride and delight as children gradually master the complexities of communication and progress from simple to more differentiated grammatical forms. The language acquisition process is a natural and effortless occurrence in all normal children. Yet a major concern of educators working with Puerto Rican populations in the United States is the native language proficiency of these children. It is an important educational concern because research on bilingualism (Cummins, 1981, 1986; Hakuta, 1986; McLaughlin, 1985) indicates that the level of native language proficiency has a definite impact on the acquisition of English as a second language: Children who have a good foundation in the native language acquire English more effectively than children with a weak native-language base.

Native language development not only impacts the acquisition of a second language, but is also related to cognitive skills (Rice & Kemper, 1984) and reading ability (Rodríguez, 1988). Thus, assertions that Puerto Rican children living in the United States initiate formal schooling with serious delays in linguistic development (Maldonado-Guzmán, in press) are a matter of great concern. Limited vocabulary, inability to use appropriate syntactical structures, language mixing, and other linguistic inadequacies are cited as major problems among Puerto

Rican school children. These unsubstantiated claims about language confusion and language deficiencies have proliferated to the point where many Puerto Rican children are referred to speech and language therapy or placed in programs for the language disordered due to perceived difficulties in their linguistic development (Ambert & Meléndez, 1985; Ambert, 1988). In many cases, consideration is not given to factors involved in acquiring language in bilingual settings.

Formation of bilingualism is a dialectical process which involves a lag-lead phenomenon. Children exhibit fluctuations in linguistic skills in the two languages. Often there occurs a period of confusion in which the child appears not to have command of either language. Finally, a resolution occurs in which the two languages are firmly established and the child can function effectively in both. The effectiveness of the process depends not only on the child's native language proficiency when entering school, but also on the quality of educational programs designed to accomplish the goal of bilingualism. Once in school, language minority children may exhibit difficulties at any stage of the process, difficulties which are attributed, often incorrectly, to deficits in native language ability.

In the present study the author has attempted to determine whether the native language skills of Spanish-speaking Puerto Rican children living in the United States were appropriate to their age upon entering Kindergarten and whether there was any evidence to sustain the language deficiency theories still proposed by some bilingual and monolingual educators.

Review of Previous Studies

Attempts have been made to document the stages of linguistic development of Spanish-speaking children. Montes-Giraldo (1971) studied the language development of his four children from birth to 51 months in Colombia. He analyzed their phonological development and followed the chronological emergence of linguistic categories. González (1970) performed a cross-sectional study on the acquisition of syntactic features and specific grammatical structures in three Spanish-speaking Chicano children, between the ages of two and five years, living in Texas. Gili-Gaya (1974) studied 50 Puerto Rican children between the ages of four and seven years to analyze the manner in which they used language as a communication tool and the syntactic structures they used in expressive language. Brisk (1972) identified deviant forms of syntax present in seven five-year-old Spanish-speaking children from New Mexico. In another study, Brisk (1976) analyzed the acquisition of Spanish gender in Spanish-speaking children in Boston and Argentina. Beléndez (1980) conducted a longitudinal study of four Puerto Rican boys living in Boston for a period ranging from three to 20 months to analyze the pattern of acquisition of the Spanish verb system. Tolbert (1978) looked into the acquisition of 12 grammatical morphemes in three Spanish-speaking children from Guatemala. Using Berko-type tests, Kernan and Blount (1966) examined the acquisition of grammatical rules in Mexican children between the ages of 5 and 12 years.

Recent ethnographic studies of children's communicative competence (Volk, in press) show that by the time they start school, Spanish-speaking children living in the United States have acquired important linguistic abilities such as turn allocation (taking turns in conversations) and using speech creatively to elicit responses from peers. Other investigators (Zentella, in press) have focused on the individual differences in linguistic competence of children who are growing up bilingual.

All these studies are helpful in understanding the acquisition of Spanish by native speakers and the impact of bilingualism on children's dual language development. It is also pertinent to investigate the language development of Spanish-speaking Puerto Rican children living in a bilingual setting, taking into account both the structural components of their linguistic production and their general communicative competence. Of particular interest were the linguistic abilities of Puerto Rican children when entering Kindergarten.

Psycholinguistic studies have evolved from structural analyses of grammatical forms towards descriptions of pragmatic abilities in language usage. However, in the everyday situations of school settings, educators and other school personnel continue to rely on children's grammatical productions in evaluation of linguistic competence. Moreover, commonly used tests administered to determine placement in special programs assess structural linguistic abilities (Alvarez, 1988). For these reasons, a description of the grammar of normally developing Spanish-speaking Puerto Rican children living in bilingual settings was considered important in the present investigation, if only to dispel the notions of ungrammatical speech patterns in the population represented in the study and to clarify the characteristics of the children's language.

Method

Purpose

The purpose of this investigation was to analyze the native language development of mainland Puerto Rican Spanish-speaking children upon entering Kindergarten.

Participants

Participants were 30 Spanish-speaking Puerto Rican children of limited English proficiency. The children were five years old and attended bilingual Kindergartens in the public schools of Hartford, Connecticut, a city of about 140,000 inhabitants. As determined by the school district's language assessment in both English and Spanish, the children were Spanish-dominant. Home language surveys indicated that the primary language of their homes was Spanish. The children were developing normally, according to teacher reports. All children qualified for free lunches and lived in low-income sections of the city.

Procedure

Spanish language samples were collected on participants' spontaneous speech production following Bloom and Lahey's language elicitation techniques (1978) in which the assessor designs a situation that the child will be willing to respond to by the presentation of specific stimuli. At least one hundred different utterances were collected for each child, using a picture story book and a set of ten pictures to elicit language. Language samples were tape recorded, transcribed, and analyzed.

Data Analysis

Analysis of each participant's linguistic performance compared both structural and pragmatic components. Structural analyses included looking into phonology (sound system); morphology (vocabulary use and development); syntax (mastery of grammatical structures and word order); and semantics (word meanings). Pragmatic analysis included an examination of meaningful verbal and nonverbal interactions, popularly referred to as communicative competence.

In analyzing the language samples, the developmental stages of Spanish language acquisition were considered. Specifically used for this purpose was Gili-Gaya's (1974) analysis of the language development of fifty Puerto Rican children between the ages of four and seven, living in a monolingual Spanish language setting in Puerto Rico. While it deals with island Puerto Ricans, it is the only available study of its kind.

Results and Discussion

Results of the study indicated that the five-year-old Puerto Rican Spanish-speaking children studied were developing language normally. An in-depth analysis of the children's linguistic and communicative competence indicated that when the children entered Kindergarten, they had a good foundation in the Spanish language. They had developed syntactic and grammatical structures consistent with their age, and they had also developed conversational skills that demonstrated their communicative competence in verbal interactions. English language influence was insignificant in the language of the children in this study. The "errors" found in the children's language were developmental in nature and to be expected of children at this stage of language development.

Furthermore, a comparison of the language development of this group of children with the Spanish-speaking language-disordered children studied by Ambert (1986), revealed that the language development of the two groups is substantially different. The language of the children participating in the present study presents none of the linguistic difficulties of the disordered group. For example, the language disordered group revealed problems in usage of gender; verb tenses; inability to understand and respond to who, what, where, when questions; and many other linguistic difficulties which do not exist in the present group of children.

The following are the grammatical structures and pragmatic competencies the children had acquired. Children's renditions are given first in Spanish, followed by a translation in English. Because of the syntactical differences between Spanish and English, the translations are as accurate as possible, though not always exact.

Syntactic Features

The linguistic features analyzed include gender, articles, pronouns, verbs, adverbs, adjectives, prepositions and conjunctions, possessives, negatives, and diminutives. According to Gili-Gaya (1974), by the age of five, children have consolidated the knowledge of these syntactic features.

Gender

Gender is learned through the association of each noun with the article, adjective, and pronoun which agrees with it; the idea of this permanent association is tied in with the meaning of the noun. Children use gender without any problem, prior to their developing a clear concept of the sexes (Gili-Gaya, 1974). This is confirmed in the present study in which all children used gender easily. In instances where noun endings did not agree with the gender, most children still made no errors. Some examples follow:

yo tengo hermanos que son nenes, no son nenas	I have brothers who are boys (they) are not girls
ellos andan solos	they walk alone
los trastes	the dishes
un traje	a dress
la nariz	the nose
una flor	a flower
la mano	the hand
un reloj	a watch

Some exceptions occurred, though. In the case of *el agua* (the water), 4 (13%) of the children said *la agua/el agua*. Furthermore, 3 (10%) used the neutral *lo* instead of the masculine *el*:

lo plato	the plate
lo cuchillo	the knife
lo viento	the wind

Both the use of *la agua* and *lo/el* are common at this stage of language development in Spanish.

When English nouns were used, 29 (97%) of the children used the correct Spanish gender marker:

un coat	a coat
muchos posters	many posters
un building nuevo	a new building

Only one child used *un* shovel, instead of *una* shovel (a shovel).

Articles, Demonstratives, and Pronouns

Use of definite and indefinite articles. All children used definite and indefinite articles *la, el, lo, los, las, un, una, unas, unos.* In the examples given below, it can be noted that the children showed mastery of both masculine/feminine concordance as well as singular/plural concordance.

le doy la leche al nene	I give the milk to the boy
a mí me gustan los conejitos	I like the bunnies
hay un lago que es de pescar	there is a lake that's to fish

Use of demonstrative pronouns. The demonstratives *éste, ésta, éstos, éstas, ésa, ése, éso* were used by all children.

éso es de papá	that is daddy's
amarillo como ése	yellow like that one

Personal, possessive, relative, and indefinite pronouns. The use of personal, possessive, relative, and indefinite pronouns was well established in all of the children's everyday repertoire.

yo tenía una guagüita y mamá me la botó porque hacía mucho alboroto	I had a little bus and my mother threw it away because it made a lot of noise
más grande que ésa	bigger than that one
si a mí me tiran algo, yo le tiro algo pa' 'tras	if some one throws something at me, I'll throw something back

Adverbs

A variety of adverbs denoting time, place, mode, quantity, order, affirmation, negation, and doubt were used by 28 (93%) of the children.

debajo de la mesa	under the table
yo me voy a quedar allá	I am going to stay there
hoy, antier dejó una trastera	today, the day before yesterday, she left a lot of dishes
dan vueltas así pa' arriba y pa' bajo	they go around like this up and down
mi mamá ningunas veces hace compra	my mother never shops
antes yo veía novelas, pero no veo más na'	before, I used to watch soap operas, but I don't watch any more
hay otro columpio que es por la primera y yo segunda	there's another swing that's for the first and I'm second
mi mamá también sabe nadar	my mother also knows how to swim
había un caballito y ahora no está	there was a little horse and now it isn't there
parece que lo mandaron pa' allá	it seems they sent him there

Adjectives

Adjectives were used by 28 (93%) of the children sampled. Some adjectives were used frequently by the children, while others were used only rarely and by a few of the participants. Commonly used adjectives were:

feo	ugly
lindo	pretty
chiquito	small
grande	big
alegre/feliz	happy
sucio	dirty
muchos	many
prieto	black

Color adjectives (black, brown, white, red, violet, blue) predominated, along with the specific adjectives (big, small, happy, ugly, and pretty). Rarely used adjectives were:

congelá'	frozen
jincho	pale
hincha'o	swollen
largo	long

Verbs

All sample children could construct sentences using the copulas *ser* and *estar* (to be).

me gusta ser maestra	I like to be a teacher
me gusta el conejo que es grande	I like the rabbit that is big
cuando yo sea grande	when I am big (grown up)
ella va a ser lo mismo que yo voy a ser	she will be the same that I will be
él está en el salón	he is in the classroom
el hombre y la dama están ahí	the man and the lady are there
ella estaba en el medio	she was in the middle

Reflexive verbs. The reflexive *se* is used with assurance by all the children.

se levantó del agua y se enfogonó	he got out of the water and got mad
la nena se arrodilló pa' meter los juguetes porque va a cerrar la caja	the girl knelt to put the toys in because she is going to close the box
un carro que se convierte en Maseen Joe	a car that becomes Maseen (?) Joe

Present indicative. The present indicative was used by all participants.

mi papá juega pelota	my father plays ball
a mí me gusta la comida	I like food
mi mamá me compra soda	my mother buys me soda
yo toco la pandereta	I play the tambourine

Imperfect tense. The imperfect was used by 26 (86.7%) of participants with assurance and with the frequency normal in the language.

la quería mucho	I loved her very much
cuando yo era bien	when I was very small
chiquitita mi mamá me	my mother would
llevaba a la playa pa'	take me to the beach
jugar con mis juguetes	to play with my toys
él siempre se metía en	he would always get
el agua	in the water

Preterit. The preterit was used by 28 (93%) of the children and appears to be firmly consolidated. It was the most frequently used verb form after the present indicative and present progressive tenses.

la recogió	she picked her up
yo cumplí años	I had a birthday
me tiró un huevo en la	he threw an egg at my
cara	face

Use of the present tense for the future. Use of the present tense for the future occurred in 26 (86.7%) of the children.

no voy	I'm not going
vamos al lago	we're going to the lake
el nene va a la tierra	the boy is going to the ground
yo no sé lo que le van a tirar en la cara	I don't know what they're going to throw in his face
yo me voy a quedar allá	I'm going to stay there

Subjunctive tense. The subjunctive was used by 25 (83%) of the children.

cuando yo vengo pa' acá	when I come here I see
veo los columpios y no	the swings and I
me canso	don't get tired
cuando yo tenga un perro	when I have a dog
parece que lo mandaron	it seems that they sent
pa' allá	him there

The gerund. The gerund was used by 24 (80%) of the children.

hay un nene sembrando banderas	there's a boy planting flags
una nena tirándose en la chorrera	a girl going down the slide

The present progressive (use of the auxiliary estar + verb). The present progressive or use of the auxiliary *estar* + verb is used by 29 (96.6%) of the children sampled.

el nene la está cogiendo	the boy is taking it
está dándole vueltas a los palos	he's going round the trees

Use of verb haber. Impersonal sentences with *haber* were used by 22 (73%) of the children.

se había ido	she had left
había un caballito y ahora no está	there was a little horse and now it isn't there

Prepositions and Conjunctions

Prepositions. The prepositions *a, con, de, en, para, sin,* and *por* were used by all children and seemed consolidated in the children's language usage.

una nena sin zapatos	a girl without shoes
yo escribo las paredes con una tiza	I write on the walls with a chalk
en el parque de piedra	in the stone park

Conjunctions. All children used conjunctions easily. The copulative *y* (and) usage is used profusely and *pero* (but) also appears very frequently. *Que* (that) is abundant and consolidated in the language. *Ni* (neither), *porque* (because), *pues* (then, since), *mas* (but), and *si* (if) are other conjunctions used.

cuando fui pa' un lago	when I went to a lake
lejos vi un tiburón	far away I saw a
que tiene alas por	shark that had
detrás	wings on its back
entonces a ella la llevaron	then they took her to
al 'pital y se golpeó	the hospital and she
aquí	got hurt here
no voy si tengo dolor de	I won't go if I have a
estómago	stomach-ache
a mí no me gusta Michael	I don't like Michael
Jackson, pero me	Jackson, but I like
gusta el coat	the coat
mi mamá me va a comprar	my mother is going to
una bicicleta pero no	buy me a bicycle but
va a ser de éstas	it will not be like
	this one
porque mi papá no tiene	because my father has
chavos	no money

Possessives, Negatives, and Diminutives

Possessives. The possessive was firmly established in all the children's language.

un hermano mío	a brother of mine
mi chinita	my little Chinese (doll)
del nene	the boy's
se metió en la finca	he went into a bull's
de un toro	farm

Negatives. Negatives are also well established and are used appropriately by all participants.

no quiere	he doesn't want to
me gusta el conejo que	I like the rabbit that's
no es grande	not big.

Diminutives. Diminutives are often used by native speakers of Spanish. All the Kindergarten children have incorporated this into their daily use. Some examples follow:

mi primito se llama Allen	my little cousin's name is Allen

una brujita chiquitita   a little witch
el perrito   the little dog

Errors

The "errors" present in the children's language were all developmental in nature and not indicative of language problems. Children at this stage of linguistic development tend to overgeneralize the rules of the grammar. The following are the overgeneralizations made by participants. They constitute normal linguistic constructions at this stage of language development.

Verb tenses. Overgeneralizations are common in the construction of verb tenses.

vinió/vino	comed/came
juegando/jugando	playeding/playing
ponió/puso	putted/put
ponieron/pusieron	they putted/they put

Phonology. At the age of five children often have difficulties with specific consonant blends and with multisyllabic words. Examples of phonological "errors" which are developmental in nature, follow:

tigere/tigre	tiger
sinera/sirena	mermaid
alimales/animales	animals
ilesia/iglesia	church
le timaron el ojo/	they hurt his eye
le lastimaron el ojo	

Semantics

The children had established word meanings. They used appropriate labels for common objects, actions, and persons. They used circumlocution when they did not know a verbal label.

la casa del pichón (jaula)	the bird's house (cage)
una máquina pa' meter el papel (maquinilla)	a machine to put the paper in (typewriter)
la casa del carro (garage)	the car's house (garage)
éso es pa' hacer casitas, lo que tú quieras hacer (bloques)	this is to make little houses, whatever you want to make (blocks)

Two of the children occasionally used *un deso* and *la deso* (a thing, the thing) when unable to produce the name of an object. When the appropriate labels were supplied, though, they used them with assurance. The difficulties observed, then, were not semantic in nature; that is, the children had no difficulty acquiring meaning or relating a verbal label to an object, action, or person. The difficulty in this respect was due to lack of exposure to the words.

Pragmatics

Participants showed strong communicative competence skills. They were able to engage in socially appropriate conversations easily. The children were not only able to tell stories, respond to questions with ease, and take conversational turns with the investigator, but they were also eager to narrate personal experiences and provide spontaneous details about events in their lives and the people that surrounded them. They were able to make inferences, request information from the investigator, and engage in discussions of future events. The following are some examples of the conversational dimensions of the children's communicative competence:

Requesting Information:

Girl:
¿El sábado tenemos clase?   Do we have class on Saturday?

Ambert:
No.

Girl:

Pues el sábado nos vamos pa' Puerto Rico con mi abuela.	Then on Saturday we're going to Puerto Rico with my grandmother.

Drawing Inferences:

Ambert:

¿Qué ves aquí?	What do you see here?

Boy:

Un bombero	A fireman

Ambert:

Muy bien. ¿Qué hacen los bomberos?	Very good. What do firemen do?

Boy:

Queman casas.	Burn houses down.

Answering Questions Appropriately:

Ambert:

¿A qué iglesia vas?	What Church do you go to?

(in a conversation about Sunday activities)

Girl:

A la ilesia de Dios Incoporada	To the Church of God Incorporated.

Logical Responses to Questions:

Ambert:

¿Cuándo salgas de la escuela que vas a hacer?	What will you do when you leave school?

Girl:

Voy a pasar de grado.	I'll be promoted.

Making Comparisons:

brinqué pa' arriba como la sinera (sirena)	I jumped up like a mermaid.

Explanations:

no me puedo doblar porque mi mamá me pone pantalones apretao y por eso no me puedo mover	I can't bend down because my mother puts tight pants on me and that's why I can't move.

Differentiation between Spanish and English:

Ella se llama Estrella y en inglés se dice star	Her name is Estrella and in English it's called star
Mi papá iba a ir un día pero no pudo porque el carro lo dejó botao en el highway, en la calle, y se fue pa' la casa y no salió más	My father was going one day but he couldn't because the car broke down in the highway and he went home and didn't go out again

English Language Influence

Contrary to popular notions, the native language of the mainland Puerto Rican children studied was well established. English language influence on the children's Spanish was scarce and most English usage limited to the use of nouns, but with Spanish syntax. No English syntactical influence could be discerned in the children's language. Although 21 (70%) of the children used English, 12 (40%) used only one English word, 5 (17%) used only two English words, and 4 (13%) used three or more words. Of all participants, 9 (30%) used no English words. That is, 26 (87%) of the children used fewer than two English words. Some of these, such as *cachear* (to catch) and *posters*, are commonly used by adult Spanish-speakers. Some other examples follow:

un coat de Michael Jackson	Michael Jackson's coat
tiene muchos zippers	it has many zippers
se metió en el mud	he got into the mud
en una cage	in a cage
en ese circle	in that circle
una cookie	a cookie

To catch was the only English verb used, in different forms:

cacharlo	to catch it
cachó	caught
cachando	catching

Suggestions for Parents and School Personnel

The following general techniques can be followed by teachers and parents to stimulate the enriched language of Puerto Rican Spanish-speaking children:

1. *You are children's linguistic models.* Remember you are children's linguistic models. Bombard them with language which is descriptive and expresses complete thoughts. When performing daily activities, talk about what you do, describing objects, events, people; making comparisons and associations.

2. *Encourage children's verbalization.* Ask children questions about their thoughts and the persons and events in their lives. What, where, how, who, why questions should be asked frequently to encourage children to talk about what they think and do.

3. *Limitations in vocabulary do not represent language deficiencies.* A paucity of vocabulary in a child simply indicates that a child has not been exposed to specific words. If a child has never heard a word, or has only heard it out of context, he or she will either not acquire it or not learn to use it appropriately. Also, a Spanish-speaking child growing up in a bilingual setting may be exposed to a word in English, usually a school-related term, but not to its Spanish equivalent. Make sure that children are exposed to words before they are expected to

use them. For example, in the present study the author found that most children did not know the word for bird cage (jaula), yet when the label was supplied, they used it immediately.

4. *Use a variety of adjectives in your conversations with children.* The children in this study tended to use adjectives sparingly compared to the children in Montes-Giraldo's study, who were the upper-class children of a linguist and were probably exposed to greater linguistic variety. Words like *bello* or *precioso* (beautiful) can be used instead of the common *bonito* and *lindo*. This researcher observed that one of the children in the study used the word *enfogonao* (angry) repeatedly. In a conversation about an angry boy, the author used the word *furioso* (furious). The child caught the word immediately and used it several times thereafter with obvious enjoyment.

5. *Be aware of the children's language community.* Puerto Rican Spanish-speaking children will use a variety of the Spanish language consistent with the language usage of their community. Linguistic differences that are dialectically motivated do not represent deviations. Acceptance of a child's linguistic variety is important. They should not be penalized for using the language to which they are exposed. For example, Puerto Ricans aspire the *s* after some vowels and at the end of words (*ehcuela* instead of *escuela* and *casah* instead of *casas*). They also tend to convert medial r's to l's (*puelco* instead of *puerco*). This does not mean that a speech impediment exists or that there is a problem with plural formation.

6. *Corrections do little to stimulate language.* Corrections may hinder a child's natural eagerness to communicate. "Errors" are part of the process by which children acquire language. Children experiment with the language, often overgeneralizing the rules of the grammar, until their language approximates adult linguistic patterns. For example, it is common for five-year old children to produce words like *juegar* instead of *jugar* (play). This is a crucial process in learning language and the more exposure the children receive to the accepted forms, the more quickly and easily they will acquire them. Purposeful exposure to appropriate linguistic forms is more

constructive than corrections and allows children to internalize the rules of the language. Furthermore, it should be taken into account that when children enter school they are still in the process of developing the native language. We should expect, then, that certain grammatical structures and conversational conventions may be in the process of acquisition.

7. *Be mindful of development stages.* Developmental stages in language acquisition must be taken into account when assessing (formally or informally) children's language. It is common for five-year-old children to overgeneralize the formation of verb tenses (e.g. *pusió/puso*, that is, putted/put) or to be unable to blend the p and l sounds (pato/plato in the Spanish word for plate) or the blend of *g* and *l* sounds (*ilesia/iglesia*, the word for church). None of these renditions reflect speech or language deviancy at this stage of language development. Again, with exposure to language and the full development of their speech musculature, most children will be able to produce an appropriate phonology and language forms.

8. *Language is mainly communication.* The purpose of language is communication. Thus, conversations are to be encouraged in the classroom and at home. Elicit as much language usage as possible. Do not dominate the conversation. While it has many virtues, silence is not conducive to maximum language development.

Summary

The purpose of the present study was to describe the linguistic abilities of normally developing Spanish-speaking Puerto Rican children who are living in the United States. An analysis of the children's linguistic structures and communicative competence indicated that when the children entered Kindergarten, they had a good foundation in the Spanish language. They had developed syntactic and grammatical structures consistent with their age, and they had developed conversational skills that demonstrated their communicative competence in verbal interaction. English language influence was insignificant in the language of the children of this study. In fact, the language skills of this group of children were very similar to the Puerto Rican children studied by Gili-Gaya (1975) who were acquiring language in a monolingual Spanish-speaking setting. In addition, a comparison with the Spanish-speaking language disordered population studied by Ambert (1986) reveals that in no way is the language of the children in the present study comparable to children with true language disorders. Furthermore, the only two areas of concern identified in this study—namely limitations in vocabulary development, such as adjective usage, and the use of English terms when the Spanish terms have not been acquired—are easily remedied in a bilingual classroom with a strong language stimulation component. Suggestions were offered to this effect.

REFERENCES

Alvarez, M.D. (1988). Psychoeducational assessment of bilingual students: Current trends and major issues. In A.N. Ambert (Ed.), *Bilingual education and English as a second language: A research handbook, 1986–87* (pp. 297–332). New York: Garland.

Ambert, A.N. (1986). Identifying language disorders in Spanish-speakers. *Journal of Reading, Writing, and Learning Disabilities International,* 2(1), 21–41.

Ambert, A.N. (Ed.) (1988). *Bilingual education and English as a second language: A research handbook, 1986–87.* New York: Garland.

Ambert, A.N., & Meléndez, S.E. (1985). *Bilingual education: A sourcebook.* New York: Garland.

Beléndez, P. (1980). Repetitions and the acquisition of the Spanish verb system. Unpublished doctoral dissertation, Harvard University Graduate School of Education.

Bloom, L., & Lahey, M. (1978). *Language development and language disorders.* New York: Wiley.

Brisk, M. E. (1972). The Spanish syntax of the pre-school Spanish American: The case of New Mexican five-year-old children. Unpublished doctoral dissertation, University of New Mexico.

Brisk, M.E. (1976). The acquisition of Spanish gender by first grade Spanish-speaking children. In G.D. Keller, R.V. Teschner, & S. Viera (Eds.), *Bilingualism in the bicentennial and beyond* (pp. 143–160). New York: Bilingual Press.

Cummins, J. (1981). Empirical and theoretical underpinnings of bilingual education. *Journal of Education, 163*, 16–49.

Cummins, J. (1986). Empowering minority students: A framework for intervention. *Harvard Educational Review, 56*, 18–36.

Gili-Gaya, S. (1974). *Estudios de lenguaje infantil.* Barcelona: Vox Bibliograf.

González, G. (1970). The acquisition of Spanish grammar by native Spanish-speakers. Unpublished doctoral dissertation, The University of Texas, Austin.

Hakuta, K. (1986). *Mirror of language: The debate on bilingualism.* New York: Basic Books.

Kernan, K., & Blount, B.G. (1966). The acquisition of Spanish grammar by Mexican children. *Anthropological Linguistics, 8*, 1–14.

Maldonado-Guzmán, A.A. (in press). Theoretical and methodological issues in the ethnographic study of teachers' differential treatment of children in bilingual bicultural classrooms. In M. Saravia-Shore & S. Arvizu (Eds.), *Ethnographics of communication in multi-ethnic classrooms.* New York: Garland.

McLaughlin, B. (1985). *Second-language acquisition in childhood: Volume 2: School-age children.* Hillsdale, NJ: Lawrence Erlbaum.

Montes-Giraldo, J.J. (1971). Acerca de la apropiación por el niño del sistema fonológico español. *Thesaurus, XXVI*(3), 322–346.

Rice, M.L., & Kemper, S. (1984). *Child language and cognition.* Austin, TX: Pro-Ed.

Rodríguez, A. (1988). Research in reading and writing in bilingual education and English as a second language. In A.N. Ambert (Ed.), *Bilingual education and English as a second language: A research handbook, 1986–1987* (pp. 61–117). New York: Garland.

Tolbert, K. (1978). The acquisition of grammatical morphemes: A cross-linguistic study with reference to Mayan and Spanish. Unpublished doctoral dissertation, Harvard University.

Volk, D. (in press). Communicative competence in a bilingual early childhood classroom. In M. Saravia-Shore & S. Arvizu (Eds.), *Ethnographics of communication in multi-ethnic classrooms.* New York: Garland.

Zentella, A.C. (in press). Individual differences in growing up bilingual. In M. Saravia-Shore & S. Arvizu (Eds.), *Ethnographics of communication in multi-ethnic classrooms.* New York: Garland.

CHAPTER 4

The Verbal Folklore of Puerto Rican Children: Implications for Promoting School Achievement

Kathryn Hill

Introduction

The task of young people everywhere is to mature, adjust, and eventually learn to function as adults. Puerto Rican children on the mainland face a particularly formidable challenge: they are not presented with a consistent and uniform mold in which to fit. Their charge is to find their place in a world where home, school, heritage, and language itself are distinct and often conflicting spheres of operation. However, as with most extraordinary challenges, the potential for reward is also of an expanded dimension. The mainland Puerto Rican child who delights in his or her own skillful adaptation to more than one language and culture is gaining an awareness, a way of thinking, a knowledge base, and a world view which are more precious than anything else schools can hope to impart to students.

Our mainland schools must enhance this process of growth and adjustment as much as possible while helping the child avoid the pitfalls inherent whenever one is learning to remain oneself yet someone else too. To explain the role of verbal folklore in meeting this challenge for educators, the author wishes to relate her experiences as an English as a Second Language (ESL) teacher in the New Haven Public Schools in Connecticut. This is done not out of unscholarly digression, but in recognition of the fact that

65

experience can provide some of the best inspirational germs for ensuing research.

Many of the games played in the author's ESL classes required the selection of which child would go first when a game began. The author automatically harkened back to her own childhood and recited "Eenie meenie minie mo" or "One potato, two potato" while pointing in turn to each student. They would squeal with glee and often began to tell their own similar rhymes (called counting-out rhymes), such as "Tin marín de los tingüé." Their response to such nonsense was surprising. With some thought, the reasons for their enthusiasm became clear. One simple activity had conveyed several important lessons.

First, English can be just as silly as Spanish. It is not reserved only for serious academic work or for transactions with the bank and the gas company. English is also used by children to play and to have fun, for purposes similar to those Puerto Rican children fulfill at times when they speak Spanish. Second, if the teacher is pleased and amused by what the child relates in Spanish, and even writes it down, the child's own language is validated, as well as the process by which the child has acquired that language. The child feels good because his/her way of learning to say things at home and with friends and relatives receives recognition in school. The child has demonstrated a kind of knowledge which is not to be viewed as a deterrent to the more important task of learning English; rather, it is valuable knowledge for appreciation on its own merits and for comparison to the kinds of things the child is learning to say in English.

The role of verbal folklore in the classroom is one of making connections for the Puerto Rican child attending school on the mainland. The elements in the child's life which must be connected are many and varied. They include the child's Puerto Rican heritage, whether or not the child ever lived on the island, and the mainland culture; Spanish and English and the relationship of the spoken to the written word for each; the worlds of home and school; and friends from the native culture and friends outside of it.

The present study is aimed at bringing verbal folklore into the classroom as a legitimate tool for linking the described areas in the lives of Puerto Rican schoolchildren on the mainland. There are few investigations on this topic, partly because it deals with informal language, transmitted primarily through casual interactions. However, "casual" need not mean insignificant. It is time for schools to capitalize on this rich resource which children bring to school.

This chapter explains what verbal folklore is and how it might be used in the classroom. The chapter summarizes the method of data collection and the major findings of a study conducted with 40 bilingual children in the public schools of New Haven. Particular attention is paid to categories or types of Children's Verbal Folklore (CVF); its processes of transmission; the roles of males and females, family, and friends in the operation of CVF; and ways in which CVF in Spanish and English reflect Puerto Rican and mainland U.S. culture. One section offers suggestions for bringing CVF into the classroom, where CVF can be used to enhance students' self-esteem, social development, and biliteracy. Throughout, examples of folkloric material are presented. Its poetic nature and humor will do more to encourage teachers to use CVF than will any amount of rational argument.

Before continuing, an explanation of the chapter's title is in order. The use of the phrase "School Achievement" does not imply that the ultimate goals for children are to do well in schools and to adjust at any cost, to schools' requirements. Rather, school achievement is seen as symbolic of the child's self-respect and acquisition of knowledge which enable the child to, first, meet success by internal and external standards and, second, attain "life achievement" when the child becomes a productive adult taking pleasure in everyday living. Thus, the real school achievement will take place when schools successfully adapt to the children they serve, not vice versa. One step in this adaptation is to draw upon—rather than ignore—the rich informal language base children bring to school.

What is Children's
Verbal Folklore?

Children's Verbal Folklore (CVF) is the body of poems, sayings, chants, rhymes, and jingles traditionally associated with children, and invoked by children or adults with children, in response to situational purposes. One such purpose might be using a counting-out rhyme when a group of children needs to decide which one will go first in a game. Other purposes might include recitations while jumping rope, or retorts, like "Sticks and stones may break my bones but names can never hurt me" and "A ruin gabazo poco caso" (To worthless garbage, pay little attention.)

One reason why this language-oriented knowledge has been relatively ignored, in any language, is that it is part of children's own culture, and flourishes with little adult intervention. At least one writer (Goodman, 1979) has lamented that anthropologists, in their extensive observation and documentation of childhood, have rarely used a child's-eye view of children's own culture, of which CVF is an important part.

Another reason for the dearth of CVF research is that naturalistic observation, the ideal method of study, has several drawbacks. First of all, an adult observer would be an intruder upon the child/child or intimate adult/child interactions in which CVF items are typically employed. Secondly, this method of data collection requires much time and patience, as the researcher waits for the folkloric item to occur.

Review of Past CVF Studies

Time constraints did not prevent Iona and Peter Opie from studying British children's folklore by observing the children in school playgrounds. The outcome was the pioneering book *The Lore and Language of Schoolchildren* (Opie & Opie, 1959). In it they proposed several distinctions among rhymes in CVF. One of these distinctions consists of rhymes that are passed along and approved by adults, as opposed to rhymes that are transmitted from child to child. Bauman (1982) also contrasted what he calls nursery lore with peer-group lore.

Researchers have distinguished between both types of rhymes and recognize the importance of parents and peers in shaping a child's language (Bauman, 1982; Hill, 1986; Hockett, 1950; Read, 1975; Ventriglia, 1982). In *The Lore and Language of Schoolchildren*, the Opies also analyzed the opposing forces guiding rhymes that regulate children's games or relationships versus rhymes that express exuberance and playfulness, and rhymes that respect tradition versus rhymes that show the conflicting desire for change and fun.

Some works have collected and discussed the verbal folklore of children in the United States (Knapp & Knapp, 1976; Larrick, 1972; Withers, 1946a, 1946b; Wood, 1940, 1952). The Children's Folklore Section of the American Folklore Society publishes a review to document research on children's folklore around the world (Sullivan, 1978-1990). By contrast, there is little research on CVF in Spanish or English for Puerto Ricans on the U.S. mainland. One anthology from Puerto Rico (Pastor, 1960) cites examples of children's folk rhymes in Spanish; another anthology of Puerto Rican folklore (Palma, 1981) contains a section on CVF in Spanish. Two record albums were also noted. One has examples of Puerto Rican and U.S. mainland CVF in Spanish and English (Hill, 1979), but deals only with counting-out rhymes. The other (Pacheco, n.d.), includes a variety of songs traditionally known to Puerto Rican children on the island. These sources record Puerto Rican children's verbal folklore, but make no attempt to analyze the dynamic elements of CVF. The lack of relevant studies and the limited resources for Puerto Rican students on the mainland is common knowledge among educators who teach these children.

The New Haven Study

Method

Due to the problems inherent in naturalistic observation, the author used structured interviews to elicit CVF. Structural interviewing calls for familiarity with the repertoire and a range of background knowledge about the subject of discussion (Bauman, 1982; Spradley, 1982). Also, printed material may be authentically folkloric, but should be verified by an informant as being part of an oral tradition (Utley, 1965).

The author, who is fluent in Spanish and English, had acquired knowledge of CVF through her contact with Puerto Rican students in the New Haven Public Schools. For several years she collected folklore and related information in the course of day-to-day interactions. In preparation for the present study, she spent many hours, under a variety of circumstances, conferring on the subject with adult Puerto Ricans living in Connecticut. She collected new CVF items and categories.

From observations and informal interviews, as well as the author's knowledge and research on U.S. folklore in English, she compiled several hundred CVF items, in Spanish and English, with which Puerto Rican children in New Haven might be familiar. She developed a framework of CVF categories in both languages. These categories include rhymes to recite the alphabet, to begin or end a story, to chant while bouncing a ball, to say to a child with hiccups, to say while touching fingers or toes, to recite on the occasion of losing a tooth, to use as a magical chant, to use while taunting someone, to say while tickling, and so forth.

Participants

Research participants were 20 third and 20 fourth graders from 8 to 11 years old. The children were of Puerto Rican background and had lived an average of 5.6 years on the mainland. Twenty-four were born in Puerto Rico, 9 in New Haven, 4 in New York City, 1 in Philadelphia,

1 in Florida. The author did not learn the birthplace of one child. Socioeconomic status is assumed to be low: all children qualified for free lunches in the schools' federally subsidized lunch programs. Participants' placement in the bilingual program meant that testing and placement procedures had found them to be dominant in Spanish and of limited English proficiency.

The two schools attended by participants represented two different types of school populations and bilingual programs common in New Haven, a city of approximately 126,000 in 1985 when this research was conducted. At that time New Haven's public school population was 56 percent African-American, 24 percent Hispanic, and 20 percent white. One school from which sample children were selected for this study had 420 students in a relatively balanced population of Puerto Ricans, African-Americans, and whites, and used a self-contained model of bilingual instruction, with one teacher responsible for instruction in both Spanish and English. The other school was much larger (703 students) and was roughly half Puerto Rican and half African-American. Its bilingual program had the pairing model of instruction in which classes alternated between two teachers responsible for either the Spanish or the English instructional component. All 20 students who comprised the third/fourth grade class of the first school described participated in the study. The 20 students at the second school were selected so that the eventual pool consisted of 10 third-grade boys, 10 third-grade girls, 10 fourth-grade boys, and 10 fourth-grade girls, for a total of 40 participants.

Procedures

Research participants met individually with the author for an informal but structured interview designed to probe the students' CVF knowledge, in Spanish and English. The interviews took place either in the back of the child's classroom or in a nearby office, as the classroom teacher wished.

Each interview began with some talk to "break the ice," in Spanish or English, as preferred by the child.

Information was recorded regarding name, age, school, grade, teacher, number of years in the bilingual program, other local schools attended, birthplace, places of residence, household composition, number of brothers and sisters and their relative ages (older or younger), and extended family in the community.

The author then guided the child through her compendium of Spanish CVF, to be followed by an exploration of CVF in English. The author's collection included those items that were, in her experience, most commonly known by Puerto Rican schoolchildren in New Haven. The author would say the first line for each rhyme or saying, and would note the child's name next to those with which the child demonstrated familiarity by saying part or all of the rhyme. The author recorded the version that the child said. The children did not see any of the printed rhymes. Interaction was aural/oral.

Categories or functions were described in such a way that children were encouraged to contribute their own items, many of which were new to the author. The author transcribed these offerings and added them to the collection of typical children's folklore for the group studied. Eventually, 1,740 instances of either familiarity with a given item or contribution of a new item were noted. Generally, Spanish was spoken when dealing with CVF in Spanish, and English when dealing with CVF in English.

All participants were asked the same questions, in the same order, from background information to CVF questions. Each interview lasted about 60 minutes. The interviews were a positive experience, emphasizing what the children knew, rather than what they did not know.

In the first two interviews, the children volunteered information on how they had learned the various CVF items they knew. Surprised by the precision of these assertions, the author asked subsequent participants (and retraced her steps with those first two girls), how they had learned the CVF items they knew.

The children's accuracy in this area was remarkable. There were many comments such as, "I heard it from José, and he learned it from a friend of his sister's." When the author later talked to José, sure enough—he said he had heard it from a friend of his sister's. There were numerous similar occurrences and never a detectable false designation of the source of the saying. If Nydia said she had learned something from Marisol, then Marisol showed that she knew the same version of the same item during her interview.

This aspect of the methodology, asking how CVF items had been learned, emerged in the beginning stages of the study itself. One principle of ethnographic research is that it can be used to explore evolving questions and hypotheses as they occur in the course of a study (Spindler, 1982). (Ethnography is a branch of anthropology based on the detailed description of different cultures.)

Data Analysis

Basic data analysis was qualitative, as befitted a study in folklore that relied on ethnographic principles and that examined cultural themes. Where appropriate, quantitative calculations were performed, such as the relative frequencies and percentages of different methods of CVF transmission.

Findings and Discussion

One of the study's research questions was: What are the processes of transmission of Children's Verbal Folklore, in Spanish and in English, among Puerto Rican schoolchildren in a mainland setting? Participants were quite specific in their designations as to how they had learned CVF items and in describing how they knew what they knew. For example, one girl knew a common nursery rhyme in English because it was printed on the curtains in a friend's bedroom. A boy had learned a magical chant in English when it was used during a magic show at a local Hawaiian restaurant.

The 40 students indicated familiarity with, or offered as new contributions, 1,740 CVF items. In order to show familiarity, participants had to say part of the rhymes. "I know that one" was not sufficient to be counted. There were only 21 instances, out of 1,740 items of folklore, of subjects saying, "I don't know" in response to the question of how a rhyme or saying was learned. Seventeen of the "don't knows" were for items in Spanish, and only 4 for items in English. This seems logical, since material in the native language was probably learned in a more natural context than material in English, the children's second language. The overall low rate of "don't know" responses is further evidence of sample children's awareness and capacity for remembering as they ascribed their sources of knowledge in this area.

How CVF is Learned

About 60% of the CVF items offered were in Spanish and 40% in English, a reasonable proportion for Spanish-dominant children in mainland schools. When looking at the transmission of CVF as a whole, without distinguishing by language, the most frequently cited ways in which CVF items were reportedly learned were mother (14%), school in the U.S. (12%), sister (12%), and female friend (12%). The frequencies and percentages are remarkably close, showing that no one method of transmission dominated. Television, especially cartoons, was responsible for 9% of the designated sources of transmission, ranking higher than books. Since CVF is mostly oral in nature, this factor is not necessarily evidence of television's having had a greater influence than books.

Several participants asserted with conviction that they had learned particular items all by themselves. Even with a rhyme recited around the world by millions, a participant would testify, "I made it up." Other collectors of children's folklore have noted this phenomenon (Henning, 1981).

An informative picture of the transmission of CVF is gained by separating the Spanish and English items and then ranking the frequencies of how participants reported they had learned CVF items. The five main ways of transmission in Spanish were mother (20%), sister (13%), female friend (11%), school in the U.S. (6%), and school in Puerto Rico (6%). In English, transmission occurred in school in the U.S. (21%), television (16%), female friend

(13%), sister (10%), and books in school (8%). The major difference was that for CVF in Spanish, people, especially family members, dominated. School and television played a greater role in the transmission of CVF in English.

For both languages, home and school were the major CVF transmitters. Other sources cited were church, a magic show, a movie, a parade, performing in a musical group, a play, private music lessons, and a sports event. These accounted only for 0.8% of the items in Spanish, and 1.8% of the items in English. These results may indicate that family, friends, school, and television play the major role in CVF transmission, rather than indicating a lack of participants' exposure to a range of activities in the community.

Language Differences in CVF Transmission

Another way to analyze the transmission of CVF is to group the data by language and by reported method of learning. Table 1 illustrates this relation. In Spanish, the order of transmission was family, friends, school and books, TV, and other. In English, the order was school and books, family, friends, TV, and other.

Table 1

How Subjects Reported that They Had Learned Items of CVF, in Spanish and in English, as Percentages of Total, by Broad Categories

Spanish				
Family	Friends	School/books	TV	Other
57%	19%	17%	4%	3%

English				
School/books	Family	Friends	TV	Other
32%	26%	22%	16%	4%

As seen in Table 1, the family played the primary role in the transmission of CVF in Spanish (57%). Family accounted for about the same percentage of items in Spanish as were learned in English through school, books, and family combined. Friends played a roughly equal role in the transmission of CVF for both languages, as "in-between" common transmitters (19% for Spanish and 22% for English). Television was responsible for transmitting a larger percentage of the items in English than in Spanish. For items in English, the family played a slightly greater role in transmission than did friends, an unexpected finding because families of students placed in bilingual programs are usually assumed to have limited command of English.

One of the main findings of this study on the processes of CVF transmission was that such documentation is possible. Sample children showed a desire to communicate how they knew what they knew; they were specific and seemingly accurate in doing so. In the transmission of CVF for both languages, the importance of the immediate and extended family, and the dominant role of females, were also key findings.

Sex Differences in CVF Transmission and Acquisition

Among participants, girls indicated familiarity with, or offered as new contributions, more CVF items than boys. This was true for material in both Spanish and English, although the amounts of CVF known by boys and girls were more similar in English.

A stronger difference in relation to sex roles was that more females than males were cited as the transmitters of CVF. For items in Spanish and English combined, 80% of the reported teachers were female and 20% were male. The dominant role of females as teachers held true for rhymes of an intimate nature, used primarily within the immediate family, as well as for rhymes thought to occur more often outside the sphere of the family.

The girls exhibited more knowledge in some but not all of the categories with which they were expected to have more familiarity than boys. They clearly knew and probably used more rhymes with a nurturant function, for example, to say with a baby or to say to a hurt or sick child. They also knew more specifically language-oriented CVF, especially how to speak secret code languages, which may be called *jerigonza* in Spanish. Another category in which the girls were dominant was the group of sayings which were openly emotional, such as, to express friendship and affection.

Boys were expected to dominate, and did, in the aggressive categories of retorts and taunts. Of the 44 CVF categories in this investigation, these were the only two in which boys were the main users and transmitters. Television also played a significant role in the transmission of aggressive material. These were the only two categories in which an adult was never mentioned as the transmitter.

Role of the Family in CVF Transmission

This study found that family members had taught more CVF items, even in English, than had friends. The strong influence of the family, both nuclear and extended, was evident even when examining categories more often thought of as material used among friends, such as handclap or jump-rope rhymes, or secret code languages. The positive aspect of this finding is the strength of the family unit for these children. The more negative side to this picture is that there may be little informal learning of English, and the related culture, by these children from other children. Some factors which may prevent free intergroup mingling are neighborhoods too dangerous for unsupervised play and racial prejudice that is fostered in the mainland culture.

The schools may also be culpable. Though bilingual programs exist for sound academic reasons, some tend to segregate students in such a way that there is little opportunity for non-native speakers of English to learn English informally from fluent peers. Bilingual programs which do segregate for most of the instruction should at least mix their students with English-dominant ones for art, music, gym, assemblies, and other activities.

Discussion

CVF as a Reflection of Culture

One of the most thought-provoking outcomes of this study was the opportunity to examine the body of folkloric material collected from Puerto Rican children on the mainland as a reflection of their culture. In her analysis, the author relied on guidelines outlined by Spradley (1982) for identifying cultural themes which are both universal and culture-specific.

A comparison of participants' CVF in Spanish and in English provided further cultural insight. Such comparative analysis can be a major strategy for generating theories which evolve from the data itself, rather than forcing the data to conform to preconceived theory (Glaser & Strauss, 1967).

The interface of culture and CVF is an area of research for which few preconceived theories are possible. There are no reliable, comprehensive, and current works describing the cultures in contact for Puerto Rican schoolchildren on the mainland. This situation is unfortunate but understandable, given the multiple issues involved and the complexity of the topic.

The Puerto Rican culture on the island is a mixture of Taino Indian, Spaniard, African, and other ethnic backgrounds. When speaking of people and their customs and values, one would have to distinguish between rural and urban people; and high, middle, and low SES. One would also take into account the enormous influence of the United States on the island.

To add to the complexity of the situation, it must be remembered that the group under study is not composed of island Puerto Ricans, but mainland Puerto Ricans, who may or may not have ever lived on the island. Those who have migrated are a self-selected group, perhaps under more stresses because of economic factors, perhaps more courageous to seek a new life, perhaps different in other ways (Figler, 1980). For Puerto Ricans on the mainland, factors such as anomie, or the breakdown of traditional social structures as they are influenced by another way of life, must be taken into account. As this complex picture emerges, it is less surprising that a definitive description of Puerto Ricans on the mainland is not available.

Overgeneralization and stereotyping should be avoided in relating CVF to culture. Dundes (1972) warned students of folklore about "folk fallacies," or invalid stereotypes. Rather than move from cultural description—likely to become stereotypes—to the folkloric items which fit in the right niches, the author preferred to let the material speak for itself. Under this approach, generalization is left to the reader, who can decide if specific items or categories of CVF "ring true" as cultural descriptors of the group studied.

To generate theory and to make cultural comparisons using the collected CVF, the author used the method of Glaser and Strauss (1967) to distill thematic categories and properties within the categories. Each folkloric item collected was coded according to the categories and properties it addressed. A category is a conceptual element of a theory; a property is one element within a category. For example, one thematic category in analyzing the CVF collected was "attitude towards formal schooling." Within that category, one property in the Puerto Rican children's folk rhymes was "respect for the teacher." According to Glaser and Strauss (1967), hypotheses are generated from the interrelations between categories and properties.

Major CVF Themes in English and in Spanish

The rich, poetic quality of CVF is best illustrated by the rhymes and sayings themselves. This section presents some of the major CVF themes that emerged in the study. Where appropriate, actual quotes of folklore material are given. (For a fuller treatment of the subject, the reader may consult Hill, 1986.)

Motherly love and affection. Some of the recurring themes of the Puerto Rican CVF in Spanish were attitudes of warmth, love, and the glorification of the mother:

La rosa cayó en el agua,	The rose fell in the water,
muy pronto se deshojó,	Quickly the petals fell off,

mamita me quiere mucho,	Mommy loves me a lot,
pero más la quiero yo.	But I love her even more.

The word "madre" (mother) has been called sacred to Puerto Ricans (Arán, Arthur, Colón, Goldenberg, & Kemble, 1973). In light of this, the common magical chant in English

Step on a crack,
And you'll break your mother's back,

would probably strike the Puerto Rican child as blasphemy. Indeed, none of the subjects recognized this saying of U.S. children. Butler (1977) noted that CVF in the United States is less reverent towards adults than is the CVF of other cultures. Typical targets in the U.S. are parents, teachers, authority figures, and political figures.

Affection for babies. A great affection for babies was expressed in the CVF in Spanish. Many poems and songs for and about babies, including lullabies, were offered.

Duérmete, mi niño,	Sleep, my child,
duérmete, mi sol,	Sleep, my sun,
duérmete, pedazo	Sleep, little piece
de mi corazón.	Of my heart.

Spanish abounds with rhymes and songs, besides lullabies, for babies. These may be for bouncing the baby on one's knee (dandling), for the baby learning to walk, for tickling, for naming facial parts or fingers and toes, or for other simple games. Sample children knew many of these in Spanish, but none in English.

Related to the Puerto Ricans' love for babies, which came through in their verbal folklore, was their fondness for the diminutive form of words. This is evident in the normal speech of Puerto Ricans, but it was the author's impression that in the CVF items, this preference was even exaggerated. The following song for a baby was an example.

Pon, pon,	Put, put,
el dedito en el pilón,	The little finger in the mortar,

acetón a la mesita	Aceton (nonsense) to the little table.
¡Ay, ay, ay, mi cabecita!	Oh, oh, oh, my little head!

The diminutive denotes smallness, but there is also a connotation of affection. This is related to the mood of warmth and love which pervaded the CVF in Spanish. *Sex role distinction.* Sex roles were clearly distinguished in the Spanish CVF. This may also be the case for CVF in other languages since folklore is traditional, historically rooted material. Clearly defined sex roles, starting at an early age, have been described as more pronounced in Puerto Rican than in mainland culture (Ibáñez de Friedman, 1978; Saville-Troike, 1978). Traditionally, men were supposed to protect, shelter, and control women, who depended upon and obeyed them (Klitz, 1980).

A rhyme which spoke directly to the idea of the male protecting the female was the following one, said to be used for both jumping rope and skipping. The last lines raise the question of who "rules the house":

Chi jí, chi já,	Chi ji, chi ja, (nonsense)
chi jí, chi já,	Chi ji, chi ja, (nonsense)
el gallo y la gallina	The rooster and the hen
se fueron a bañar	Went swimming.
La gallina se ahogó,	The hen started to drown,
el gallo la salvó.	The rooster saved her.
Que sí, que no,	Yes, no,
la casa la mando yo.	I rule the house.

Religion. Spanish CVF alluded frequently to religious figures. The following song was known by 23 of the 40 participants:

Que llueva, que llueva,	Let it rain, let it rain,
la Virgen de la cueva,	The Virgin of the cave,
los pajaritos cantan,	The little birds sing,
las nubes se levantan,	The clouds rise,
que sí, que no,	Yes, no,
que llueva el chaparrón.	It's a shower.

The Virgin Mary even steps in to help a baby learning to walk in this song:

Andando, andando,	Walking, walking,
que la Virgen	The Virgin
te va ayudando	Is helping you.

The active intervening God so evident in Puerto Rican children's folk rhymes and songs can also be seen in the Puerto Rican custom of following a compliment with the hope that God will take care of whatever has been admired, as in:

Qué lindo vestido,	What a pretty dress,
que Dios te lo guarde.	May God take care of it
	for you.

Without the disclaimer, it is feared that the receiver of the compliment might think the speaker covets the object or wishes harm.

The influence of religion is much less apparent in Anglo children's CVF in English. The author knows of only one common folk rhyme in English with a religious reference and it is an oblique reference at that:

This is the church,
This is the steeple,
Open the doors,
And see all the people.

It may be that this finger play's original invention and subsequent popularity had to do with the wonderful rhyme of "steeple" and "people," rather than interest in a church.

Closeness to nature. Another theme in Spanish CVF was a closeness to nature. This closeness may have resulted from exposure to rural life in parts of Puerto Rico. Although animals are favorite characters in all children's folklore, they were particularly frequent in the Spanish CVF. There were bees, birds, cats, chickens, dogs, donkeys, ducks, elephants, frogs, goats, hens, horses, mice, rabbits, roosters, spiders, wolves, and the popular *coquí.*

Some of the lullabies in Spanish created a mood of idyllic peace in a rural setting:

Duérmete, mi niño,	Sleep, my child,
duérmete, mi sol,	Sleep, sun,
duérmete, pedazo	Sleep, little piece
de mi corazón.	Of my heart.
Este niño lindo	This lovely child
se quiere dormir,	Wants to sleep,
háganle la cama	Make his bed
en el toronjil.	In the grapefruit tree.
Y de cabecera	And on his head
pónganle un jazmín,	Put a jasmine,
para que se duerma	So he sleeps
como un serafín.	Like an angel.

The indication of a closeness to nature in these rhymes does not mean that this is a current aspect of life for the participants in this study. It merely demonstrates part of their cultural heritage. After all, though the cradle is on the tree top in "Rock-a-bye, baby," such an arrangement is hardly common in the present-day United States.

English/Spanish dynamics. A theme of more recent evolution, which may reflect the participants' lives, was the mixing of Spanish and English. One common song, often learned in school in Puerto Rico, used direct translation:

Pollito, chicken,
gallina, hen,
lápiz, pencil,
y pluma, and pen.
Ventana, window,
piso, floor,
maestra, teacher,
y puerta, and door.

The most striking similarity between this study's collected CVF in Spanish and CVF in English was in the categories or purposes for which the folkloric material had evolved. Of the study's 44 common categories of CVF, for which first lines of rhymes were said in the structured interviews, only 6 categories did not elicit corresponding items in both languages. In other words, there are rhymes in Spanish and English for deciding who goes first in a game, for clapping hands in a rhythm, for counting off fingers and toes, and so on. These universal aspects of CVF are more impressive than any differences. In this regard folklore is like children's literature, and adult literature as well, which has been characterized as centering around basic recurring themes (Butler, 1977).

One obvious likeness in particular items in the two languages was when the same rhyme occurred in rough translation. The following counting-out rhyme probably appeared first in English, since Mickey Mouse was a U.S. character, and since "mouse" and "house" rhyme in English:

> Mickey Mouse built a house,
> How many nails did he need?
> One, two, three,
> Out goes he.

Subjects in this study knew both the English version and the Spanish one, which was probably devised later, but still preserved the rhyming and rhythmic quality of the original:

Mickey Mouse iba a hacer	Mickey Mouse went to build
una casita	A little house.
¿Cuántos clavos necesita?	How many nails does he need?

Mickey Mouse and Popeye are cartoon characters who originated in the United States, but now figure in the CVF of Puerto Rican children in both Spanish and English. There were also cases of characters similar in personality, but different in their specific related lore. In English, the fool or simpleton is Simple Simon. Poems about Simple Simon typically relate several verses of his hapless escapades. The popular foolish character for the Puerto Rican children was Juan Bobo:

Pasé por la casa	I went by the house
del pobre Juan Bobo,	Of poor Juan Bobo
	(Juan the Fool),
y allí lo encontré,	And there I found him,
hablándose solo.	Talking to himself.

There are many stories in Spanish about the hilarious misadventures of Juan Bobo. Juan Bobo is probably a better known character for Puerto Rican children, more pervasive in folklore, than Simple Simon is for Anglo children. One could speculate that the fool who behaves stupidly has a special function, similar to that of a scapegoat, in a culture where preserving one's dignity and not losing face are important. These characteristics of Puerto Rican culture have been described in other sources (Arán et al., 1973; Klitz, 1980).

Threatening folkloric figures. For Anglo and Puerto Rican children alike, there is a scary figure who "gets them" if they misbehave. This is "the boogeyman" in English and "el cuco" in Spanish. However, the Puerto Rican character seemed more fully developed and figured more largely in the awareness of the Puerto Rican children, than the English equivalent. Almost all sample children had heard of el cuco and most knew a bedtime poem or lullaby, such as the following, about him:

Duérmete, nene,	Sleep, little boy,
duérmete y no llores,	Sleep and don't cry,
porque si el cuco viene,	Because if el cuco comes,
viene y te come.	He'll come and eat you.

It is hard to classify the above poem with lullabies, which are usually gentle and soothing. One reason for el cuco's continuing presence in Puerto Rican children's CVF must be his value to parents as a threat of potential punishment. The participants reported that they believed in el cuco until ages four, five, or six, when they decided he wasn't real. Still, as third and fourth graders, they spoke of him with a smile and a shudder.

Humor. Children's Verbal Folklore is playful. One of the most delightful aspects of CVF in both Spanish and

English is its humor. One type of humorous poem is sheer nonsense, as in "Hey, diddle, diddle!" in English. Sample children offered many nonsensical items in Spanish, such as this song which entailed linguistic manipulation to substitute all the vowels:

La mar estaba serena,	The sea was serene,
serena estaba la mar.	Serene was the sea.
La mar astaba sarana,	(Nonsense until all
sarana astaba la mar.	the vowels have been
Le mer estebe serene,	used, then the first
serene estebe le mer.	two lines repeat.)

Another nonsense song known to the children was:

Jíngüili, jíngüili	Jinguili, jinguili
	(nonsense)
está colgando.	Is hanging.
Jóngolo, jóngolo	Jongolo, jongolo
	(nonsense)
está mirando.	Is watching.
Si jíngüili, jíngüili	If jinguili, jinguili
se cayera,	Should fall,
jóngolo, jóngolo	Jongolo, jongolo
lo cogiera.	Would catch him.

A different type of humor common to CVF in Spanish and English asks or states the obvious, as in the following riddles:

Who is buried in Grant's tomb?	
¿De qué color es el	What color is
caballo blanco	Napoleon's
de Napoleón?	White horse?

Parody and impropriety in general are beloved sources of humor for most children. Anglo and Puerto Rican youth are no exception. Children take special delight in poking fun at the religious, the formal, the pompous historical figure. Instead of saying or singing, "While shepherds watched their flocks by night," Anglo children sometimes substitute:

"While shepherds washed their socks by night."

Children enjoy spoonerisms:

"The Lord is a shoving leopard" for
"The Lord is a loving shepherd."

A parody in Spanish of a well-known marching song about the heroic Duke of Marlborough is:

Mambrú se fue a la guerra,	Mambru went to war,
montado en una perra,	Mounted on a dog,
la perra se cayó,	The dog fell down,
y Mambrú se escocotó.	And Mambru broke his neck.

Interestingly, some participants knew the following equivalent parodies in both languages:

Ladies and Jellyfish	
Ladies and Germs	(for Ladies and Gentlemen)
Damas y Caballos	Ladies and Horses
(for Damas y Caballeros)	(for Ladies and Gentlemen)

Tricks, retorts, and taunts. There is one type of CVF which is often humorous, but has an aggressive intent. This type includes tricks, retorts, and taunts. The fact that this study found no examples of tricks (also called "catches") in Spanish, although they may exist, is probably related to the importance of maintaining one's dignity in Puerto Rican culture (Arán et al., 1973; Klitz, 1980). One source states specifically that many Puerto Ricans find practical jokes, insult humor, and self-ridicule offensive to their dignity and image (Arán et al., 1973).

Love and romance. Romantic love was observed in both Spanish and English CVF. Poems and sayings about love were equally known by both boys and girls. The view of love was both serious and comic and had positive and negative aspects. The children knew these autograph rhymes in English:

Roses are red,
Violets are blue,
Sugar is sweet,
And so are you.

* * *

Roses are red,
Violets are blue,
Pity the woman
Who marries you.

Many participants could say these autograph rhymes in Spanish about love:

Pan es pan,	Bread is bread,
queso es queso,	Cheese is cheese,
no hay amor,	There is no love,
si no hay un beso.	Without a kiss.

* * *

Pan es pan,	Bread is bread,
jalea es jalea,	Jelly is jelly,
no hay amor,	There is no love,
si no hay pelea.	Without fighting.

Many also knew the following gentle, loving rhyme which was usually used for counting out. One child said her mother played a circle game using it; another said her father sang it to her mother.

Manzanita colorada,	Little red apple,
que del cielo te cogí,	That I took from the sky,
si no estás enamorada,	If you're not in love,
enamórate de mí.	Fall in love with me.

One jump rope rhyme in English, known by several female subjects, seemed to convey a veiled warning about pregnancy. The jumper skips rope until she misses, and that is the number of babies she will have:

Last night, the night before,
I met my boyfriend at the candy store,
He bought me ice cream,
He bought me cake,
He brought me home with a stomach ache.

I said, "Mama, Mama,
Call the doctor quick,
Cake and ice cream
Make me sick."
How many babies did she receive?
One, two, three. . . .

It is interesting that a study of jump rope and clapping rhymes among a group of mostly African-American girls in Detroit (Henning, 1981), found versions very similar to those used by this study's Puerto Rican girls in New Haven.

Magic and superstition. Another common theme in both Spanish and English CVF is superstition or belief in magical forces. There were oracles about love in both languages. One might expect this aspect to be more prevalent in the CVF of Puerto Ricans than in the CVF of Anglos, since the Puerto Rican world view has been described as fatalistic, with people controlled by exterior forces, in contrast to the mainland view that people shape their own destinies (Klitz, 1980).

In fact, children's lore in Spanish and English is so imbued with magical belief that it is impossible to say it is emphasized more in one culture than the other. Sample children had learned, usually from television cartoons, magical chants, such as Abracadabra and Open Sesame, in both languages:

Abracadabra	Abracadabra,
pata de cabra	Goat's foot.
* * *	
Abrete Sésamo.	Open Sesame.

One belief among Puerto Ricans with no equivalent for Anglos is the danger associated with a compliment. The following saying wards off ideas of wishing harm, or coveting:

Que lindo vestido,	What a pretty dress,
que Dios te lo guarde	May God take care of it
	for you.

The custom of the *azabache* is a manifestation of this attitude and expresses a fatalistic outlook. The *azabache* is a black onyx amulet which Puerto Ricans place on their babies to ward off *mal de ojo* (the evil eye). The *azabache* is often given by the godparents. Even educated Puerto Ricans may follow this practice. The *azabache* guards against the potentially harmful consequences of compliments to a baby.

Tooth/Good Fairy. Both Anglo and Puerto Rican children have a body of lore related to losing a tooth. The Anglo child puts the tooth under the pillow upon going to bed for the tooth fairy or good fairy to leave money in replacement. Sample children said they put the tooth under the pillow or under the bed, or simply tossed it outside. They would chant not to the tooth fairy, but to a mouse, saying this rhyme or a variation:

Ratoncito, ratoncito,	Little mouse, little mouse,
te doy este dientito,	I give you this little tooth,
para que me dejes	So you'll leave me
unos chavitos.	Some little money.

Schools and schooling. Like the themes of humor, love, and magic, the subject of school appears in the CVF of both Puerto Rican and Anglo children, since schooling is a common experience. The similarity is only surface level; the actual content in the two languages is different. The rhymes in English deride schooling; those in Spanish glorify it. Sample children knew the poem in English to say at the end of the school year:

No more pencils,
No more books,
No more teachers'
Dirty looks.

In contrast, the following loving song in Spanish about school was known by all the children as well:

Mi escuelita,	My little school,
mi escuelita,	My little school,
yo la quiero con amor,	I love it dearly,
porque en ella,	Because in it,
porque en ella,	Because in it,
yo aprendo mi lección.	I learn my lesson.
Cuando vengo en la	When I arrive in the
mañana,	morning,
lo primero que yo hago,	The first thing I do,
saludar a mi maestra,	Is greet my teacher,
y después a mi trabajo.	And then, to my work.

A parody version, known by some of the study's adult informants in the beginning of this investigation, was:

Mi escuelita,	My little school,
mi escuelita,	My little school,
yo le pego dinamita,	I set it with dynamite,
pa' que explote,	So it will explode,
pa' que explote,	So it will explode,
y se vea más bonita	And look prettier.

Thus, although the standard version of "Mi escuelita" was by far the most common, there was evidence that Puerto Rican children have also reacted against the constraints of formal schooling in their verbal folklore.

Stylistic Differences in Spanish and English CVF

Songs vs. recitations. Some of the differences in Puerto Rican and Anglo CVF are obvious even on the surface level. More of the material in Spanish seemed to be sung, as opposed to spoken. Of 255 different folkloric items in Spanish collected from Puerto Rican adults and children for this study, 55 (22%) were songs. Of 174 items in English, 6 (3%) were songs.

Body contact in CVF. Another difference between the English and Spanish folkloric material was that more items in Spanish were meant to be accompanied by physical contact between people than was the case for English. This finding supports the opinion of several investigators (Ibáñez de Friedman, 1978; Klitz, 1980) that touching is more important for human relations and communication among Latin Americans than among U.S. Anglos. Though such rhymes exist for both languages, there are more in Spanish than in English for eliciting clapping, for bouncing a baby on one's knee, for playing with the fingers and toes, and for naming the parts of a baby's face.

The following song is an example of a rhyme in Spanish which involves touching the child:

Chichirí cantando,	Chichiri singing,
se quedó dormido,	Fell asleep,
y vino un mosquito,	A mosquito came,
le picó su ombligo,	And bit his bellybutton.

The author identified few rhymes in English to accompany tickling, such as the following:

Round and round the garden,
Goes the chocolate bear,
One step, two steps,
Get him right there.

In contrast to the apparent relative lack of popularity of tickling rhymes in English, 33 of the 40 subjects knew rhymes for tickling in Spanish. Most giggled as they recalled being tickled, usually by their mothers. One common rhyme, which had many variations, was:

Cuando compres carne,	When you buy meat,
no la compres de aquí,	Don't buy it from here,
ni de aquí, ni de aquí,	Or from here, or from here,
sólo de aquí.	Only from here.

Protection from discomfort. A desire in the Puerto Rican CVF to save the child from harm and spare the child any discomfort, manifested itself in two special categories of CVF in Spanish. The author does not know of any equivalent categories or equivalent rhymes for them in CVF in English. If they do exist, they are not so common.

The first of these categories is rhymes for a child with the hiccups. The purpose of these is obviously to distract children from the hiccups, perhaps even to make the hiccups go away. Participants reported that it was usually the mother who said these rhymes to them, while often touching them to get their minds off the hiccups:

Hipo, hipo,	Hiccups, hiccups,
mandorico,	Mandorico, (nonsense)
¿quién te dio	Who gave you
el tamaño pico?	Such a big beak (nose)?

* * *

Ayer pasó por mi casa	Yesterday a gentleman
un caballero,	Passed by my house,
vendiendo romero,	Selling rosemary,
le pedí un poquito,	I asked for a little,
para mi pollito.	For my chicken.
No me lo quiso dar,	He wouldn't give it to me,
y me eché a llorar,	And I started to cry,
cogió un garrotito,	He took a little club,
y me hizo callar.	And made me be quiet.

Another category with a protective purpose noted in the Spanish, but not in the English material, was that of rhymes said to a hurt or sick child. Again, it was the child's mother who usually said the following rhyme, or a variation thereof, which was known by 28 of the 40 children. A word which sounds like *colita* but has a more earthy meaning is often used in this rhyme:

Sana, sana,	Get well, get well,
colita de rana,	Little frog's tail,
si no sanas hoy,	If you don't get well today,
sanarás mañana,	You'll get well tomorrow,
y si no,	And if not then,
cuando te dé la gana.	Whenever you choose.

Prominence of riddles in Spanish. Riddles, or *adivinanzas*, were more prominent in Spanish CVF than in English CVF. Although riddles exist in English, whether Anglo children know and actively use riddles is open for investigation. This study noted 32 common Puerto Rican riddles. Some examples are:

Cien damas	A hundred ladies
en un castillo,	in a castle,
y todas visten	And all of them dress
de amarillo	In yellow.
(el árbol de chinas)	(an orange tree)

* * *

Soy pequeñita	I am little
como un ratón,	Like a mouse,
y guardo la casa	But I guard the house
como un león.	Like a lion.
(la llave)	(a key)

* * *

Plata no es,	It isn't silver
oro no es,	It isn't gold,
abre la canasta,	Open the basket,
y verás qué es.	And you'll see what it is.
(el plátano)	(a plantain)

There is a marvelous flavor of complexity and subtlety in these Spanish riddles, while they pique the children's curiosity. One reason why the riddle seems to be more highly developed for Puerto Ricans than for Anglos may be related to Puerto Ricans' use of language generally. Latin Americans are described as more subtle and less frank; they believe that some things are better left unsaid. Anglos want to get to the point and state matters directly (Klitz, 1980).

Anglos are said to socialize based on a mutual activity, while Hispanics rely more on talk and discussion. *Relajo* is a kind of playful kidding with language, an important part of socializing for Hispanics (Klitz, 1980). The attitude that oral language is a form of recreation may relate to the fact that riddles are an important CVF category for Puerto Ricans.

This discussion examined reflections on the culture of the Puerto Rican child on the mainland, using the children's verbal folklore as the mirror. Recurring themes of Puerto Rican CVF in Spanish were described, as well as similarities and differences of Puerto Rican CVF in Spanish and mainland CVF in English.

The comments and comparisons made regarding Puerto Rican CVF represent conclusions reached by the author on the basis of the data gathered in this study.

She does not wish to give the impression, however, that relevant sources about CVF are not available. There have been excellent studies of Puerto Rican folklore on the island (Cabrera, 1972; Cadilla de Martínez, 1933; Canino Salgado, 1968; Deliz, 1952; Feliciano Mendoza, 1972; Marrero, 1967; Ramírez de Arellano, 1928; Rosa-Nieves, 1967). Consulting these more historical folkloric analyses was gratifying for the author because, in some cases, they corroborated ideas, such as the importance of music and songs in Puerto Rican CVF, and the riddle as a highly developed poetic form in Puerto Rican culture (Asociación de Maestros de Puerto Rico, 1985).

Suggestions for Educators

This chapter has described the verbal folklore of Puerto Rican children on the mainland, the ways in which it is transmitted, and the ways in which it highlights aspects of the culture. The first step in helping educators use CVF in the classroom is to heighten their awareness by explaining what Children's Verbal Folklore is, how it is learned, how it operates, and how it relates to the child's world and background.

Next, educators can take heart in the rich store of informal language that Puerto Rican children bring with them to school. Furthermore, the importance of the family, especially mothers, as prime transmitters of this material suggests that much verbal interaction is taking place in the Puerto Rican home and that this interaction is usually accompanied by warmth and affection.

The following recommendations are primarily geared towards teachers and school personnel. Yet, they can also be of interest to counselors, psychologists, social workers, and other people seeking to promote the optimal development of Puerto Rican children:

1. *Use CVF to help children make connections.* Teachers who wish to capitalize on this resource need to learn to use it to establish connections for the child. A classroom collection of these offerings in Spanish and English, already known by the students and compiled in

a computer, "big book," or ordinary notebook, would serve several functions. The children would see concrete validation in school of the language they know and of what their family and friends say outside of school.

This would help break down the idea in a child's mind that there are separate entities of "home language" and "school language," and the concomitant sense of unworthiness because the home language is not respected in school. The things the child's parents and grandparents have said and taught would become items for appreciation, delight, and amusement, when collected in a classroom anthology. Also, these key figures in the child's life would themselves gain a more positive attitude towards the school when they feel they have a contribution to make to classroom activities. This would in turn help the child.

2. *Use CVF to promote positive feelings and social harmony.* Children's Verbal Folklore can play a role in helping children in general to deal with the anxieties and tensions of childhood, while promoting social harmony. Paredes (1968) has explored ways in which folklore can be useful to ethnic groups in the United States. He suggests that folklore can help ease conflicts and tensions, can create intra-group unity and homogeneity, and can enhance a group's dignity and confidence.

The warm, loving attitude and emphasis on the traditional values of family, religion, and schooling conveyed in much of this study's collected CVF may serve to fortify the Puerto Rican child who is often faced with another society's varying values and cultural norms. This study also noted the soothing, protective function of many of the Spanish sayings, e.g., rhymes for a child who has the hiccups or is hurt or sick.

Another benefit of direct teaching with verbal folklore is that many of its rhymes and songs strengthen the child and promote intra-group unity by expressing pride in being Puerto Rican, whether or not the child lives on the island:

| De las flores, la violeta, | Of flowers, the violet, |
| de los colores, azul, | Of the colors, blue, |

de las islas, Puerto
   Rico,
y de mis amigos, tú.
	Of the islands, Puerto
	   Rico,
	And of my friends, you.

One rhyme was touching in its expression of homesickness, yet it let some children know that they were not alone if they longed to escape unfamiliar surroundings and return to Puerto Rico:

El canto del gallo no se oye aquí, tampoco se conoce la voz del coquí Si quieres tú esta música oir, al campo de Borinquen tendremos que ir	The rooster's crowing Is not heard here, Nor is known The voice of the coqui. If you want To hear this music, To the land of Borinquen We'll have to go.

3. *Use CVF to help release tension and anxiety.* The psychological value of giving words or a name to feelings that would otherwise go unexpressed could also be seen in a type of CVF in Spanish which mocked the English language. This material clearly provided an outlet for tension as the child struggled to learn a new language. It should be noted that the items about English were not just in children's verbal folklore, but were also told with much enjoyment by adult Puerto Ricans, who must at times feel like children when they first try to speak and negotiate in English.

The following examples make fun of English or of the imperfect fit in translation between Spanish and English:

Apio verde to you.	Green celery to you. (sounds like Happy Birthday to you)

* * *

El hielo grita.	The ice screams. (like the English "ice cream")

* * *

Mantequilla con moscas.	Butter with flies. (like the English "butterfly")

* * *

Yo abrigo la esperanza   I am hopeful.
                                (in English say, "I
                                overcoat the
                                grasshopper.")

Another way in which verbal folklore can help release anxiety and tension is when it allows the expression of things that could be classified as indecent or scatalogical in nature. It was the author's impression while conducting interviews with Puerto Rican children and adults that obscenity in varying degrees was quite common in their store of verbal folklore. Sometimes in the interviews, a child could not state a particular phrase or rhyme which came to mind because it was "very bad." The classroom teacher, like this researcher, would probably choose not to transcribe or highlight this type of material, which may be allowed to remain the province of children themselves. The existence of this risqué material might reflect the need for an outlet from a certain amount of repression in the strong devotion to mother, family, and religion, and obedience to adults, which have been seen to characterize Puerto Rican culture. This idea corroborates Abrahams' description of folklore as a "steam valve" for aberrant and potentially divisive impulses, institutionalizing some degree of guiltless rebellion (Abrahams, 1972).

4. *Use CVF to promote self-esteem and self-growth.* Another reason for using verbal folklore in the classroom is that students could learn to become possessors of valued knowledge, and could enjoy the status of skillful performers. Awareness of Puerto Rican CVF in Spanish would help them socially within their immediate cultural group. The same kind of knowledge of CVF in English could assist them in reaching out to new friends from the Anglo or African-American mainland cultures.

Abrahams (1972) proposed that if folklore is composed of a group's wisdom, anxieties, and values, then the people who know and perform this traditional material have a key to power and status within their community. Indeed, it was the author's impression while conducting her interviews that those children who knew the most folkloric material, and had taught others, were also the most popular members of their classes. There was a certain reverence in the way children would speak of other children who had taught them a CVF item.

One participant, a third-grade girl, insisted on copying some of the rhymes in the author's collection. She was permitted to do so when all the interviews had been completed, and attacked her project with such zeal that she worked at the task even through her lunch time. It seemed that she was exhibiting not only an appreciation for traditional rhymes and sayings, but also a wish to obtain the kind of power this material represented.

The relationship between folklore and power is not a simplistic one in which a child knows CVF items and, therefore, has extra status. The cause and effect process is more complex. Yet, raising the issue of CVF as a tool for power does offer an intriguing area for future ethnographic research. Part of the picture, which invites investigation, is the way in which girls, who dominate as users and teachers of CVF, employ CVF as a way to attain status. One collection of clapping and jump rope games and rhymes, gathered from 18 six- to ten-year-old female informants in Michigan, analyzes the power which children gain in relation to adults, through the use of folk rhymes (Henning, 1981).

One of the present study's adult informants told how, when she was growing up in Puerto Rico, knowledge of verbal folklore brought status even to the illiterate. She remembered one old man in particular, who could not read but could recite the longest, most beautiful rosaries. The poor and illiterate people without books relied on oral language to teach the children. Riddles were an important part of this teaching. She recalled as a young girl passing many hours of this type of instruction and entertainment with the old men who had finished for the day in her grandparents' sugar cane fields.

5. *Use CVF to promote academic learning.* Although verbal folklore can become the specialty of those without much formal schooling, it can also have special applications for directed classroom instruction. One function of CVF is to impart knowledge in a way that is fun for the child

as well as memorable. Alphabet songs and counting rhymes exist in both Spanish and English. Letters and numbers, their subject matter, are generally accepted as essentials for a child to know. Less consciously, adults are also instructing when they use finger and toe plays, or facial feature naming rhymes, with babies and children. These teach counting and labeling attached to objects. CVF items can help children remember historic dates:

> In fourteen-hundred and ninety-two
> Columbus sailed the ocean blue.

There are also mnemonic devices for such facts as the number of days in each month, as in "Thirty days hath September" and "Treinta días trae septiembre."

Children are usually quite enthusiastic about this type of language, and experience with CVF in Spanish and English increases their overall linguistic ability, including vocabulary development, in the native and second languages. A classroom teacher might, after discovering the categories of CVF which have emerged in the class collection in Spanish, pair the students with those in another classroom and let the students conduct interviews with English-speaking peers. They could ask, "How do you decide who will go first in a game?," "What do you say to make a wish?," etc.

Another educational value of CVF in the classroom is that it can be used to promote literacy. Whenever the child makes the connection between the printed word and language that offers meaning or enjoyment, literacy development is enhanced. Many CVF items develop preliteracy skills by requiring specific attention to language itself and involving linguistic manipulation. Even what adults think of as nonsense syllables can be quite useful. These syllables train the young learner to distinguish among different phonetic elements. The child has fun saying silly things while the rhyme and rhythm are training the ear for eventually learning to read.

It was interesting to observe the superiority exhibited by girls in language-oriented CVF, since it is generally thought that girls experience less difficulty in learning to read than boys. Girls knew more poems, songs, and variations of the alphabet and the vowels, such as the alphabet song:

A E I O U	A E I O U
más sabe el burro	The donkey knows more
que tú.	than you.

They liked to practice the vowel manipulations of "La mar estaba serena," described earlier.

Twice as many girls as boys knew tongue twisters, or *trabalenguas* in Spanish. Usually they had learned these from female relatives—mothers, sisters, aunts, or female cousins. Another type of linguistically-oriented CVF that emerged in this study was secret code languages, or *jerigonza*. These dictate special rules of transposition ("isthay" for "this" in Pig Latin) or syllable insertion ("thoppis" for "this" in "Oppo;" "thithigis" for "this" in "Ithig"). None of the subjects had heard or knew how to use secret languages in English. This is not surprising, given the linguistic skill required and the fact that English was their second language.

Examples of secret code languages in Spanish are "Chi," "Papepipopu," and "Agara, eguere, iguiri, ogoro, uguru." Another formula in Spanish uses only one vowel, like saying *jaraganza* for *jerigonza*. Nine boys had heard these languages in Spanish, but none could speak them. Twelve girls had heard them and most of the twelve could also speak them, some with great skill. All of the reported teachers of *jerigonza* were female—friends, sisters, and cousins. Fluency in secret code languages requires awareness of segmenting the consonants and vowels in the language which is being manipulated and, thus, relates closely with readiness for reading or with the ability to read.

6. *Use CVF to promote cognitive development.* In addition to imparting concrete knowledge and literacy skills to their students, educators are concerned with training them in critical thinking skills or reasoning. Verbal folklore lends itself to the enhancement of skills in this area. The highly developed form of riddles in Spanish is an example,

as trying to figure out correct answers involves ascribing attributes, using logic and creativity, and so forth.

When the author had finished her interviews with one class, she put the questions for all the collected riddles on pieces of paper in a riddle box. Students took turns reaching in and reading a riddle to the class. The contributor of an item was not allowed to answer. After some random guessing at first, the students began to really think about the riddles. Later they practiced creating their own riddles, when given the answer (e.g., "an egg") and told to make up the question.

The humorous subtlety of much of the CVF in Spanish exposes children to a kind of intelligence which is part of their own verbal heritage. The following rhyme jokes about the antisocial (and uncharacteristic for Puerto Ricans) desire to save something for oneself rather than sharing, without stating this directly:

Cinco, diez,	Five, ten,
quince, veinte	Fifteen, twenty,
tapa la olla,	Cover the pot,
que viene gente.	Company's coming.

An adult informant offered the following subtle rhyme used often for a child suspected of stealing something. She remembered saying it as a young girl in school, in Puerto Rico, when her pencil was missing and she thought another child had taken it:

Chucho andaba,	Chucho was walking,
comiéndose un mangó,	Eating a mango,
y a todos nos dijo,	And he told all of us,
que en la marqueta	That he bought it
lo compró	In the market.

This kind of rhyme, though simple, offers children an introduction to indirect statement, poetics, and the use of metaphor. Best of all, it is from the child's native culture.

Summary

Researchers and teachers have paid little attention to the content and classroom applications of CVF, a type of material comprised mainly of orally transmitted rhymes, sayings, and chants. The situation is unfortunate. It is hoped that this chapter has convinced the reader that CVF has unique applications for improving students' self-esteem and skills in the first and second languages, while laying a foundation for literacy.

The chapter is based on a study of the verbal folklore, in Spanish and English, of 40 Puerto Rican third- and fourth-grade bilingual program students in New Haven, Connecticut. Perhaps the study's method of data collection, which was individual interviews structured according to specific categories of folklore, will provide a framework for gathering data and using this material. One reason why CVF is a relatively untapped resource may be that there is no established methodology for its collection and analysis.

This chapter has compared cultural themes in the collected CVF to indicate how important insights can be gained from this seemingly childish and trivial material. Particular items of CVF have been presented to illustrate directly what CVF is and to increase the reader's enthusiasm for this area of study by giving examples of the wit and poetry in Children's Verbal Folklore.

In documenting 1,740 instances of participants' awareness of verbal folkloric items, the investigation produced a preliminary main finding that CVF is alive and well among the children studied. The study also yielded important findings regarding the processes of CVF transmission and the roles of males and females, family, and friends as teachers and users of CVF. An ethnographic approach in analyzing the collected CVF allowed the material to speak for itself, rather than imposing preconceived limited and inflexible thematic categories, and produced provocative insights regarding Puerto Rican and Anglo cultures.

Finally, Children's Verbal Folklore was examined as a tool that can be brought into the classroom to promote personal development and academic achievement for Puerto

Rican children in mainland schools. This body of rhymes and songs is uniquely suited for establishing the connections Puerto Rican children need to make in order to meet with success. These include the connection between home and school; between the Puerto Rican island heritage and the new mainland culture; between Spanish and English; between the spoken and the written word, in the development of literacy in the two languages; and between the children themselves and friends of similar and different backgrounds.

The need to unite these disparate elements in the Puerto Rican child's life in a meaningful way is an immense challenge for the child and for mainland schools. The beauty of using verbal folklore to help meet this challenge is that it springs from the child's own interests and experiences and from the child's own cultural heritage.

REFERENCES

Abrahams, R.D. (1972). Personal power and social restraint in the definition of folklore. In A. Paredes & R. Bauman (Eds.), *Toward new perspectives in folklore* (pp. 16–30). Austin, TX: University of Texas Press, for the American Folklore Society.

Arán, K., Arthur, H., Colón, R., Goldenberg, H., & Kemble, E. (1973). *Puerto Rican history and culture. A study guide and curriculum outline.* New York: United Federation of Teachers.

Asociación de Maestros de Puerto Rico (1985). Cancionero escolar y juegos populares puertorriqueños. Edición Especial de *Asoma, el periódico del maestro puertorriqueño.* Año XIII, Núm. 01-15. Hato Rey, PR: Autor.

Bauman, R. (1982). Ethnography of children's folklore. In P. Gilmore & A.A. Glatthorn (Eds.), *Children in and out of school* (pp. 172–186). Language and Ethnography Series, No. 2. Washington, DC: Center for Applied Linguistics.

Butler, F. (Ed.) (1977). *Sharing literature with children: A thematic anthology.* New York: Longman.

Cabrera, F.M. (1972). *Literatura folklórica de Puerto Rico*. Ciclo de conferencias sobre la literatura de Puerto Rico. San Juan: Instituto de Cultura Puertorriqueña.

Cadilla de Martínez, M. (1933). *La poesía popular en Puerto Rico*. Madrid: Cuenca.

Canino Salgado, M.J. (1968). *La canción de cuna en la tradición de Puerto Rico*. San Juan: Instituto de Cultura Puertorriqueña.

Deliz, M. (1952). *Renadío del cantar folklórico de Puerto Rico*. Madrid: Grafispania.

Dundes, A. (1972). Folk ideas as units of world view. In A. Paredes & R. Bauman (Eds.), *Toward new perspectives in folklore* (pp. 93–103). Austin, TX: University of Texas Press, for the American Folklore Society.

Feliciano Mendoza, E. (1972). *Literatura infantil puertorriqueña*. Ciclo de conferencias sobre la literatura de Puerto Rico. San Juan: Instituto de Cultura Puertorriqueña.

Figler, C.S. (1980). *A comparative study of Puerto Rican families with and without handicapped children*. Unpublished doctoral dissertation, University of Massachusetts, Amherst.

Glaser, B.G., & Strauss, A.L. (1967). *The discovery of grounded theory: Strategies for qualitative research*. Chicago: Aldine.

Goodman, M.E. (1979). *The culture of childhood: Child's-eye views of society and culture*. Anthropology and Education Series. New York: Teachers College.

Henning, B. (1981). *There's a hole in the wall where the children see it all: Clapping, jump rope, and other songs*. Detroit, MI: Wayne State University Folklore Archive. Accession Number 1984 (41).

Hill, K. (1979). *Who goes first? ¿Quién va primero? Children's counting-out rhymes in Spanish and English*. Folkways Record Album No. 7857. New York: Folkways Records.

Hill, K. (1986). *Playing with words: The verbal folklore of Puerto Rican schoolchildren in a mainland setting*. Dissertation Abstracts International, 47, 02A, 623A. (University Microfilms No. DA8607862.)

Hocket, C.F. (1950). Age-grading and linguistic continuity. *Language, 26*, 451–452.

Ibáñez de Friedman, G. (1978). A comparison of cultural factors: North American and Puerto Rican. In *International year of the child: A New England prelude: Selected papers from the 1978 New England kindergarten conference*. Cambridge, MA: Lesley College Graduate School.

Klitz, S.I. (1980). *Crosscultural communication: The Hispanic community of Connecticut. A human services staff development training manual.* A Title XX Project. Storrs, CT: University of Connecticut.

Knapp, M., & Knapp, H. (1976). *One potato, two potato . . . The secret education of American children.* New York: Norton.

Larrick, N. (1972). *The wheels of the bus go round and round: School bus songs and chants.* San Carlos, CA: Golden Gate Junior Books.

Marrero, C. (1967). *Tierra y folklore.* San Juan: Cordillera.

Opie, I., & Opie, P. (1959). *The lore and language of schoolchildren.* London: Oxford University.

Pacheco (n.d.). *Rin-ran las canciones de San Juan.* Record album. San Juan: Nomar.

Palma, M. (1981). *Muestras del folklore puertorriqueño.* San Juan: Edil.

Paredes, A. (1968). Tributaries to the mainstream: The ethnic groups. In T.P. Coffin (Ed.), *Our living traditions: An introduction to American folklore* (pp. 70–80). New York: Basic Books.

Pastor, A. (Ed.) (1960). *Campanillitas folklóricas: Decires y cantares de los niños de Puerto Rico.* River Forest, IL: Laidlaw.

Ramírez de Arellano, R. (1928). *Folklore puertorriqueño: Cuentos y adivinanzas recogidos de la tradición oral.* Madrid: Junta de Ampliación de Estudios, Centro de Estudios Históricos.

Read, A.W. (1975). Family language. In S. Rogers (Ed.), *Children and language: Readings in early language and socialization* (pp. 125–134). London: Oxford University.

Rosa-Nieves, C. (1967). *Voz folklórica de Puerto Rico.* Sharon, CT: Troutman.

Saville-Troike, M. (1978). *A guide to culture in the classroom.* Rosslyn, VA: National Clearinghouse for Bilingual Education.

Spindler, G. (Ed.) (1982). *Doing the ethnography of schooling: Educational anthropology in action.* New York: Holt, Rinehart & Winston.

Spradley, J.P. (1982). *The ethnographic interview.* New York: Holt, Rinehart, & Winston.

Sullivan, C.W., III (Ed.) (1978–1990). *The Children's Folklore Review,* formerly *The Children's Folklore Newsletter.* Greenville, NC: East Carolina University, The Children's Folklore Section of the American Folklore Society.

Utley, F.L. (1965). Folk literature: An operational definition. In A. Dundes (Ed.), *The study of folklore* (pp. 7–24). Englewood Cliffs, NJ: Prentice-Hall.

Ventriglia, L. (1982). *Conversations of Miguel and Maria. How children learn a second language: Implications for classroom teaching.* Reading, MA: Addison-Wesley.

Withers, C. (1946a). *Eenie, meenie, minie, mo and other counting-out rhymes.* New York: Oxford University.

Withers, C. (1946b). *A rocket in my pocket.* New York: Holt.

Wood, R. (1940). *The American Mother Goose.* New York: Lippincott.

Wood, R. (1952). *Fun in American folk rhymes.* New York: Lippincott.

CHAPTER 5

Motivational Orientations, Learning, and the Puerto Rican Child

María Rosa Tapia

Introduction

Competition and cooperation are commonly observed interpersonal behaviors and have been extensively studied since the early twentieth century (Maller, 1929; May & Dobb, 1937). Early studies were mostly based on the theoretical assumption that individuals tend to act primarily in their own best interest and tend to maximize their own personal gains. That is, given some valued commodity, individuals tend to obtain as much as possible of it for themselves. Therefore, regardless of whether individuals cooperate or compete, the main motive was assumed to be the same: To maximize personal gains. However, in the past two decades, phenomenological and empirical data (Kagan, 1977; Kohn, 1986; McClintock, 1972, 1977; Triandis, 1983) have indicated that individuals may cooperate or compete even when it is not in their best interest to do so. These studies underscore the complexity of the motivational bases of cooperative and competitive behavior and the importance of distinguishing cooperative and competitive motivational orientations from cooperative and competitive strategies. These insights led to a different experimental paradigm in the study of cooperation and competition.

    The recent body of scientific literature has documented the existence of three major motivational orientations (referred to as orientations in this chapter) in interpersonal behaviors. These orientations are individualistic, cooperative, and competitive. The individualistic orientation reflects a tendency to maximize one's own gains regardless of the outcome afforded others who are affected by one's behaviors. Individualistically oriented (Ind/O) people cooperate or compete when such behaviors are required to maximize their own gains. Cooperation and competition are only strategies used to maximize personal gains. The cooperative orientation reflects a preference to attain the highest collective gain, that is, a tendency to maximize joint gains. Cooperatively oriented (Coop/O) individuals forgo their own gain maximization, if this is necessary to maximize joint gains. Finally, the competitive orientation reflects a tendency to maximize relative gains to one's own advantage, that is, a tendency to obtain as much more of a given valued commodity than someone else as is possible. Competitively oriented (Comp/O) individuals forgo their own gains maximization, if this is necessary to maximize relative gains.

Data on the orientation of Puerto Rican children is important for educational practitioners. The pattern of substandard academic achievement observed among Puerto Rican children attending schools in the U.S. is well documented. There is evidence of serious underachievement at different levels. In a study conducted by the Education Commission of the States (Brown, Rosen, Hill, & Olivas, 1980), Puerto Ricans were found to be significantly below the national average for the three age groups studied (9, 13, and 17) in the areas of English reading, social studies, math, and career development. More recent figures on school attendance reinforces the findings mentioned above. For example, in cities like New York almost 70% of Puerto Rican students drop out of high school before the tenth grade. In other major cities, the dropout rate for Puerto Ricans is between 45 and 65% (Fernández & Vélez, 1989). Furthermore, the placement of Puerto Rican and other Hispanic children in special education programs is high (Dew, 1984; Willig, 1986). A question that arises in analyzing the academic achievement data on Puerto Rican students is whether serious cultural conflicts exist between

Puerto Rican students' motivational preferences and the schools' interpersonal outcome structures. These conflicts could exacerbate the emotional strain suffered by Puerto Rican children due to migration, poverty, and clash of cultures in U.S. society. As Canino, Early, and Rogler (1980) state:

> The school becomes a source of stress for children when they come to school with community and family roles, concerns, and values markedly different from those of the school system. Such confrontations may serve as a continual source of stress for the child throughout his school years. (p. 32)

In view of these conditions, it is important to determine whether Puerto Rican children's motivational orientations are sufficiently inconsistent with the way educational activities are structured in U.S. schools as to hinder their academic achievement. In order to do so, it is necessary to identify the motivational orientations of Puerto Rican children and to compare them to the orientations of Anglo-American children.

Research Findings

Research findings have indicated that motivational orientations are established in children between the ages of 8 and 10 (Knight, Dubro, & Chao, 1985; McClintock & Moskowitz, 1976). However, studies on the effects of gender on orientation have been inconclusive (Kagan & Zahn, 1983; Kagan, Zahn, & Gealy, 1977; Knight, 1981; Knight & Kagan, 1981).

Findings indicate wide group differences in the proportion of Ind/O, Coop/O, and Comp/O children as a function of social variables, such as socioeconomic status (Knight & Kagan, 1977; Knight, Kagan, & Buriel, 1981) and cultural background. Cross-cultural investigations on this topic have been extensive and have included children from several countries (Graves & Graves, 1977; Kagan &

Madsen, 1972; Toda, Shinotsuka, McClintock, & Stech, 1978); as well as U.S. children from Anglo-American and Mexican cultures (Kagan & Zahn, 1983; Kagan, Zahn, & Gealey, 1977; Kagan, 1986; Kaplan, 1988; Knight, Kagan, & Buriel, 1981; Knight, Kagan, & Buriel, 1982; McClintock, 1974).

Implications for School-Aged Children

The existence of motivational orientations is of importance to educators and other professionals working with children as young as eight years of age. School activities usually operate in an interpersonal outcome structure in which consequences exist for students as a result of their classmates' performances. That is, school activities are individualistically, cooperatively, or competitively structured. In the competitive structure, a student's success necessitates another's relative failure. Students seek an outcome most beneficial to themselves and most detrimental to the other students. In the cooperative structure, one student's success helps another to be successful. Students seek an outcome that is beneficial to all participants. Finally, in the individualistic structure, the students' goal achievements are unrelated to each other. Students seek the outcome that is best for them regardless of whether other students achieve their goals. The spelling-bee contest, group project, and mastery program are examples of the competitive, cooperative, and individualistic structures, respectively.

The degree to which students like the interpersonal outcome structure in which they are required to operate affects their emotional response toward the school experience and their motivation to do the assigned tasks. In turn, this situation affects students' emotional well-being and learning. Research findings have confirmed the relationship between the interpersonal orientation structure operating in the schools and students' motivational preferences.

In a study in the Cook Islands of the South Pacific, where the educational system stresses competitiveness, Graves & Graves (1975) found that competitive orientation in children was positively related to school achievement. Mostly Mexican-American minority students, who are known to have a cooperative motivational orientation, were included in a study by Lucker, Rosenfield, Sikes, and Aronson (1976). They found that when classroom structures were switched from individualistic to cooperative, there was a significant improvement in the academic performance of minority students. Bryant and Arnold (1977) argue that a child well socialized in the Mexican culture encounters strain when confronted with the competitive values of the mainstream U.S. educational system. Ramírez and Castañeda (1974) indicated that Mexican-American children tend to perform poorly in situations that demand competition. Ramírez (1988) studied culturally determined learning styles and concluded that the failure of many Mexican-American children in U.S. schools may result from their field-sensitive learning styles. Delgado-Gaitan (1987) did an ethnographic study of Mexican children at home and at school in California. She found discontinuity among the home, community, and school in three areas: collectivity-competitiveness, authoritarian-egalitarian, and multidimensional-unidimensional. The author concludes that the strengths of Mexican children are overlooked in U.S. classrooms.

The impact of stress on children's academic performance is an important consideration when one examines the anxiety produced by conflict between a school's interpersonal outcome structure and students' motivational preferences. Johnson and Johnson (1974) discuss several studies which demonstrated that individuals who experience high levels of anxiety suffer a loss in efficiency in processing information, a loss in the ability to abstract, and a loss in other flexibilities of intellectual functioning. Gougis (1986) describes findings from a study which suggest that anxiety can impair cognitive functioning among minority students.

In general, the research points to the existence of different motivational orientations or preferences to maximize joint, relative, or own gains in children. As the research findings suggest, alternative outcome structures which depend on students' motivational preferences, rather than set interpersonal outcome structures, are optimal for efficient learning. For Ind/O students, individualistic structured activities are highly functional. For Coop/O and Comp/O students, such individualistic efforts are not optimal. Cooperatively structured activities are optimal and competitively structured activities are not optimal for Coop/O students. The reverse is true for Comp/O students.

Research findings have shown wide group differences in motivational orientations as a function of culture; therefore, alternative outcome structures, as those described above, can be said to be optimal learning strategies for different cultural groups.

A review of the literature revealed that Puerto Rican children had never been assessed in terms of motivational preferences, nor had Puerto Rican and Anglo-American children been compared in this area. Cross-cultural investigations in the U.S., though extensive, had been limited to comparisons of orientations between children from Anglo-American and Mexican cultural backgrounds. In general, these investigations indicate that Mexican-American children are more cooperative and less competitive than their Anglo-American counterparts. Even though Mexican-American and Puerto Rican children in the U.S. share a common Hispanic heritage, there are enough differences in history, culture, and language between the two groups to prevent any extrapolation of findings.

Cultural differences in the cooperative and competitive orientation between Anglo-American and Puerto Rican children were thought to be likely. In terms of the cooperative orientation, expectations were based on the theoretical and empirical link between affiliative tendencies and the cooperative orientation, on one hand (Bennett & Carbonari, 1976), and on the existence of stronger affiliative tendencies in the Puerto Rican than in the Anglo-American population, on the other hand (Murrillo-Rhode, 1976; Ross, 1974). Regarding the competitive orientation, the expectations were based on the theoretical link between active-type aggression and the competitive orientation, on one hand (Kagan & Carlson, 1975; Romney & Ramsley, 1963), and on the stricter control of active-type aggression in the Puerto Rican than in the Anglo-American population, on the other hand (Leavitt, 1974; Ramos-McKay, Comas-Díaz, & Rivera, 1988; Ross, 1974). For the individualistic orientation, there is no a priori basis for expecting any cultural differences.

It was thought that a cross-cultural study comparing Anglo-American and Puerto Rican children would be not only of scientific, but also of practical importance considering the educational implications of these orientations. Hence, a study was conducted to assess and compare, in an experimental setting, the individualistic, cooperative, and competitive orientations of Anglo-American and Puerto Rican children.

The Study

Purpose

The study addressed several research questions formulated as a result of the above discussion.

1. Do Anglo-American children differ in their preferences for maximizing own, joint, and relative gains? Do Puerto Rican children differ in their preferences for maximizing own, joint, and relative gains? These questions were geared to determine the existence of the three orientations in each cultural group.

2. Is the proportion of Coop/O Puerto Rican children larger than that of Coop/O Anglo-American children?

3. Is the proportion of Comp/O Puerto Rican children smaller than that of Comp/O Anglo-American children?

4. Is there any difference in the proportion of Ind/O Anglo-American and that of Ind/O Puerto Rican children?

5. Is there any difference in the proportion of Ind/O Anglo-American boys and that of Ind/O Anglo-American girls and in the proportion of Ind/O Puerto Rican boys and that of Ind/O Puerto Rican girls?

6. Is there any difference in the proportion of Coop/O Anglo-American boys and that of Coop/O Anglo-American girls and in the proportion of Coop/O Puerto Rican boys and that of Coop/O Puerto Rican girls?

7. Is there any difference in the proportion of Comp/
O Anglo-American boys and that of Comp/O Anglo-
American girls and in the proportion of Comp/O Puerto
Rican boys and that of Comp/O Puerto Rican girls?

Research Participants

A sample of 42 Anglo-American and 42 Puerto Rican
children participated in the study. The Anglo-American
children were born in the continental United States. Only
English was spoken in their homes. Persons of Hispanic
ancestry identified by Spanish surnames were excluded
from this group. The Puerto Rican children were born either
in Puerto Rico or on the mainland. Those born on the
mainland were of Puerto Rican parentage who had been
on the island at least once. The children ranged in age
from 10 to 12 years. Within each cultural group, half of
the children were boys and half were girls. Children were
from low socioeconomic status and had achieved at least
a fourth-grade math level. The minimum recommended
sample size of 84 was used because of feasibility
considerations.

The children's motivational orientations were assessed
by means of their performance in a set of decomposed
games, a standard technique in studies of this nature. The
games have well established test-retest reliability (Kagan
& Zahn, 1983) and criterion-related validity (Bem & Lord,
1977; Khulman & Marshello, 1975b; Knight, 1981). Each
game in the set required the child to choose from a group
of three alternatives the one he or she liked the best. The
three alternative choices in each game were structured to
lead to different outcomes representing the motivational
systems under study. To the extent that the child had a
given orientation, the child should have selected game
alternatives consistent with that orientation. Verbalizations
of children during the game indicated that they understood
the nature of the various outcomes and that they made
their choices based on that understanding. For example,
verbalizations often heard when selecting the individualistic
alternative were: "I want to get the most for me" and "I
want the largest number for myself." Verbalizations heard

when selecting the cooperative alternative included: "I want to be nice" and "I've to think about my classmate too." In contrast, verbalizations when selecting the competitive alternative included: "I want to beat my classmate" and "I want to get more than the other."

Each child was classified in a specific orientation based on game choices. To be categorized as Ind/O, Coop/O, or Comp/O the child had to choose a predetermined minimum number of choices consistent with either the individualistic, cooperative, or competitive orientation. Otherwise, the child was classified as Inconsistent. To statistically support the existence of a given orientation, a minimum of two children had to be categorized in that orientation.

A multidimensional categorical analysis using a logistic regression (Agresti, 1984) was carried out to determine the effect of gender and culture on these orientations. The analysis used the .05 level of significance.

Findings and Discussions

Differences in Orientations do Exist

One of the goals of the study was to determine the existence of the individualistic, cooperative, and competitive orientations in Anglo-American and Puerto Rican children. Results of the study indicate that these orientations exist in both populations. In the Anglo-American group, 16 children were categorized as Ind/O, 9 as Comp/O, and 9 as Coop/O. In the Puerto Rican group, 13 were categorized as Ind/O, 6 as Comp/O, and 15 as Coop/O. Eighty-one percent of the children in each cultural group were categorized for orientations. Only 19% of the children in each cultural group were categorized as Inconsistent. A summary of the numbers and percents of children categorized by orientation, culture, and gender is given in Table 1. Figure 1 shows a bar graph of the percentages.

The existence of the individualistic orientation, that is, that persons act in their own best interest, has always

Table 1

Numbers and Percents of Children Categorized by Orientation, Culture, and Gender

Gender	American				Puerto Rican			
	Ind/O	Comp/O	Coop/O	Inc	Ind/O	Comp/O	Coop/O	Inc
Boys	7[a] (33.3)[b]	6 (28.5)	6 (28.5)	2 (9.5)	7 (33.3)	3 (14.2)	7 (33.3)	4 (19)
Girls	9 (42.8)	3 (14.2)	3 (14.2)	6 (28.5)	6 (28.5)	3 (14.2)	7 (38.0)	4 (19)
Total	16 (38.0)	9 (21.4)	9 (21.4)	8 (19.0)	13 (30.9)	6 (14.2)	7 (35.7)	4 (19)

[a]Number of children.   [b]Percents of children.

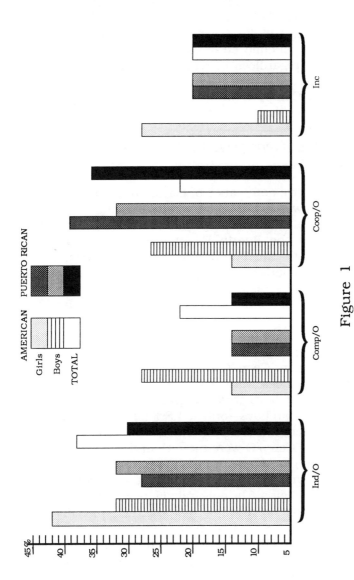

Figure 1

Percents of Children Categorized by Orientation, Culture, and Gender

been assumed. However, its exclusivity has been challenged recently (Kagan, 1977; Kohn, 1986; McClintock, 1972, 1977; Triandis, 1983). The present study supports that challenge. Not all children in this study acted in their own best interest regardless of what happened to others. In fact, close to 50% of the children in each group were Coop/O and Comp/O, which indicated that they tended to act with a social dimension in mind.

Culture and Gender Differences in Orientations

The relative dominance of certain orientations within each culture was analyzed. It was interesting to note the dominance of the cooperative over the competitive orientation in the Puerto Rican group. This finding is compatible with the Puerto Rican set of values, which emphasizes affiliative relations and control of active-type aggression.

Another goal of the study was to determine the effect of culture on each of the orientations and that of gender within each cultural group. In the cooperative orientation category, Puerto Rican children were not found to be significantly more Coop/O than Anglo-American children. Cultural differences were relatively small in boys (33.3% of Puerto Rican boys were Coop/O, compared to 28.5% of Anglo-American boys—only a 4.8% difference). However, cultural differences were greater in girls. Puerto Rican girls categorized as Coop/O were more than double the percent of Coop/O Anglo-American girls. Therefore, Puerto Rican girls were found to be significantly more Coop/O than Anglo-American girls. The cultural differences between boys, even though not significant, were in the same direction as that of girls, as had been predicted.

In the competitive orientation, the percent of Puerto Rican boys categorized as Comp/O was half that of Anglo-American boys, a large enough difference to consider further, even though in this sample size it did not reach the standard .05 level of significance.

In the individualistic orientation category, no significant cultural differences were found. This was even the case when cultural differences were analyzed according to gender.

The effect of gender on orientations within each cultural group was analyzed. The findings indicate no gender differences within the Puerto Rican group in any of the orientations. Even though there had been no basis on which to make predictions in this respect, it would not have been surprising if gender differences had been found to exist. The Puerto Rican culture holds different standards and values for both genders in several social dimensions, such as sexuality, obedience, and childrearing (Díaz-Royo, 1974; Leavitt, 1974; Vázquez-Nuttall & Romero-García, 1989; Ramos-McKay, Comas-Díaz, & Rivera, 1988). However, it seems that the cultural values of affiliative relations and of control of active-type aggression, assumed to be related to the development of cooperative and competitive orientations respectively, are basic values of the Puerto Rican culture. These values are apparently held to a large extent by both genders.

Although in the Anglo-American group no significant gender differences were found in any of the orientations, an interesting pattern emerged. In the cooperative orientation category more boys were Comp/O than girls. In the competitive orientation category, boys were again more Comp/O than girls. In the Inconsistent category, more girls were Inconsistent than boys. This pattern suggests that Anglo-American girls may be less Coop/O and Comp/O, but more Inconsistent than boys. There may be several reasons for the resulting pattern. One consideration is the stability of men's social roles as compared to those of women, who, because of their changing roles, have had to develop nurturing and affiliative skills, on the one hand, and aggressive and assertive behavior, on the other. It is possible that because of the multiplicity of roles Anglo-American women must assume in the home and the workplace requiring different skills, socialization practices with young girls do not follow a consistent pattern that facilitates the emergence of either the cooperative or the competitive orientation, resulting in more inconsistent social behavior in girls than in boys.

Not all the expected cross-cultural findings were significant. More importantly, not all the cross-cultural differences found were in the predicted directions. These unexpected findings raise the possibility that the culture of Puerto Rican children living on the mainland may have diffused somewhat. The literature indicates that the Puerto Rican culture on the mainland is constantly reinforced due to specific socioeconomic variables related to migration (Colón, 1986; Rodríguez, Sánchez-Korrol, & Alers, 1980; Wagenheim, 1975). However, the findings in this study raise questions regarding the degree of maintenance of the Puerto Rican culture on the mainland.

Implications of the Study

As mentioned earlier, the existence of preferences for maximizing joint, relative, or own gains, suggest that alternative outcome structures may be more optimal for school activities. For Ind/O students, individualistic activities are highly functional. For Coop/O and Comp/O students individualistic efforts are not optimal. Cooperative activities are optimal for Coop/O students, and competitive activities not optimal. The reverse is true for Comp/O students. However, it is unrealistic to think that school activities can be personalized to such an extent as to structure them according to each child's motivational orientation. Furthermore, even if it were possible, this would not be wise. Children should learn how to perform within all outcome structures in order to better function in school and society.

Traditionally, the U.S. educational system has used competitive and individualistic structures. Cooperative structures have been absent for the most part from the school scene (Coleman, 1972; Johnson & Johnson, 1975; Johnson, Johnson, & Bryant, 1973; Kohn, 1987). Johnson and Johnson (1975) have done extensive research on cooperative structure learning. In a study with sixth-grade boys, they found that 70% of the children perceived their classrooms as competitively structured (Johnson & Johnson, 1973). Based on their research, they depict the U.S. classroom as a place where students are pitted against each other in a contest for attention, approval, and achievement. Or, as an innovative alternative, the teacher may create a classroom structure that separates students from each other and individualizes their lessons.

The educational implications of the cross-cultural findings are important. This study indicates that Puerto Rican girls are more Coop/O than Anglo-American girls. The study also suggests that it is possible that Puerto Rican boys are more Coop/O and less Comp/O than Anglo-American boys. Current educational practices of structuring school activities exclusively on a competitive or individualistic basis may not be facilitating the emotional well-being and/or the academic performance of Puerto Rican children. Consequently, the findings in this study would suggest to educators in schools with large numbers of Puerto Rican children, that they should implement changes in the way school activities are traditionally structured. By adding cooperative activities to basic learning experiences, offering options to students for participating in cooperative as well as individualistic and competitive activities, and providing feedback on group performance, educators will be accommodating cultural differences in interpersonal orientations. In so doing, they will likely affect positively Puerto Rican children's well-being in school. This is of immediate importance, considering that Puerto Rican children constitute a substantial portion of the enrollment in some of the largest school systems of the U.S. and that their academic achievement lags behind that of their Anglo-American counterparts. In addition, Puerto Rican children tend to suffer from the emotional strain that results from the clash of cultures.

Recommendations

1. *Use of different interpersonal outcome structures in classroom activities.* The existence of different orientations cannot be denied. Educators should use all three structures in classroom activities at different times and not rely on one or two, as is usually done in U.S. schools, where individualistic and competitive structures predominate (Coleman, 1972; Goldman & McDermott, 1987; Johnson

& Johnson, 1975; Johnson, Johnson, & Bryant, 1973; Kohn, 1986). An approach to using the three structures could be providing children with time and opportunity for participation in cooperative, as well as individualistic and competitive, activities.

2. *Determine children's motivational preferences.* Educators should identify children's motivational preferences through informal observation and evaluation, as an important component of cognitive assessment. With this information, the teacher can personalize educational planning by matching children's motivational preferences with interpersonal outcome activities. For example, Comp/O students will obtain the most information and potential reinforcement from information on how well they have done in relation to their peers. Ind/O students will obtain the most relevant information from knowledge about what proportion of the material they have mastered and from data concerning their improvement over time. Coop/O students will be provided the most relevant information when given data concerning how well the group as a whole has performed and, perhaps, how it has improved through time.

3. *Counseling and psychotherapeutic activities should also take into account Puerto Rican students' motivational preferences.* Individual counseling and psychotherapy is basically structured on an individual basis. The probability that a patient receives a reward (feels and functions better) is unrelated to the probability that any other patient receives a reward. Group counseling and group therapy, on the other hand, are structured mainly in a cooperative manner. Through interaction of all group members, all members in the group benefit, and there are joint gains. Since counseling and psychotherapeutic activities are limited and of a personal nature, counselors and psychologists should favor one of the above modalities over the other, according to the student's motivational orientation. Since Puerto Rican children are predominantly Coop/O, group approaches are preferable.

4. *Recreational activities should also take into account Puerto Rican students' motivational preferences.* In

considering outcome structure, recreational activities can be individualistically structured as the "solitary" card game, competitively structured as the "tic-tac-toe" game, or cooperatively structured as choir singing. Recreation implies enjoyment. Therefore, recreational activities, more than any other type of activity, require a match of children's motivational preferences and the corresponding interpersonal outcome structure. Again, since Puerto Rican children tend to be predominantly Coop/O, group recreational activities should be used most of the time.

5. *Further research on the motivational orientation of Puerto Rican children is needed.* Future research needs to explore whether differences exist between the motivational orientations of Puerto Rican children on the mainland and those living in Puerto Rico. Research efforts should attempt to determine whether Puerto Rican children have developed motivational orientations by the age of 8 to 10. If young Puerto Rican children have determined orientations, school activities, compatible with the orientations the children bring to school, may contribute to the formation of Puerto Rican children's positive impressions of their school experience from the beginning. This, in turn, may serve to increase motivation and the likelihood of academic success. Research is also needed to determine the extent of the mismatch between Puerto Rican children's motivational orientations and the orientations of educational activities in U.S. schools.

Summary

Recent scientific literature points to the existence of three different motivational orientations in the interpersonal behavior of children. These are: (a) individualistic; (b) cooperative; and (c) competitive. They are described as a preference for maximizing own, joint, or relative gains, respectively.

The existence of these orientations has important educational implications. Classroom activities are structured either individualistically, cooperatively, or competitively. In the competitive structure, a student's success necessitates another's relative failure. In the cooperative structure, a student's success helps another to be successful. In the individualistic structure, students' goal achievements are unrelated to each other. Research data indicate that the degree to which students like the interpersonal outcome structure in which they are required to operate affects their emotional response toward school experiences and their motivation to do the assigned tasks. In turn, this situation affects students' emotional well-being and learning.

The wide range of orientations evident as a function of culture require alternative classroom structures, as those described in this chapter that can be optional learning strategies for different cultural groups. This is important to Puerto Rican students in the United States who show a pattern of substandard academic achievement perhaps because, on the one hand, the U.S. classroom is mostly structured on a competitive basis and, on the other, there are theoretical bases to expect that Puerto Rican children are less competitive and more cooperative than their Anglo-American counterparts. Hence, a question that arises is whether serious conflict exists between Puerto Rican students' motivational preferences and the schools' outcome structures, thus hindering their academic performance. To shed some light on this important issue, an experimental study was done to identify the orientation of Puerto Rican children and compare them to Anglo-American counterparts.

The study was conducted with 42 Puerto Rican and 42 Anglo-American children, ages 10 to 12. The orientations were assessed by the children's performance on a set of decomposed games. Findings show that orientations exist in both cultural groups. Based on these findings, two basic recommendations are drawn for educators working with Puerto Rican children:

(a) To provide children wide opportunity for participating in cooperative, as well as individualistic, tasks. This applies not only to classroom activities, but also to counseling, psychotherapy, and recreational activities.

(b) To identify children's motivational preferences so as to include this component in the educational planning of individual children.

REFERENCES

Agresti, A. (1984). *Analysis of ordinal categorical data*. New York: Wiley.

Bem, D., & Lord, C. (1979). Template matching: A proposal for probing the ecological validity of experimental settings in social psychology. *Journal of Personality and Social Psychology, 37*, 833–846.

Bennett, R., & Carbonari, J. (1976). Personality patterns related to own, joint, and relative gain maximizing behavior. *Journal of Personality and Social Psychology, 34*, 1127–1134.

Brown, C., Rosen, N., Hill, S., & Olivas, M. (1980). *The condition of education for Hispanic Americans*. Washington, DC: National Center for Education Statistics.

Bryant, B., & Arnold, M. (1977). School-related problems of Mexican-American adolescents. In S. Chess and A. Thomas (Eds.), *Annual progress in child psychiatry and development* (pp. 677-692). New York: Brunner/Mazel.

Canino, I., Early, B., & Rogler, L. (1980). *The Puerto Rican child in New York City: Stress and mental health.* (Monograph No. 4.) New York: Fordham University, Hispanic Research Center.

Coleman, J. (1972). The children have outgrown the schools. *Psychology Today,* May, pp. 72–75.

Colón, D. (1986). Relational value-orientations and achievement potential modes of mainland and island college freshmen Puerto Ricans. *Dissertation Abstracts International, 48*, 1134A.

Delgado-Gaitan, C. (1987). Traditions and transitions in the learning process of Mexican children: An ethnographic view. In G. Spindler & L. Spindler, (Eds.), *Interpretive ethnography of education: At home and abroad.* Hillsdale, NJ: Lawrence Erlbaum Associates.

Dew, N. (1984). The exceptional bilingual child: Demography. In P.C. Chinn (Ed.), *Education of culturally and linguistically different exceptional children.* Reston, VA: Council for Exceptional Children.

Díaz-Royo, A. (1975). The enculturation process of Puerto Rican highland children. *Dissertation Abstracts International, 35*, 7646A.

Fernández, R.R., & Vélez, W. (1989). Who stays, who leaves?: Findings from the Aspira five cities high school dropout study. Working Paper No. 89-1. Washington, DC: Aspira Institute for Policy Research.

128 PUERTO RICAN CHILDREN ON THE MAINLAND

Goldman, S., & McDermott, R. (1987). The culture of competition in American schools. In G. Spindler (Ed.), *Education and cultural process*, 2nd ed., (pp. 282–299). Prospect Heights, IL: Woodland.

Gougis, R.A. (1986). The effects of prejudice and stress on the academic performance of Black Americans. In U. Neisser (Ed.). *The school achievement of minority children*. Hillsdale, NJ: Lawrence Erlbaum.

Graves, N., & Graves, T. (1975). *The impact of modernization on Polynesian society: Or how to make an up-tight rivalrous Westerner out of an easy-going generous Pacific islander* (No. 7). Auckland, New Zealand: South Pacific Research Institute.

Graves, T., & Graves, N. (1977). *Altruism in Aitutaki: Development of rivalry in a cooperative society* (No. 15). Auckland, New Zealand: South Pacific Research Institute.

Johnson, D., & Johnson, R. (1974). Instructional goal structure: Cooperative, competitive, or individualistic. *Review of Educational Research, 2*, 213–240.

Johnson, D., & Johnson, R. (1975). *Learning together and alone: Cooperation, competition, and individualization*. Englewood Cliffs, NJ: Prentice-Hall.

Johnson, D., Johnson, R., & Bryant, B. (1973). Cooperation and competition in the classroom: Perceptions and preferences as related to students' feelings of personal control. *Elementary School Journal, 73*, pp. 306–313.

Kagan, J. (1965). Personality and the learning process. *Daedalus*, Summer, 553–563.

Kagan, S. (1977). Social motives and behaviors of Mexican-American and Anglo-American children. In J.L. Martinez (Ed.), *Chicano psychology* (pp. 45–86). New York: Academic Press.

Kagan, S. (Ed.) (1986). Cooperative learning and sociocultural factors in schooling. In Evaluation, Dissemination and Assessment Center. *Beyond language: Social and cultural factors in schooling language minority students*. Los Angeles, CA: California State University.

Kagan, S., & Carlson, H. (1975). Development of adaptive assertiveness in Mexican and U.S. children. *Developmental Psychology, 11*, 7–78.

Kagan, S., & Madsen, M. (1972). Rivalry in Anglo-American and Mexican children of two ages. *Journal of Personality and Social Psychology, 24*, 214–220.

Kagan, S., & Zahn, L. (1983). Cultural differences in individualism? Just artifact. *Hispanic Journal of Behavioral Sciences, 5,* 219–232.

Kagan, S., Zahn, L., & Gealy, J. (1977). Competition and school achievement among Anglo-American and Mexican-American children. *Journal of Educational Psychology, 69,* 432–441.

Kaplan, R. (1988). Cultural thought patterns in inter-cultural education. In J. Wurzel (Ed.). *Toward multiculturalism.* Yarmouth, ME: Intercultural Press.

Khulman, M., & Marshello, A. (1975a). Individual differences in the game motives of own, relative, and joint gain. *Journal of Research in Personality, 9,* 240–251.

Khulman, M., & Marshello, A. (1975b). Individual differences in game motivation as moderators of preprogrammed strategy effects in Prisoner's Dilemma. *Journal of Personality and Social Psychology, 32,* 922–931.

Khulman, M., & Wimberly, D. (1976). Expectations of choice behavior held by cooperators, competitors, and individualistics across four classes of experimental games. *Journal of Personality and Social Psychology, 34,* 69–81.

Knight, G., & Dubro, A. (1984). Cooperative, competitive, and individualistic social values: An individualized regression and clustering approach. *Journal of Personality and Social Psychology, 46*(1), 98–105.

Knight, G., Dubro, A., & Chao, C. (1985). Information processing and the development of cooperative, competitive, and individualistic social values. *Developmental Psychology, 21,* 37–45.

Knight, G., & Kagan, S. (1977). Development of prosocial and competitive behaviors in Anglo-American and Mexican-American children. *Child Development, 48,* 1385-1394.

Knight, G., & Kagan, S. (1981). Apparent sex differences in cooperation-competition: A function of individualism. *Developmental Psychology, 17,* 783–790.

Knight, G., Kagan, S., & Buriel, R. (1981). Confounding effects of individualism in children's cooperation-competition social motive measures. *Motivation and Emotion, 5,* 167–178.

Knight, G., Kagan, S., & Buriel, R. (1982). Perceived parental practices and prosocial development. *The Journal of Genetic Psychology, 141,* 57–65.

Kohn, A. (1986). *No contest.* Boston: Houghton Mifflin.

Kohn, A. (1987). It's hard to get left out of a pair. *Psychology Today,* October, pp. 53–56.

Leavitt, R. (1974). *The Puerto Ricans: Cultural change and language deviance.* Albuquerque, AZ: University of Arizona Press.

Lucker, G., Rosenfield, D., Sikes, J., & Aronson, E. (1976). Performance in the interdependent classroom: A field study. *American Educational Research Journal, 13*, 115–123.

Maller, J. (1929). Cooperation and competition: An experimental study in motivation. *Contribution to education* (No. 384). New York: Teachers College.

May, M. & Dobb, L. (1937). *Cooperation and competition.* New York: Social Science Research Council.

McClintock, C. (1972). Social motivation: A set of prepositions. *Behavioral Science, 17*, 438–454.

McClintock, C. (1974). Development of social motives in Anglo-American and Mexican children. *Journal of Personality and Social Psychology, 29*, 348–54.

McClintock, C. (1977). Social motivations in settings of outcome interdependence. In D. Druckman (Ed.), *Negotiations, social-psychological perspectives* (pp. 49–77). Beverly Hills: Sage.

McClintock, C., & Moskowitz, J. (1976). Children's preferences for individualistic, cooperative, and competitive outcomes. *Journal of Personality and Social Psychology, 34*, 543–555.

McClintock, C., Moskowitz, J., & McClintock, E. (1977). Variations in preferences for individualistic, competitive, and cooperative outcomes as function of age, game class, and task in nursery school children. *Child Development, 48*, 1080–1085.

Murrillo-Rhode, I. (1976). Family life among mainland Puerto Ricans in New York City slums. *Perspective on Psychiatric Care, 14*, 174–179.

Ramírez, M. (1988). Cognitive styles and cultural democracy in action. In J. Wurzel (Ed.) *Toward multiculturalism.* Yarmouth, ME: Intercultural Press.

Ramírez, M., & Castañeda, A. (1974). *Cultural democracy, bicognitive development, and education.* New York: Academic Press.

Ramos-McKay, J., Comas-Diaz, L., & Rivera, L. (1988). Puerto Ricans. In L. Comas-Díaz & E. Griffith (Eds.), *Clinical problems in cross-cultural mental health* (pp. 204–232). New York: Wiley.

Rodríguez, C., Sánchez-Korrol, V., & Alers, J. (Eds.) (1980). *The Puerto Rican struggle.* New York: Migration Research Consortium.

Romney, K., & Ramsley, R. (1963). The Mixtecans of Juxtlahunca, Mexico. In. B. Whiting (Ed.), *Six cultures: Studies of child rearing* (pp. 655–688). New York: Wiley.

Ross, C. (1974). Identification of cultural characteristics of young Puerto Rican children in mainland schools: A survey of the reference literature and a study and analysis of teacher's perceptions. Unpublished doctoral dissertation, Rutgers University, New Jersey.

Stern, J.D., & Chandler, M.D. (1987). *Condition of education.* Washington, DC: National Center for Education Statistics, U.S. Department of Education.

Toda, M., Shinotsuka, H., McClintock, C., & Stech, F. (1978). Development of competitive behavior as a function of culture, age, and social comparison. *Journal of Personality and Social Psychology, 36,* 825–839.

Triandis, H. (1983). *Allocentric vs. idiocentric social behavior: A major cultural difference between Hispanics and mainstream subjects* (Tech. Rep. No. 1226). Urbana: University of Illinois, Department of Psychology.

U.S. Bureau of the Census (1985). *Nosotros . . .We. . . .* Washington, DC: U.S. Government Printing Office.

U.S. Bureau of the Census (1988). The Hispanic population in the United States: March 1988. *Current Population Reports* (Series P-20, No. 431). Washington, DC: U.S. Government Printing Office.

Vázquez-Nuttall, E., & Romero-García, I. (1989). From home to school: Puerto Rican girls learn to be students in the United States. In C.T. Garcia-Coll & M.L. Mattei (Eds.) *The psychosocial development of Puerto Rican women.* (pp. 61–83). New York: Praeger.

Wagenheim, K. (1975). *Puerto Rico: A profile,* 2nd ed. New York: Praeger.

Willig, A.C. (1986). Special education and the culturally and linguistically different child: An overview of issues and challenges. In A.C. Willig & H.F. Greenberg (Eds.) *Bilingualism and learning disabilities* (pp. 191–209). New York: American Library Publishing, Inc.

PART III

Schools and Schooling

CHAPTER 6

Promoting the Academic Growth of Puerto Rican Children

María D. Alvarez

Introduction

It is often said that Puerto Rican students are underachievers. Yet the study reported in these pages found that schools, not the students nor their families, are the real underachievers. The present chapter deals with academic achievement among Puerto Rican first graders and the variables which facilitate and hinder academic growth among this group. It summarizes a study by Alvarez (1983) conducted in three public schools of New York City's Spanish Harlem. The schools served a largely Puerto Rican population.

Academic Underachievement and the Puerto Rican Child

Although much literature documents Puerto Rican student underachievement, a smaller body of research aims at explaining it quantitatively. This chapter summarizes a multivariate quantitative study of the correlates of differential achievement among inner-city Puerto Rican students (Alvarez, 1983).

The extent to which socioeconomic and cultural backgrounds affect underachievement is a long-standing debate. The relative influence of three sets of variables—home, person, and school—has been at the core of the debate, not to mention academic planning: How educators design and set up programs and curricula depends on whether group achievement results largely from manipulable variables, over which educational planners have some control, or from nonmanipulable variables, over which they have little or none.

Within the group of underachievers there are those who standardized tests and past records suggest are successful learners (so-called positive deviants) and those who tests and records suggest are not (negative deviants). If positive deviance is a function of either domestic or personal variables, then whatever programs schools adopt are still likely to fail. If, however, positive deviance is primarily a function of school-related variables, then instructional planning and modification may improve the situation.

Current educational situation. A large proportion of Puerto Rican children in urban U.S. schools are serious underachievers. The problem encompasses nearly all grades and subjects. The 1988 National Education Longitudinal Study (cited in De La Rosa & Maw, 1990), which focuses on eighth grade student achievement nationwide, finds the situation of Puerto Ricans seriously compromised in just about every subject category studied: reading, writing proficiency, mathematics, science, and classroom grades. Statistics released by individual school districts every year further document the alarming proportions of Puerto Rican students performing below grade level. In New York City, for instance, some 60% of students in predominantly Puerto Rican districts are below grade level in English reading ("Scores on Reading Tests," 1983).

Figures for school attendance further reinforce this bleak picture. By March 1988 about 2.4% of adults in the United States had completed less than five years of school; of the Puerto Ricans on the U.S. mainland, 9.6% had completed less than five years. Nationally, the percentage of adults 25 years old and over who have completed high school is 76.2%; the percentage of Puerto Ricans on the mainland is 50.7% (U.S. Bureau of the Census, 1988).

Evidence from empirical research. The literature on the schooling of Puerto Rican children has great breadth.

Many researchers have analyzed large-scale survey research and/or census data (Brown, Rosen, Hill, & Olivas, 1980; De La Rosa & Maw, 1990; USCCR, 1976; Veltman, 1980a, 1980b, 1981). Others have done cumulative work, what some Puerto Rican educators (Anglada, n.d., p. 57) refer to as "research based on previous research." A sizeable number of investigators have made comparative or predictive research studies (Alvira-Benítez, 1976; Borges, 1975; Chang, 1971; Kleiber, 1974; McCollum, 1980; Prewitt-Díaz, 1983; also Tapia, in this volume).

The research has identified several determinants and correlates of low achievement. The most prevalent include: limited command of English (Bedotto, 1973; Chang, 1971; De La Rosa & Maw, 1990; Morrison, 1958); bilingual background (Strong, 1973; Summers & Wolfe, 1976); perceptual dysfunction (Cohen, 1966); low self-concept (Meléndez, 1978; Prewitt-Díaz, 1983); unresponsiveness and inflexibility of schools (Bucchioni, 1965; Nazario, 1980); discordance resulting from differences between mainstream and Puerto Rican cultures (Elam, 1960; Fitzpatrick, 1987); poverty and low SES (Coleman et al., 1979; Cordasco, 1967; De La Rosa & Maw, 1990); low parental education (De La Rosa & Maw, 1990); minority status and discrimination (Fuentes, 1980; Rodríguez, 1974; 1989); isolation and stigmatization (Zanger, 1987); incompatibility between home and school (Lucas, 1971; Montalvo, 1974; Morrison, 1958); and conflicts between parents and children (Lucas, 1971). Canino, Earley, and Rogler (1980) pointed out that schools have become stress-inducing rather than socially supportive settings for children whose community and family roles, concerns, and values differ from or conflict with those established by the school.

The factors contributing to high achievement are varied but generally not surprising: sex—girls do better than boys (Chang, 1971); intelligence (Borges, 1975); reading ability (Kleiber, 1974); availability of positive reinforcement in the classroom (Ansell, 1976); school-based motivational strategies (Baker & Sanson, 1990); parental education (Brown et al., 1980; Veltman, 1981); high SES (Borges, 1975); the educational environment at home (Alvira-Benítez, 1976; Prior, 1974); and two-parent families

(Brown et al., 1980). Curricular modifications involving bilingual schooling and parental involvement (Ambert, 1980; Aspira of New York, 1973; Plante, 1977; Torregrosa Díaz, 1986; Troike, 1978) have yielded impressive results for academic achievement. However, not all studies find curricular modifications to be unqualified successes (Layden, 1972; Zirkel, 1972), or for that matter, successes at all (cf. Paulston, 1977; 1980).

Unanswered questions. The literature shows that particular variables—in isolation or in combination—can influence achievement, and that these variables may stem from characteristics of the individual, the homes, or the learning environments. Yet little of the literature shows the relative importance of these sets of variables. The answer to the question posed earlier—is positive deviance attributable more to personal and/or domestic variables or to school-related variables?—may provide a workable foundation for improvement.

A major study of the relation of sets of variables, the "Equality of Educational Opportunity Survey" (Coleman et al., 1979), suggested that the order of influence was home-person-school. Several investigators examined the Coleman data for low-income and minority group children (Gordon, 1975; Madaus, Airasian, & Kellaghan, 1980). Their analyses, as well as Thorndike's (1973) results for students in less-developed countries (a population roughly analogous to low-income students in industrialized societies), suggest that the order of influence is school-person-home or school-home-person. Strong connections with educational and/ or behavioral attainments and secondary school characteristics were found by Rutter and colleagues (1982); these investigators dealt with several outcome variables and with process variables that emphasized the characteristics of schools as social—rather than merely educational—institutions.

Method

Purpose of the Study

The goal of the study was to assess the relative and differential impact of three sets of variables (biopersonal, domestic, and school), in a sample of Puerto Rican bilingual first graders enrolled in bilingual/biliterate programs.

Research Questions

Using multiple regression techniques, the present study addressed the following research questions:

1. What are the relative contributions of person, home, and school variables to reading, spelling, and arithmetic achievement?

2. What personal, domestic, and school variables show the strongest associations with reading, spelling, and arithmetic achievement?

Setting

Data were collected at three New York City public schools located within 20 blocks of one another. The schools belonged to a largely minority, low-income district and were representative of the district: Their average enrollment of Puerto Rican students was 68% (vs. 65% for the district); and 21% of the students read at or above grade level in English (vs. 18% for the district). In addition, the schools offered bilingual/biliterate instruction. Teachers were Puerto Rican and exhibited near native-speaker competency in the two languages. All three schools were headed by Puerto Rican principals and catered to a mostly Puerto Rican and African American student population. There seemed little difference in equipment, materials, and instructional aids.

The data were collected under the auspices of the Bilingual Supportive Learning Centers (BSLC), a federally funded project of the Puerto Rican Family Institute of New York City, during three school years. The BSLC's goal was to prevent academic failure in Puerto Rican first- and second-graders through early identification and remediation of incipient difficulties. The project used a pretest/intervention/posttest design. Intervention consisted of two different treatments: (a) a direct service small group resource room instruction; and (b) an indirect service consultation to classroom teachers. Children were randomly assigned to one condition or the other.

Standardized instruments and observation measures were used to identify at-risk children. Children were considered at-risk if (a) they scored at least one standard deviation below their classmates in both English and Spanish reading, or (b) they fell one standard deviation below their peers in teacher evaluations of problematic learning behaviors. Children who otherwise qualified as high-risk, however, were excluded from this category if their maladaptive academic performance or behavior resulted from lack of previous schooling or low intelligence.

Research Participants

Essentially, the sample for this investigation is made up of a native-born first generation parent population and a largely mainland-born child population. Many of the parents in the sample came to the U.S. as teenagers and young children accompanying their own parents in this venture. Others are recent immigrants. Fathers and mothers average 15.4 and 13.1 years in the U.S., respectively, with a range of 1 to 31 years for both groups. Thus, all except five of the parents are island-born Puerto Ricans, the majority of whom came from small towns and rural communities representing some 46 localities within the five major island regions. By contrast, most (75%) of the children were born in the U.S., specifically in New York City. Parents are relatively young in age. Mean age for fathers is 34.9 (range = 21–50), while mothers average 31.5 years (range = 22–51). Their educational attainments correspond to an elementary education: Fathers have completed 6.8 years of school and mothers 8.0 years. The range in schooling is wide, spanning grade 1 through grade 12, with eight parents reporting at least one year of college. Research participants belong to households falling within the lowest socioeconomic stratum in New York City.

Though most households have adults with blue collar employment histories, only 27% of the families reported having at least one employed adult, generally a male (only six mothers were employed). Thus, most families are dependent—either totally or partially—on one or another form of public assistance.

A direct result of the low income affecting families is their rather deteriorated living quarters. Most families live in public housing and walkup buildings whose upkeep is extremely deficient. Homes were rated on 10 different aspects on a 1 (poor) to 5 (excellent) scale and "Condition of the Building"—a variable over which families have little control—received a mean rating of 2.7. By contrast, variables over which families can act upon (e.g., cleanliness, order, furniture, personal appearance) received average ratings of 3.8 points or more.

The internal composition of the households themselves presents patterns worthy of note. In all cases the domestic units have at least one adult female, but some 4 out of 10 units have no coresident adult male. Despite these patterns of widespread male absenteeism, families are not small. The mean number of residents per household is 5.0. This figure reflects the presence not only of siblings (who average 3.6), but also of grandparents, collateral relatives, and non-kin visitors, as 16% of the children live in extended households. By contrast, space is at a premium (mean bedrooms per household = 2.3). Eighty-five percent of children share bedrooms and 26% share beds with either parents or siblings.

Mothers are the more prominent figures in the day-to-day functioning of families, and this holds true even for two-parent families. They are the disciplinarians in most homes (76%), and they are also the family member more apt to help children with their school work (over 60% do). They also constitute the links between the home and the schools.

The child sample consisted of 98 children—56 boys and 42 girls. They ranged in age from 5 years, 7 months to 7 years, 3 months and were spread out almost evenly between the three schools (31, 34, 33).

Measuring Instruments

School and teacher records were used for variables such as sex, age, and attendance. Standardized tests were used to measure academic achievement, intelligence, and oral language. Instruments for assessing school functioning and home environment were developed and/or modified from published measures and are described in more detail in Alvarez (1983).

Academic achievement measures. The *Examen de Aprovechamiento Escolar* (Canabal & Ferisin, 1973) measured ability to read in and spell in Spanish. The *Examen* parallels the Wide Range Achievement Test (WRAT), the test used to measure English reading and spelling (Jastak, Bijou, & Jastak, 1976). The Mathematics section of the WRAT—administered in the child's dominant language—was used to assess performance in arithmetic. Both the Examen and the WRAT are individually administered paper-and-pencil tests that assess performance in word recognition, spelling from dictation, and arithmetic computation.

Intelligence measures. Cognitive development was assessed by the Goodenough-Harris Human Figure Drawing Test (Harris, 1963). Either group-or individually-administered, this paper-and-pencil test has the advantage of minimizing language and literacy skills; it is thus especially serviceable for use with bilingual preliterate populations.

School function and learning behaviors. Teachers rated students' cognitive, visual-motor, academic, and bilingual oral and written language skills on a scale from 1 (poor) to 5 (excellent) using the Teacher Referral Form. They also used a checklist to indicate whether certain learning-related, social/emotional, and interactional behaviors were present or absent in each child.

Biopersonal and domestic data. Health histories of children and their mothers were compiled through a structured interview: the Personal-Social Survey. The Survey uses fixed-alternative, open-ended, and scale items; it consists of two major parts. The first part explores pregnancy, birth, and medical history of children and mothers; the second part explores domestic demographic variables, developmental milestones, socialization, and language use patterns.

Oral language measures. Language competency was established by combining teachers' oral language ratings with results on the Listening/Speaking sections of the Language Assessment Battery, LAB (Polemeni, 1976). Teachers rated each child's receptive and expressive oral language in English and Spanish on a rating scale; the LAB yielded a combined Listening/Speaking score for each language. Taking both these measures into account, each child was assigned a "Lau" category, ranging from A (monolingual speaker of other language) to E (monolingual speaker of English).

Design

The present study was based on a correlational model using three sets of predictor variables and five criterion variables. The predictor variables were clustered along three dimensions—person, home, and school. The criterion variables represented achievement measures for English and Spanish reading, English and Spanish spelling, and arithmetic.

The predictor variables were scrutinized and factor analyzed in order to reduce the number of variables and to form more reliable clusters. The relative importance of the three major sets was ascertained through multiple regression techniques, using hierarchically ordered sets: person, home, and school variables. The contributions of the variables within a set were also explored through multiple regression.

The Criterion Variables

As seen on Table 1, the criterion variables consisted of Normal Curve Equivalents (NCE) scores for English reading, Spanish reading, English spelling, Spanish spelling, and mathematics.

Table 1

The Criterion Variables

Variables	How measured
English reading achievement	NCE on WRAT reading
Spanish reading achievement	NCE on Examen reading
English spelling achievement	NCE on WRAT spelling
Spanish spelling achievement	NCE on Examen spelling
Mathematics achievement	NCE on WRAT Math

The Predictor Variables

Initial clustering. Predictor variables fall into three sets. The person set included two clusters of three variables each, plus three predictors. The home set included three clusters of five, four, and three variables each; the school set consisted of three major predictors. Their names and how they were measured appear in Table 2.

Table 2

The Predictor Variables After Reclustering

Variables	How measured
Biopersonal	
Sex	Boy or girl
Age	C.A. in September of grade 1
Lau category	Score on LAB test & teacher ratings
School skills cluster	
Learning behaviors	Score on Behavioral Checklist
School function	Score on Teacher Referral Form
IQ	Score on Goodenough-Harris Drawing Test
Health cluster	Responses to Personal-Social Survey
Pregnancy/Birth problems	Total reported pregnancy problems
Brain Insults	Total reported brain-related problems
General Health	Total reported current problems

Domestic

Household quality cluster	Responses to Personal-Social Survey
Mother's years of school	Grades completed by mother
Employment	Whether someone at home is employed
Father presence	Single or two-parent family
Mother's years in U.S.	Years residing in the U.S.
Home condition	Ratings of home condition
Household density cluster	Responses to Personal-Social Survey
Household size	Number of residents at home
Bedrooms	Number of bedrooms
Sibsize	Number of siblings living at home
Sibling rank	Rank among siblings at home
Language cluster	Responses to Personal-Social Survey
Household dominance	Reported dominance of home members
Language with parents	Language(s) child speaks with parents
Language with siblings	Language(s) child speaks with siblings

School

School	Attended school A, B, or C
Program	Resource room or consultation
Attendance	Days in attendance for grade 1

Variable clustering through factor analysis. Variable-reduction was achieved through factor analysis followed by Varimax rotation to approximate simple structure. With the exception of age, sex, school program, and attendance, all variables (totaling 19) entered the analysis.

After considering various criteria (e.g., dimensionality of the space, a scree test, percentage of variance accounted for, and interpretability), it was determined that four factors best defined the space. Factor loadings of the predictor variables are given in Table 3. Only variable loadings with absolute values $\geq$ .35 were considered meaningful. Those values that are underlined identify the variables that make up the factors: one biopersonal factor (III, named Well Child) and three domestic factors, Household Density (Factor I), Pull towards English (Factor II), and Household Quality (Factor IV).

Table 3

Loadings on Varimax Rotated Principal Factors of Predictor Variables

	Factor loadings				
Variables	I	II	III	IV	Communality
Sibsize	.84	.07	.31	.11	.79
Household size	.78	.06	.28	.23	.74
Sibling rank	.74	.13	.05	-.15	.59
Bedrooms	.63	-.03	-.03	-.07	.41
Mother school	-.47	.17	.14	.16	.30
Mom yrs in US	.22	.74	-.12	.14	.63
Language w/par	-.20	.70	.07	.05	.53
Lau category	.02	.66	.02	-.02	.43
Language w/sibs	.00	.63	.03	-.21	.44
Home dominance	.01	.57	.11	.08	.34
School function	-.05	.24	.65	.01	.49
IQ	.03	.13	.58	.18	.39
Brain insults	-.11	.14	.51	.03	.30

Variables	I	II	III	IV	Communality
Learning beh.	.05	.11	.49	.06	.26
General health	.02	.06	.42	.11	.19
Pregnancy/Birth	-.12	.01	.25	.19	.11
Father presence	.03	-.04	.06	.82	.67
Employment	-.02	-.02	.03	.59	.34
Home condition	-.13	.16	-.31	.38	.29

Note. Eigenvalue for unrotated Factor 1 = 3.36; Factor 2 = 2.88; Factor 3 = 2.16; Factor 4 = 1.91; Factor 5 = 1.18; Factor 6 = 1.12; Factor 7 = .93; Factor 8 = .78; Factor 9 = .71; Factor 10 = .66.

Factor I, Household Density, describes how crowded a home is. Factor II, Pull towards English, groups all language measures plus Mother's Years in the U.S. Factor III, Well Child, relates school functioning to health measures and is an index of a child's learning skills and health. Factor IV, Household Quality, is an index of the general socioeconomic status of a home and of the support systems available for child rearing.

Final clustering. The four factors obtained through factor analysis and the five predictor variables—sex, age, school, program, and attendance—were used in the multiple regression analysis. As seen on Table 4, each set was reduced to three predictors.

Table 4

Major Predictor Variables and Factors

Variables/factors	How measured
Biopersonal	
Sex	Boy or girl
Age	C.A. in September of grade 1
Well Child	Factor III
Domestic	
Household Quality	Factor IV
Household Density	Factor I
Pull towards English	Factor III
School	
School attended	Attended school A, B, or C
Program	Resource room or consultation
Attendance	Days in attendance for grade 1

Results

Overall Contribution of the Sets to Achievement

Table 5 presents the significance levels and the percent of variance accounted for by each criterion measure. Every measure except Spanish Spelling reached the pre-established .05 level for significance. Corresponding analysis of variance source tables and the intercorrelation matrix for these variables appear in Alvarez (1983).

Table 5

Percentage of Variance and Significance Levels for Five Criterion Measures

Criterion measure	Percent of variance accounted for	Significance levels
English Reading	37.0	.003
English Spelling	29.1	.030
Spanish Reading	27.1	.050
Spanish Spelling	15.0	.495
Mathematics	34.3	.007

Individual Contributions of the Sets to Achievement

English Reading. As seen in Table 6, School was the only set that contributed significantly to English Reading. In fact, school alone accounted for 21% of the variance, a noteworthy percentage, for this set was entered into the regression last. The contributions of the domestic and personal sets were similar. Each explained about 8% of the total variance, but neither reached significance.

Table 6

Summary Table of Multiple Regression Predicting English Reading Achievement from Biopersonal, Domestic, and School Sets

Set	Multiple R	R^*	R^* change	F for R^* change
Biopersonal	.282	.080	.080	1.756
Domestic	.395	.156	.076	1.331
School	.608	.370	.214	2.736**

** $p < .01$.

English Spelling. As shown in Table 7, the situation for English Spelling was similar to that for English Reading: The school set contributed the most—and significantly—to the total variance.

Table 7

Summary Table of Multiple Regression Predicting English Spelling Achievement from Biopersonal, Domestic, and School Sets

Set	Multiple R	R^*	R^* change	F for R^* change
Biopersonal	.278	.077	.077	1.708
Domestic	.337	.113	.036	.593
School	.540	.291	.178	2.033*

* $p < .05$.

The total variance was smaller for English Spelling than for English Reading; however, it was higher than that for Spanish Reading and almost double that for Spanish Spelling, as the next two tables indicate.

Spanish Reading. The total variance explained by the sets for Spanish reading achievement was smaller than for English Reading, 27% vs. 37% (Table 8). Although the school set again contributed most to the total variance, its impact here was not significant. The domestic set explained 10.2% of the variance, but again it did not reach significance. The biopersonal block's impact was a modest 4.8%.

Table 8

Summary Table of Multiple Regression Predicting
Spanish Reading Achievement from
Biopersonal, Domestic, and School Sets

Set	Multiple R	R^*	R^* change	F for R^* change
Biopersonal	.219	.048	.048	1.027
Domestic	.387	.150	.102	1.755
School	.521	.271	.171	1.348

Note that while each individual set did not reach significance, the three sets as a whole did (see Table 5).

Spanish Spelling. None of the sets in isolation contributed significantly to Spanish Spelling (Table 9). In addition, the relative contributions of the various sets differed from those observed for other subjects. For Spanish Spelling, the biopersonal—rather than the school block—explained the largest percentage of variance. School and domestic sets made approximately equal contributions.

Table 9

Summary Table of Multiple Regression Predicting
Spanish Spelling Achievement from Biopersonal,
Domestic, and School Sets

Set	Multiple R	R^*	R^* change	F for R^* change
Biopersonal	.270	.073	.073	1.599
Domestic	.328	.108	.035	.571
School	.387	.150	.042	.402

Mathematics. The school set once again accounts for the largest variance (22.7%), significant at $p < .01$. The biopersonal set accounts for a variance of 10.9%, which was significant at p <.07. Remarkably, the domestic set accounted for no variance at all.

Table 10

Summary of Multiple Regression Predicting Mathematics Achievement from Biopersonal, Domestic, and School Sets

Set	Multiple R	R^*	R^* change	F for R^* change
Biopersonal	.331	.109	.109	2.500*
Domestic	.341	.116	.007	.167
School	.585	.343	.227	2.789**

* p < .07.
**p < .01.

The preceding tables show that where significance obtained, the school set contributed most to achievement, followed by the biopersonal set. The domestic set made the most modest contribution to the total achievement variance. The prominent contribution of school variables is noteworthy because it was the last block introduced into the regression framework.

Discussion

What Promotes Academic Achievement: Person, Home, or School?

The order: school-person-home. The order of prominence for the sets in this study, school-person-home, agrees with findings of cross-national investigations of elementary school children in developing nations (Thorndike, 1973), a population similar to low-income students in industrialized societies. The prominence of school in influencing academic achievement is consistent across countries. The order of person and home shifts from one developing country to another, but in general the order is person-home. Reanalyses of the Coleman data for low-income and minority children in the U.S. (Gordon, 1975; Madaus et al., 1980) corroborate the preeminent influence of school, as do investigations with secondary school students in England (Rutter et al., 1982).

However, the school does not dominate achievement for middle- and upper-income students or in general for students of industrialized societies. For such students, particularly at the elementary level, family backgrounds and domestic environments are the keys to achievement. For older students, personal attributes and school factors begin to play important roles. The order of prominence appears to be home-person-school rather than school-person-home.

Dynamics underlying Spanish spelling. Total variance for Spanish spelling was conspicuously low. A qualitative analysis of test protocols provided clinical insights into the aspects that may have spuriously lowered individual scores and restricted the range of Spanish spelling scores. In addition, this analysis highlighted some of the struggles beginning writers and speakers have when learning to read and write a standard version of the spoken language.

Dialect interference was a major source of "error" in the Spanish spelling protocols. Many of the distinctions of standard written Spanish are not incorporated in the spoken language of Caribbean speakers and take a longer time to master: (a) the distinction between the voiced bilabial stop /b/ and the voiced labiodental fricative /v/ (which explains why children would write ben/ven or bas/vas; (b) interchanging of soft /c/, /s/, and /z/ and of /y/ and /ll/ (e.g. *felis/feliz, palasio/palacio, eyos/ellos*); and (c) dialectical substitutions (e.g., r/l as in *leel/leer, reil/reir*). In fact, one child, obviously torn between his own sense of language and what was taught in school wrote /*dorlmil, jugarl,* and *leerl*/ for /*dormir, jugar,* and *leer*/. While the latter is the "correct" standard form, the spoken version among certain dialect speakers sounds more like /*dolmil, jugal,* and *leel*/.

Also prominent in spelling protocols were orthographic interferences most likely resulting from the simultaneous acquisition of literacy skills in two languages. Such interferences were noted in both Spanish and English protocols, but especially in Spanish. For example, (a) the use of /y/ as a vowel in Spanish and the failure to use it in English (e.g., *reyr/reir*, or boi/boy); and (b) the writing of English following Spanish cues (e.g., sey/say) or vice versa (e.g., *thetho/dedo, kien/quién*). The misuse of /h/ further illustrates the struggle of incipient writers. In Spanish the /h/ is silent unless preceded by /c/; in English it is roughly analogous to the Spanish /j/. A child thus wrote *dijo* as *diho*, attributing to the Spanish word sound properties of English. Another child read *him* and *how* as /im/ and /au/, an obvious overgeneralization from the Spanish silent /h/ rule.

Other "errors" (e.g., reversals, distortions, omissions, transpositions, inversions) typical of beginners and especially of high-risk learners seem to have been more evenly distributed across languages and skills; they did not seem to affect exclusively the Spanish spelling and reading measures. Yet, these miscues did not have as great an effect on Spanish reading. Why? Most likely the answer lies in the nature of spoken and written language. A child's oral rendition of *dormir* as *dolmil* can hardly be marked incorrect. However, criteria applied to written language are stricter; the global scores do not discriminate between dialect-based errors and no response. The investigation of no response, however, exceeds the scope of this discussion.

Identifying the Best Predictors of Achievement

The specific research questions aimed to identify the best predictors of achievement. Most conclusive findings settled on the school set: It contributed more than did the other sets, and it was significant for three subject matters. This section discusses primarily School Attended, the major predictor within the school block. It also discusses significant variables in the biopersonal block. Finally, certain trends for domestic variables are briefly discussed. The sequence person-home-school will be followed in this discussion, even though a more accurate order, given the statistical findings, would be school-person-home.

What personal attributes promote achievement? Of all the person variables, the Well Child factor had the largest impact on achievement. Well Child consisted of the general health of the child, the neurological intactness, the school skills, the classroom behaviors, and intelligence. Individually, these variables relate positively to learning tasks (Bloom, 1964; Otto, McMenemy, & Smith, 1973).

A thought-provoking trend was noted in the contributions of sex to achievement in English vs. Spanish reading. Being a girl was associated with higher achievement in Spanish; being a boy was associated with higher achievement in English. This was in line with differences observed in Lau categories: Boys were more English dominant at the oral level than girls, who were more Spanish dominant. Thus, 55.6% of the boys are rated bilingual as compared with 26.6% of girls; and 69% of the girls are Spanish dominant in contrast to 48.2% of boys. Additionally, boys reportedly used more English than girls when interacting with parents (30% vs. 16%) and with siblings (57% vs. 46%) at home. Incidentally, these differences are also present among adults: Based on the self-reported speaking proficiency in English and Spanish of adult household members, adult males were rated as more proficient in English than adult females [3.1 vs. 2.3 on a scale from 1 (poor) to 5 (excellent)] though they were equally proficient in Spanish (4.2 vs. 4.1).

What home variables promote achievement? Of the three domestic factors, knowledge and use of English (i.e., Pull towards English), was the variable with the strongest association with achievement and was associated with higher scores in English Reading and lower scores in Spanish Reading. (The converse would have been true if the data had been analyzed in terms of Spanish dominance.) English language knowledge had more of an impact on achievement than Household Density or Household Quality. Pull towards English was associated not only with the English spoken at home (with parents and siblings), but also with Mother's Years in the U.S. The latter is as much a linguistic measure as it is a measure of acculturation, and of the general know-how available to parents in interacting with their environment.

What school variables promote achievement? While Attendance and Program contributed virtually nothing to variance in achievement, School Attended correlated powerfully with academic growth or lack of it. School B was associated with the largest differentials in achievement for *all* academic subjects, but especially in the English and mathematics measures. School A was associated with large differentials in English, modest differentials in arithmetic, and a detraction in Spanish, especially in Spanish reading. School C took third place, with the lowest associations for all English measures and mathematics; in Spanish it fared somewhat better.

To illustrate, the adjusted means on English reading, English spelling, and mathematics for School B are 65.9, 46.7, and 59.6, respectively; for School A, 42.6, 42.2, and 44.1; and for School C, 21.7, 25.9, and 39.9. The inference is that children in School C are achieving less in English reading and English spelling than children in schools A and B, and in mathematics they are achieving less than children in School B.

The schools are similar in several ways: location, student population, faculty, administration, and bilingual/biliterate curriculum. What characteristics distinguished them from one another? First of all, the schools differed in attendance patterns and in the degree of parental involvement. In fact, the order for both these indicators corresponded to the academic rank: School B first, A second, and C last.

Other differences noted among the schools in many ways align A and B together and leave C in a class apart. These differences appear both in status characteristics and in process-oriented observations. Table 11 provides information on each school's standing on a number of status characteristics, based on Board of Education (1976) data. School C is apparently an older, more crowded school that spends less per pupil, exhibits a higher rate of teacher absence, and is staffed with less experienced and less trained teachers. And while it serves the poorest families—

based on the percentage of students that qualify for free lunch—the difference is rather small, especially in relation to the most effective, School B.

Table 11

Statistics on Different Characteristics
of Project Schools

	School		
Variable	A	B	C
Year of Construction	1961	1968	1907
Cost per pupil	$1,058	$1,003	$960
Size of school	589	529	626
Utilization	51.7%	64.7%	65.8%
Pupil/teacher ratio	16.6	18.0	19.1
Teacher absence rate	5.4	7.0	8.3
Teachers ≥ 5 years experience	85.1%	80.6%	71.0%
Teachers with ≤ B.A. + 30	23.5%	12.9%	32.3%
Teachers over B.A. + 30	76.5%	87.1%	67.8%
Free lunch students	89.1%	94.5%	97.4%
Departure rate	31.9	24.6	24.3

Note. The data corresponds to the 1974–1975 school year (Board of Education of the City of New York, 1976).

Other observed differences are more process oriented. Both Schools A and B were headed by females; School C by a male. The leadership style of each principal differed. School C's leadership tended to be autocratic; frequent unpopular decisions irritated parents and lowered teacher morale. For example, all bilingual classes were moved to the top third floor with no bathroom facilities (especially troublesome for the first graders); a huge warning was displayed at the entrance of the school that parents were *not to proceed beyond that point* without stopping at the office.

In Schools A and B decisions about difficult matters were made more democratically: Administration consulted the affected parties. For instance, at the beginning of the project's third year, some changes took place in the Resource Rooms. In School C the changes were effected autocratically. The Resource Teacher came to her room one morning and found all her belongings packed in a box and another teacher at her desk; no one was there to explain. In fact, several weeks of negotiation passed before she settled into another room; the result, of course, was a loss of instruction time for the children. In School A, a change of rooms also occurred, but the principal took care to explain what would happen, and a room—though less adequate than the previous one—was emptied for the teacher, who was given the chance to dismantle the bulletin boards and other decorations that had adorned her classroom. About the same time these changes occurred, School B's principal called in the resource teacher and the project director soliciting their advice for extending the program beyond its third year of funding.

The principals' involvement in the day-to-day activities of teachers and children also differed. At the beginning of the school year, the first-grade classes were screened and high-risk learners identified; both principals at A and B wanted to be kept abreast of the process and the results and attended meetings about project results; several times they stopped by during an Open House for parents and community members. By contrast, the principal of School C would be conspicuously absent at the same or similar events. Perhaps most importantly, Schools A and B both had special commitments. School B was committed to the education of young children: It shared a building with another school that housed Grades 3 through 6, but School B's actual enrollment included pre-school through Grade 2, so it focused on the young learner. Its pre-school programs were innovative; a number of them catered to youngsters with special needs. School A was also somewhat special in that it was a "school within a school." While it served the bilingual children in the surrounding community, it was also dedicated to expanding their creative abilities through the arts. School C was the most conventional school: It offered the usual K through 6 curriculum, with no particular emphasis on any one aspect of a child's development. None of its offerings set it apart from the other primary schools in the area.

Each school had quite distinct curricula. School A emphasized English over Spanish and allotted most of its time to teaching English skills. School C conducted instruction heavily in Spanish. School B offered the most balanced program, allocating about equal time to instruction in the two languages.

Clearly, school effectiveness is a multi-faceted phenomenon. It is impossible to sort out which, if any, of the various school characteristics affected achievement. The features associated with the high achieving schools may be summed up as follows: (a) higher attendance for both students and teachers; (b) increased parental participation; (c) newer buildings; (d) less crowding in school and classrooms; (e) more highly trained and experienced teachers; (f) democratic leadership style; (g) more principal involvement in day-to-day activities of teachers and children; (h) a specific focus or topic to set it apart from other elementary schools. Only School B, the most effective school, allocated equal instruction time to the two target languages.

But if the schools differed in their effectiveness in fostering academic achievement, they also differed in their effectiveness in fostering bilingual achievement. In the two effective schools, differentials were higher in English than in Spanish; in the least effective school, scores in both English and Spanish fell to about the same level. The school with the most balanced bilingual teaching was the one with the largest differentials in the two languages, particularly in English.

The "bilingual/biliterate" programs vary a great deal from one school to another. Even schools in the same district differ in their understanding and implementation of bilingual schooling. Variety may be a strength if it reflects the linguistic competencies of learners and the wishes of a community. Yet this same variety may be a weakness if it reflects primarily the whims and preferences of teachers and administrators.

Implications of the Study

Generally, most of the burden for substandard achievement experienced by certain low-income groups falls on the home environments and on the personal attributes of the children themselves. This study indicates the burden is misplaced: The impact of individual traits and family background appears minimal compared to the impact of school. Despite personal attributes and domestic characteristics, students respond to adequate learning environments and appropriate academic support. In short, good institutions enable youngsters to transcend personal or domestic difficulties and enhance their academic achievement.

That schools carry the largest weight in a student's scholastic performance should alert educators to the value and importance of educational settings. A child's home environment is basically a non-manipulable variable; it can be altered only through major societal changes. To a certain extent, the same can be said of a child's personal attributes. But if the learning needs of bilingual Puerto Rican children from the lowest socioeconomic stratum are found to be adequately addressed through schools, then the schools that serve them are to be more responsive to their obligations towards them. The helplessness experienced by some educators at these children's substandard achievement can be converted into positive action and energetic planning. If achievement varies so strongly with schools, then the schools can be credited with positive as well as negative outcomes.

Findings about the impact of schools on the achievement of low-income students directly oppose those on middle- and upper-income students, particularly at the elementary level. For the latter, schools add little to what their homes already provide. However, when the support of the home for scholastic pursuits is less prominent, then the contributions of the school become increasingly more relevant to children's academic performance. Schools must offer their best services and resources to low-income youth: Schools *can* make a difference; they should try to.

Summary

This chapter summarized a study which explored the relation between academic achievement and several biopersonal, domestic, and school variables among 98 first grade Puerto Rican students attending bilingual programs in three public schools. Academic achievement was represented by measures of English Reading, English Spelling, Spanish Reading, Spanish Spelling, and Arithmetic. Predictor variables consisted of five major variables (Age, Sex, Attendance, School Attended, and Program Attended) and four factors identified through factor analysis (Well Child, Household Quality, Household Density, and Pull towards English). The predictors were grouped in three sets representing Person, Home, and School variables.

Major findings of the study can be summarized as follows: (a) the School set exerted the largest contribution to achievement for all criterion measures except Spanish Spelling, and these contributions were significant for English Reading, English Spelling, and Mathematics; and (b) within the School Set, the School Attended by the child was the best predictor of achievement in both English and Spanish; the evidence showed two of the schools to be more effective than the third in terms of the achievement differentials exhibited by the children.

Major implications of the study stem from the finding that schools are the major contributors to achievement among low-income Puerto Rican children. If the major determinants of children's achievement had been found to reside in their personal attributes or in their domestic situations, the interventions open to educators would be limited. But given that major differentials were associated with the institutions charged with the children's education, efforts can focus on making these institutions more responsive learning environments.

REFERENCES

Alvarez, M.D. (1983). Puerto Ricans and academic achievement: An exploratory study of person, home, and school variables among high-risk bilingual first graders. Unpublished doctoral dissertation, New York University.

Alvira-Benitez, S. (1976). Selected factors in the home environment and Puerto Rican fourth grade pupils' reading achievement. Unpublished doctoral dissertation, Temple University.

Ambert, A.N. (1980). Language disorders in Spanish-speaking children: A language intervention program. Unpublished doctoral dissertation, Harvard Graduate School of Education.

Anglada, M. (n.d.). Statement by Puerto Rican educators: A response to the multicultural education task force of the National Institute of Education. *Rican* (vol. and p. nos. unavailable).

Ansell, P.N. (1976). Psychological differentiation, social reinforcement, and task performance with Black, White, and Hispanic first and second grade children. Unpublished doctoral dissertation, New York University.

Aspira of New York. (1973). *Annual report 1972–1973*. New York: Author.

Baker, J., & Sanson, J. (1990). Interventions with students at risk for dropping out of school. *Journal of Educational Research, 83*, 181–186.

Bedotto, M.J. (1973). The effects of non-native speech upon the reading achievement of Spanish-speaking students at different levels of intelligence and upon their ability to use syntactic clues to meaning in reading English. Unpublished doctoral dissertation, New York University.

Bloom, B.S. (1964). Human characteristics and school learning. New York: McGraw-Hill.

Board of Education of the City of New York (1976). *Community and high school profiles 1974–1975*. New York: Author.

Borges, F. (1975). *Variables associated with successful learning to read experiences of children when they enter school in Puerto Rico.* (ERIC Document Reproduction Service No. ED 122–237).

Brown, G.H., Rosen, N.L., Hill, S.T., & Olivas, M.A. (1980). *The condition of education for Hispanic Americans.* Washington, DC: National Center for Education Statistics.

Bucchioni, E. (1965). A sociological analysis of the functioning of elementary education for Puerto Rican children. Unpublished doctoral dissertation, New School for Social Research.

Canabal, J., & Ferisin, A. (1973). *Examen de aprovechamiento escolar.* New York: Puerto Rican Family Institute.

Canino, I.A., Earley, B.F., & Rogler, L.H. (1980). *The Puerto Rican child in New York City: Stress and mental health.* New York: Fordham University, Hispanic Research Center.

Chang, W.L. (1971). A comparison of certain structures written in English by monolingual and bilingual sixth graders. Unpublished doctoral dissertation, Boston University.

Cohen, A.S. (1966). Some learning disabilities of socially disadvantaged Puerto Rican and Negro children. *Academic Therapy Quarterly, 2*(1), 37–41; 52.

Coleman, J.S., Campbell, E.Q., Hobson, C.J., McPartland, J., Mood, A.M., Weinfeld, F.D., & York, R.L. (1979). *Equality of educational opportunity.* New York: Arno (originally published 1966).

Cordasco, F. (1967). Puerto Rican pupils and American education. *School and Society, 95,* 116–119.

De La Rosa, D., & Maw, C.E. (1990). *Hispanic education: A statistical portrait 1990.* Washington, DC: National Council of La Raza.

Elam, S.L. (1960). Acculturation and learning problems of Puerto Rican children. *Teachers College Record, 61,* 258–264.

Fitzpatrick, J. (1987). *Puerto Rican Americans: The meaning of migration to the mainland,* 2nd ed. Englewood Cliffs, NJ: Prentice-Hall.

Fuentes, L. (1980). The struggle for local political support. In C.E. Rodríguez, V. Sánchez Kennol, & J.O. Alers (Eds.), *The Puerto Rican struggle: Essays on survival in the U.S.* (pp. 111–120). New York: Puerto Rican Migration Research Consortium.

Gordon, E.W. (1975). New perspectives on old issues in education for the minority poor. *ICRD Bulletin, 10*(1), 5–17.

Harris, D.B. (1963). *Children's drawings as measures of intellectual maturity: A revision and extension of the Goodenough Draw-A-Man Test.* New York: Harcourt, Brace, Jovanovich.

Jastak, J.F., Bijou, S.W., & Jastak, S.R. (1976). *Wide Range Achievement Test, 1976 Edition.* Wilmington, DE: Guidance Associates of Delaware.

Kleiber, W.C. (1974). Academic achievement and aspects of acculturation among Puerto Rican male community college students. Unpublished doctoral dissertation, New York University.

Layden, R.G. (1972). The relationship between the language of instruction and the development of self concept, classroom climate, and achievement of Spanish speaking Puerto Rican children. Unpublished doctoral dissertation, University of Maryland.

Lucas, I. (1971). *Puerto Rican dropouts in Chicago: Numbers and motivations.* Washington, DC: Office of Education, Bureau of Research.

Madaus, G.F., Airasian, P.W., & Kellaghan, T. (1980). *School effectiveness: A reassessment of the evidence.* New York: McGraw-Hill.

McCollum, P.A. (1980). Attention-getting strategies of Anglo-American and Puerto Rican students: A microethnographic analysis. Unpublished doctoral dissertation, University of Illinois.

Meléndez, S.E. (1978). A review of the literature on the self-concept of Puerto Rican children in bilingual education and monolingual education. Qualifying paper, Harvard Graduate School of Education.

Montalvo, B. (1974). Home-school conflict and the Puerto Rican child. *Social Casework, 10,* 100-110.

Morrison, J.C. (1958). *The Puerto Rican study, 1953–1957: A report on the education and adjustment of Puerto Rican pupils in the public schools of the City of New York.* New York: Board of Education of the City of New York.

Nazario, I. (1980). Intervention in the development of negative attitudes of fourth grade Puerto Rican children toward school. Unpublished doctoral dissertation, Rutgers University.

Otto, W., McMenemy, R.A., & Smith, R.J. (1973). *Corrective and remedial teaching,* 2nd ed. Boston: Houghton Mifflin.

Paulston, C.B. (Ed.), (1977). Research viewpoint. In Center for Applied Linguistics. *Bilingual education: Current perspectives. Vol. 2, Linguistics.* Arlington, VA: Center for Applied Linguistics.

Paulston, C.B. (1980). *Bilingual eduction: Theories and issues.* Rowley, MA: Newbury House.

Plante, A.J. (1977). Connecticut pairing model proves effective in bilingual education. *Phi Delta Kappan, 58,* 427.

Polemeni, A.J. (1976). *Language Assessment Battery, Level 1.* New York: Board of Education of the City of New York.

Prewitt-Díaz, J.O. (1983). A study of self-esteem and school sentiment on two groups of Puerto Rican students. *Educational and Psychological Research, 3,* 161-167.

Prior, D.R. (1974). Inner city elementary pupil mobility, reading achievement, and environmental process variables. Unpublished doctoral dissertation, Fordham University.

Rodríguez, C. (1974). The structure of failure II: A case in point. *Urban Review, 7*(3), 215–226.

Rodríguez, C. (1989). Puerto Ricans born in the U.S.A. Winchester, MA: Unwin Hyman.

Rutter, M., Maughan, B., Mortimore, P., Ouston, J., & Smith, A. (1982). *Fifteen thousand hours: Secondary schools and their effects on children.* Cambridge, MA: Harvard University Press.

Scores on reading tests given in public schools. (1983). *The New York Times,* January 4.

Strong, L. (1973). Language disability in the Hispano-American child. *Bulletin of the Orton Society, 23,* 30–38.

Summers, A.A., & Wolfe, B.L. (1976). Which school resources help learning? Efficiency and equity in Philadelphia public schools. *IRCD Bulletin* (ERIC Clearinghouse on Urban Education, Teachers College, Columbia University), *11*(3), 1–15.

Thorndike, R.L. (1973). *Reading comprehension education in fifteen countries: An empirical study.* New York: Wiley.

Torregrosa Diaz, V. (1986). Biliteracy and its effects on reading achievement among bilingual Puerto Rican and Mexican American students in grades two through four. Unpublished doctoral dissertation, Wayne State University.

Troike, R.D. (1978). Research evidence for the effectiveness of bilingual education. Rosslyn, VA: National Clearinghouse for Bilingual Education.

U.S. Bureau of the Census (1988). *The Hispanic population in the United States: March 1988* (Advance Report). Current Population Reports, Population Characteristics Series P-20, No. 431. Washington, DC: Author.

U.S. Commission on Civil Rights (1976). *Puerto Ricans in the continental United States: An uncertain future.* Washington, DC: Author.

Veltman, C.J. (1980a). *Relative educational attainments of minority language children, 1976.* Washington, DC: National Center for Education Statistics.

Veltman, C.J. (1980b). *The role of language characteristics in the socioeconomic attainment process of Hispanic origin men and women.* Washington, DC: National Center for Education Statistics.

Veltman, C.J. (1981). Relative educational attainments of Hispanic-American children, 1976. *Metas, 2,* 36–51.

Zanger, V.V. (1987). The social context of second language learning: An examination of barriers to integration in five case studies. Unpublished doctoral dissertation, Boston University.

Zirkel, P.A. (1972). An evaluation of the effectiveness of selected experimental bilingual education programs in Connecticut.Unpublished doctoral dissertation, University of Connecticut.

CHAPTER 7

Researching Research:
A Student-Teacher-Researcher
Collaborative Project

Carmen I. Mercado

Introduction

This chapter chronicles the first year of a collaborative project that I initiated with a former graduate student in September 1989. I met Marcy and discovered her interest in research during the Spring semester when she was enrolled in the advanced reading course I teach at Hunter College. She caught my attention, close to the end of the term, when she described in one of the session logs, how she was applying "inference training" strategies discussed in an assigned article by Pearson and Dole (1987). Soon thereafter, I arranged to visit her class in the South Bronx to observe how this was being accomplished. It was on that visit in June that, energized by her initiatives and her willingness to try "new ideas," I proposed that we collaborate on a project in September. The various phone calls I received from Marcy during the summer convinced me that her commitment was firm. With the start of the academic year, I began what turned into regular Friday visits. My goal was to engage Puerto Rican and other minority students in doing ethnographic research the way Brice-Heath (1985) had done, although I later discovered that Marcy expected that we would continue with the inference training activities she had begun to apply. Considering that what we both wanted was to form a partnership, this was a minor discrepancy.

As one of the few Hispanic females on the Hunter College faculty, my interest in this project went beyond that of experimenting with innovative instructional practices that I had read about in the research literature. For some time now, I have been concerned about the dismal statistics which document the high dropout rate and the general educational failure or underachievement of our youth. My partnership with Marcy, who like me is Puerto Rican, was part of a personal commitment, however small, to addressing this unacceptable situation. The Latino Adopt-a-Class Program provided a legitimate mechanism for accomplishing this goal as it was designed to provide "students who are at a critical stage in the development of their academic purpose, with role models and examples of opportunities that could be available to them after successful completion of their education" (Board of Education, n.d.). As a drop-out prevention program, Adopt-a-Class afforded me another legitimate explanation for my presence in schools. Therefore, I adopted Marcy's class to share my world as an educational researcher.

It should be clear from the outset that this project was important to me for professional reasons. Participation in it would enable me to focus my attention over a period of time on one activity, and its documentation would lead to presentations and publications, while at the same time providing direct services to the classroom. Reciprocity was thus an essential ingredient, which may explain why Marcy and I have taken the lead in this project in different ways and at different times. I did at first in charting a course for collaborative activities, but she and the students also have as the journey has gotten underway. Reciprocal needs have brought us together and affinity, admiration, and trust have kept us from moving apart.

Purpose of the Study

I have employed a case study approach to document issues that surface when innovations are introduced into a traditional classroom structure. Specifically, the study was intended to describe what happens when minority students—many of whom are Puerto Rican—are initiated into the world of educational research, gathering and analyzing data, and making presentations at forums and conferences where researchers share their findings. As a participant-observer, I documented our activities using ethnographic procedures, the same procedures that I demonstrated to students during our sessions together as a means of modeling research practices.

Through participation in these activities, it was expected that students would (a) learn to value and understand the work of researchers; (b) gain competence in communicating and thinking like researchers; and (c) develop confidence in their ability to do more advanced work than they are typically exposed to in schools.

Data were gathered from a variety of sources, including, (a) my field notes of observations and conversations with the students and the teacher within and outside of the school; (b) notes in the students' research folders; (c) student responses to assignments completed in class and at home; and (d) scores on the standardized reading exam administered in the Spring. Qualitative data analysis required going back and forth between these different data sets, developing summaries, and generating and testing hypotheses/categories that surfaced from the data. Quantitative analysis involved comparing gains made on the Degrees of Reading Power (DRP) test between 1989 and 1990.

Description and Procedure

On Fridays, students in Marcy's official class remained with her for all but two 45 minute periods—Spanish and Dance. This allowed us the luxury of devoting two 90 minute sessions—one in the morning and one in the afternoon—to discussions, conferences, and independent activities related to students' research work, which is unusual as far as scheduling at this level goes.

Since our first encounter in September, the 28 remaining sixth graders, down from a register of 40 in September—18 males and 10 females—have been involved in gathering data from a variety of sources, including family and peers, on topics they identified in response to the question: "What would you like to learn about (as part of this research project)?" Chart 1 contains a listing of student responses, with repetitions reflecting the number of students who copied the same topic from the list of elicited responses I wrote on the board. I rephrased the first item as I made sense of the student's utterances, but all the others are their actual words.

During our second session, students formed research teams with peers who had similar interests or who wanted to work together, even if they had different topics, as Angel, Wilton, and Garland had done. Collaboration was an important aspect of the instructional approach, as students were expected to learn by doing with the help of more capable others, reflecting a Vygotskian perspective. It took three sessions to establish the relational and interactional structure for these types of activities as it was the beginning of the academic year.

The students voted to name our class project "World-Wide Researchers" or WWR, voting down my suggestion—the title that I had submitted to the Ethnography in Education Conference and which serves as the title of this chapter: "Researching research. . . ." Individual teams chose to have their own identities, as well, selecting far more powerful names than I could have dreamed of: the "drug" group called themselves D.E.A.D. or Drugs End All Dreams. It is worth noting that giving this project a name arose out of a real need I had to make reference to our activities to one of the supervisors in the school, who asked, "What do you call it?" Giving the project a name established our identity and legitimized what we were doing to others, including me!

During our Friday meetings, I usually shared my work as well as the work of other researchers in areas of concern to the students. Demonstrating or modeling how research is done is a distinctive feature of this project. By my showing students how I am documenting the research activities of this class, we have the opportunity to reflect on and discuss what occurred during our previous meeting, as well as to explore how ethnographic procedures may be used by the students in their own work. In addition, bringing in copies of my typed field notes/logs and data summaries for their examination, allowed me to validate my recorded data and obtain additional perceptions of and reactions to occurrences I had noted. The significance of this procedure had been discussed, and students were well aware that ethnographic researchers must verify the accuracy of their information. In fact, they enjoyed "correcting" my data, as they referred to it. The students derived much pleasure from correcting the document: Sources of Data (Chart 2), prepared for the Ethnography in Education Conference held in March of 1990 at the University of Pennsylvania.

Occasionally, I brought copies of articles from newspapers and research journals that were relevant to our work. No effort was made to keep materials from students because they might be too difficult, a procedure I had learned from Brice-Heath (1985). In fact, I read from and showed students the article by Ed Farrell (1989) and his high school collaborators that appeared in the *American Educational Research Journal*, not only because of similarities in methodology, but also because we were to be co-presenters at the Ethnography in Education Conference.

Class discussions have focused on topics such as the following: (a) Planning Our Study; (b) Different Ways of Learning; (c) Examining Student Interviews and Surveys; (d) The Project Chronology; (e) Writing Bibliographic References; and (f) Assessing our Presentations. Typically, these discussions were in response to group and individual concerns that surfaced from involvement in activities, rather than being pre-planned to coincide with a particular sequence.

As I was both participant and observer, it was difficult for me to record events during class discussions. I requested the assistance of volunteers to be "scribes" and take notes

Chart 1

WHAT DO YOU WANT TO LEARN ABOUT? RESPONSES
FROM STUDENTS IN 6M23 ON FRIDAY,
SEPTEMBER 13TH, 1989

How can we the citizens get more money for food and
housing for the poor and homeless?

What is the government's responsibility to its citizens?
What is the government's responsibility to its citizens?
What is the government's responsibility to its citizens?
          homeless warfare

Why does the government spend so much money on nuclear
weapons while there are homeless people?

Why is the government wasting so much money on guns,
and many other weapons, and homeless are dying of
starvation on blocks and on trains?

How government can help the homeless?

Where do we get our supplies for army weapons, first aid
and gears?

Where do we get money from?

Who pays for the city mortage?

Why are there so many bad things in the world and why do
they raise taxes on people who can't pay it?

— —

Why more people every day are taking drugs?

How can we stop drug abuse?

How can we stop the drug problem in the world and the
U.S.?

How can we stop the drug problem in the U.S. and the
world?

How can we prevent AIDS and drugs?

Why do people like to use drugs?

Why is there so many drinking problems and car crashes?

— —

Where do diseases come from and what can we do about it (or how can we)?

Where do diseases come from and what can we do about it?

Where do diseases come from and what can we do about it?

Where do diseases come from and what can we do about it or how can we prevent them?

Where do diseases come from and how can we prevent it?

— —

Why is there so much abuse and abandonment and why are there so many murders. How can we stop it?

Why is there so much abuse and abandonment? And how can we stop it? Why are there so many murders?

Why is there so much abuse and abandonment? How can we stop it?

How can we stop people from being abused and why do they abuse?

What can we do to prevent child abuse?

How can we prevent murders, rapes, robberies?

How can we protect our children from kidnappers?

— —

Why are girls getting pregnant at an early age?

"The facts of life"

Learning facts of life

tell them what's right and wrong

Why do men and women have different jobs?

How can we increase our children's grades?

How can we stop food shortage in other countries?

I want to learn more about love.

Chart 2

SOURCES OF DATA

1.0 Interviews and Conversations with Authorities/Informants

  1.1 family members and friends who had babies in their
teens
Kim interviewed Njeri mother
Shannon interviewed his cousin and aunt
Gloria and Malika interviewed Gloria's aunt
Njeri interviewed Mrs. Jones
Adrianna interviewed her girlfriend J.

  1.2 people we met outside school
Sonia talked to a lady she knows who has AIDS;
She attempted to interview a doctor during visit to
clinic;
She spoke to her counselor
Angel interviewed a homeless woman in the street
John talked to his grandparents about drugs in their
days
Maigen interviewed a 15 year old who has two kids.

2.0 Field Visits and Observations

  2.1 Observations on the block
Ming observed drug dealers from his window
Amaury observed the way drug dealers and addicts
communicate
Adrianna observed the girls on her block who had
kids in their teens

  2.2 Observations at other places
Rebecca, Maigen, Idalia, and Sonia visited a hospital
which provides special services to babies with
AIDS, after school with the teacher

3.0 Reading

  3.1 Library books
Angel read *The Homeless* by Elaine Landau
Jerell read his cousin's book about having babies
Rebecca read *Children Having Children* and *Sexually
Transmitted Diseases*

3.2 Pamphlets and Brochures

3.3 Newspaper and Magazine Articles
Article Dr. M. gave out: "Coke Study: Drug Users at 11"
News clippings M.T. gave students
Articles students found on their own:
Samuel
Angel read: "Homeless Mom Felt Unable to Care for Two"
"Tompkins Park Flap"

4.0 Viewing Special TV Programs and Films and Radio Programs out of school

4.1 Viewing television programs that provide information ("True Stories)"
Samuel looked at the news
Wilton saw two movies about child abuse and sexual abuse
watching the show "Cop"
Idalia watched "America's Most Wanted"
Diana watched "When He's Not A Stranger"
Maigen also watched "The Reporters"
Adrianna watched shows like "The Oprah Winfrey Show"
Shannon saw a movie called "Intermediate Family"

5.0 Listening to Guest Lectures and Watching Videos in School

5.1 Watching the video "It Only Takes Once" with guest speaker Mrs. Ramos, from Kingsbridge Heights Community Center

5.2 Weekly visits by Mrs. Benitez, a police officer who works with SPECDA program (School Program Educate Control Drugs Abuse)

of our Friday meetings. Samples of notes taken by Salvador, one of the most consistent scribes, appear on Chart 3. With this record, as well as my sketchy notes, I was able to reconstruct our activities after leaving the setting. Although Marcy kept a log of events, I regularly depended on the students' notes to preserve a record of what we accomplished each session. More importantly, these notes allowed us the additional advantage of seeing what we were doing through the eyes of students, an essential part of the ethnographic approach I was demonstrating. Sharing my own notes with students and calling attention to details, such as the date and the time when things occur, was a means of guiding this activity.

Students were given the opportunity to brief me on what occurred during the week and to request assistance or consult with others about their work—with the entire class, in small groups, and individually. Throughout, students were encouraged to consult peers and "to help each other out," as students expressed it. As I have done with my work, I brought in copies of computer printouts of students' interviews and questionnaires for these discussions. In general, I sought to help students document the details of their activities or the research process. I avoided direct discussions of "drug abuse" and "teenage pregnancy" in light of Board of Education regulations which stipulate that discussions of these topics may be conducted only by individuals trained in these areas. Through special programs in the school as well as the teacher's vast network of community resources—her "funds of knowledge," as Moll and his colleagues (1989) refer to it—students were given access to a wide range of specialists in the major topic areas of their research.

Research teams were asked to write and submit brief progress reports on what they had accomplished during the week, which included telling us (a) how they were getting their information; (b) what they were learning; (c) how we could be of help; and (d) what they planned to do the following week. In a long term project of this nature, it is important for students to synthesize their accomplishments and plan what they will do next on a regular basis.

Findings and Discussion

Although our journey together is not yet over, we have already made many exciting discoveries—a word we all use with great regularity—since this adventure began. Students are learning that (a) they can conduct research, (b) that research is fun but hard, (c) that research is a way of learning, (d) that others, including adults, can learn from students, and (e) that researchers help others. Each of these will be described in turn.

"We can do research!" (Sonia, 01/05/90)

Late in October, I asked students to complete a one-page survey of their perceptions of research which I developed (see Chart 4). At that time, not all acknowledged that they would consider themselves as researchers. Angel, who has become one of our most serious researchers, was one of eight (out of 22) who said, "I won't consider myself a researcher because I don't explore for important things." However, as the students became aware that they were engaged in "authentic activities" (Brown, Collins, & Duguid, 1989), that yield useful knowledge, their perception of themselves as researchers appears to be changing. Students are becoming aware, from my reactions as well as the reactions of audiences they have addressed, that they have access to information that others may not have. ("We have friends who can tell us what it's like.") Consequently, they can contribute to other's understanding of real problems. In preparing for the presentation at Fordham University, I asked students, sometimes individually and sometimes in groups, "What have you learned?" Sonia's response was most memorable for its emphatic delivery: "I *can* research!" She repeated this point to our audience the next day. Maigen, Miguel, and others stated similar views. Both Angel and Malika have now said that they want to become "real researchers," as Malika phrased it, and Maigen has indicated that she wants to be "a researcher and a dancer," a rather unusual, but not impossible, combination!

Chart 3

10-30-89

Today on the 10-20-89 Dr. Mercado was
speaking to the class about what our
Project name should be one of the same
was RIOS, Research, In, our, schools, another
was RIF, Research, Is, Fun, another "Researching
Research: a student and teacher collaborative
Project". The class were taking in the work
series but not all some were looking
around but as I said some are taking
It series, at 1:21 the teacher was saying
what we were doing right and what
we were doing wrong, she said we should
not only read that we should ask people
who experience, at 1:08 she asked for a little
at 1:20 the teacher was talking about the ...
of ... at 1:44 the teacher was asking
if we had improve at 2:04 we were voting
on our project name.

BRIVADES

1-12-90

Dr mercado come to our class on the 1-12-89 at 9:40 to our class to do research at 10:00 we were talking about what happened at the fordham university and how can that conference help us for our next conference at philadelphia and how many weeks we got left to go to our conference we had only 6½ weeks left at 10:30 we were saying that they think there research work was good they said that it was good because people liked it they were laughing taking pictures they were impressed by the research they sounded professional and they also invited us to a radio station. to say more about our research Dr mercado said that to do better we need to get over our nervousness Projecting our voice and also to trie eye contact at 10:47 Dr mercado gave out papers that she typed that said how good we were and how can we improve she also teached us a new word assess - means evaluate you say whats good and what can be better. to improve we need to avoid saying the same Information over and over, we also need to devolep a list of references : books, articles, and programs at 10:56 Dr mercado gave us another shet that she gave to the Researchers of the conference she also gave us the shets on the 1-12-89 at 11:04 Dr mercado gave us another shet that had the chronology she said that a chronology Is important because then you know whats going on those days or maybe things that already went on those days at 11:14 Dr mercado wanted us to look on her chronology to look for the day's she already came to our class since the 9-15-89 to know. at 11:20 we were looking for types on her chronology we found typos on the 11-20-89 fund raising 9-15-89 round table 10-27-89 most 10-27-89 ysee at 1:10 Dr mercado said we had to do a letter for Mrs Eva Collazo we were writing to her because we needed money to go to philadelphia to make our other presentation Shannon said that the cake sale was to go to philadelphia Dr mercado told him that the cane sale was not enough then Mrs. torres said that writing the letter maybe Mrs Eva Callazo would help us to go to philadelphia at 1:30 Mrs Mercado was melting with people in the back of the class at 1:48 mrs Torres was also helping Dr mercado by going around the class reading letters and correcting letters. at 1:52 Dr mercado was packing to leave. I do not want her to leave but she had to go home I cannot wait for new friday.

X Salvador

"Research is fun, but hard!" (Kim, 01/04/90)

Many students have said that research is "fun" and "interesting" because they are "researching the topic they want to research." "We love doing work. With Dr. Mercado, 'our research teacher,' we do lots of work, but we love and enjoy it." "We get to go out in order to get information and we get to work in groups, and that's fun."

However, doing research also "takes time" and is "hard work." "You have to go deeper into it." "It wasn't easy finding information," as "books don't have all the information." Researchers have to use different sources of information. "It's hard to find answers." Sonia indicated (see Chart 4) that she got nervous when she had nothing to write, suggesting that students were negotiating their work for a grade.

Some students indicated that you have to be observant and take careful notes. "It's hard to interview people," particularly when dealing with topics such as drugs or when you don't have the means to record conversations. Kim, Njeri, and Shannon honestly admitted difficulty in writing down what people said, realizing the need for a tape recorder. Rebecca admitted in early March, much to my surprise, that she sometimes wrote in her own words what people said as she could not take everything down.

Yet students have learned that research is fun because you do not have to work alone. Receiving "help" and support from peers, as well as others who are interested in their work, is essential. Marcy was impressed when she discovered that students were "giving each other advice on what to do" on their own. Furthermore, Rebecca moved and surprised me when she stated publicly during our presentation at Fordham University, that "(Dr. Mercado) showed me I could do it (research) with the help of my friends, my research helpers."

However, Rebecca noted that "it wasn't easy working together." Thus, while groups were organized as a supportive structure for students so that they would be able to gain from the benefit of interaction, as suggested by Vygotsky (1978) and others, relationships between and among group members sometimes got in the way of learning. This possibility is seldom considered by researchers on collaborative learning.

"When you research, you find out things you don't know." (Angel, 10/20/89)

Many students claim that they have "learned a lot from doing research," as Adrianna and others have said. By focusing their attention on one topic over a period of time, students have gained greater knowledge about their topics, which is evident from the effortless manner in which they are able to conduct themselves during formal presentations. However, what I found most affecting were students' revelations of how research was helping them "with their own problems." Adrianna was especially compelling when she said during our Fordham presentation that, "people tell us never to get pregnant, and we girls say why is it so important never to get pregnant? Working on the topic we learn why it is bad for us to get pregnant." Her sentiments were echoed by Maigen, who went on to say that, to her, "research is exploring the life of a teenager." Jerrel said that doing research (on drugs) helped students "find out information so they won't make the same mistake early in life."

Sonia made an insightful discovery when she realized that you have to know about something in order to do research. Thus, while research yields knowledge, it also takes knowledge to be able to ask pointed questions during an interview and to know what is important when you read and when you talk to people. What Sonia did not know was that this was the main point of a recent article by Roth (1989). Sonia had discovered that knowledge and process are inseparable! Some students have commented that they are learning "new words and to talk more intelligent." As Shannon said with pride "we sixth graders are doing college work."

Chart 4

OCTOBER 20, 1989

1. What is research?

Reserch is kids (or) teacher's
that pick a certain topic and
work on it until they got all of the information
they need.

2. What does a researcher do?

A reasercher tries to get
information on there topic
and write it down.

3. Would you consider yourself a research?

yes. Becouse I have
look around for my topic.
And I writting it down to get information on it.

4. What are you learning about research?

I am leanning alot. Becouse
Before I started I didn't know that
Much about aids and drugs so it's realy helping me

5. How is our research project helping you with other assignments?

By. Giving the noledge and information
on what to do and what
not

6. Would you like to share what we are doing in this project with

   (a) other students and teachers in this school?

   (b) teachers and students in other schools?

   (c) teachers and researchers at special meetings?

7. What do you find interesting about our research project?

That we get to go out in order
to get nfy info and also
get to work in groups and that's fun.

8. What do you find difficult about our research project?

What I find difficult is
that when I don't got
any thing to write about I get norwause.

OCTOBER 20, 1989

1. What is research?

research is something you want to explores. and something.

2. What does a researcher do?

A researcher is like a scientist. It looks for or explores for important things.

3. Would you consider yourself a researcher?

I won't consider myself a researcher because I don't expir for important things.

4. What are you learning about research?

I'm learning that research is fun. When you rises. you find out things you don't know.

5. How is our research project helping you with other assignments?

It is helping me with other assignments by giving me understanding.

6. Would you like to share what we are doing in this project with
   (a) other students and teachers in this school?
   (b) teachers and students in other schools?
   . ⬤ **teachers and researchers at special meetings?**

7. What do you find interesting about our research project?

I find interesting because i learning things I don't know

8. What do you find difficult about our research project?

We have to work.

"It felt good for people to listen to us and want to see us again." (Njeri, 01/25/90) *". . . so people can learn what we learn."* (Miguel, 01/05/90)

Thirteen students have now experienced the excitement of sharing their work at two major conferences and at presentations with teachers and prospective teachers that are part of the City University of New York teacher training programs. These conferences have served several important purposes. I have become increasingly aware that formal presentations at legitimate research forums have played a critical role in "enculturating" students into the world of research, to borrow an expression from Brown, Collins, and Duguid (1989). As part of this process, students have grown to understand that they are capable of contributing to the knowledge base, and that they are responsible for sharing their discoveries with teachers and researchers from other settings. Moreover, these presentations have given us the opportunity to reflect upon our data in the company of informed others, and to validate our interpretations or to consider alternative interpretations of our findings, essential to the research process. With each new presentation, I have gained new insights from students about the work they are doing. As an aside, the professional jealousies that are displayed over who received the most attention at the end of our session at the Ethnography in Education Conference made it quite clear that students had been initiated into the competitive nature of research!

The presentations have also served another very important purpose, which I had not entirely anticipated. They have been a vital means of rekindling interest in our work when enthusiasm has waned from time to time, as may be expected in a long-term project of this nature.

"Researchers help others." (John, 10/20/89)

Perhaps the most surprising finding to date is that students are conducting research with the goal of doing something about the problems of their communities, not just for the sake of gathering information. Information gained through research must serve some valuable purpose, as Miguel and Shannon emphasized during the presentation at Fordham University. Miguel added, "I'm planning to write a letter to the drug association and the President." Both Angel and Sonia have expressed the urgency of doing something about the attitudes that people have toward the homeless and the victims of AIDS.

These five main trends have surfaced from preliminary qualitative data analyses. Findings from achievement data are as impressive.

Recommendations

Marcy and I have also learned a great deal through our collaborative research. In particular, we have learned that (a) collaboration takes time and requires constant negotiation; (b) students can learn about research from doing "real" research; (c) data generated from collaborative classroom research provides important insights for teachers and teacher educators; (d) there are many resources within the school/community that may be used in a systematic manner to promote classroom learning; and (e) some level of funding is essential to accomplish a project of this nature.

Collaboration Takes Time and Requires Negotiation

It is not easy to accomplish collaborative research between university-based faculty and classroom teachers. There are many factors that get in the way of collaboration, even with the most willing of participants. I sometimes found my attention distracted by meetings and other activities related to my college responsibilities and professional interests. Similarly, Marcy's attention was drawn away most frequently by problems related to students, which required immediate attention and sometimes involved others in the school. Exhaustion and interruptions were common. I suspect that this is the way it is and will always be when working within school settings.

However, our biggest enemy may have been "routine." In school, everything becomes routine, as one of my graduate students wrote in Spanish in her research log ("Todo se vuelve rutina"). Marcy and I had to work at keeping the excitement of this project alive. Activities such as research that are meaningful and real to adults may not be real and meaningful to students. As Brown, Collins, and Duguid (1989) argue, everything that is done in school is considered school work and, therefore, unauthentic. Angel's revelation that "at first I thought research was boring" came as a real surprise, particularly since Marcy and I considered him to be one of our most serious researchers from the very beginning.

Had it not been for the relational fabric between Marcy and me—our mutual admiration and trust, our love of learning, and the energizing effect we had on each other—the momentum required for this collaboration would not have been sustained. Marcy has rekindled my interest in our work when other concerns pulled my attention away, as I have done for her. Similarly, students have also had a key role in keeping the excitement alive, as Angel has done when he has called me at the office or at home "just to say hi," and Jackie, who in her eagerness to see me inquired, "When is that lady coming again?" I agree with McDermott (1977) that this relationship is at the heart of what individuals are able to accomplish together.

Learning from Doing "Real" Research

Both Marcy and I have come to recognize the power of guided activities as a means of learning as opposed to learning, "by being told." This is what students meant when they said that they are learning a lot from me, a statement I first found surprising, as I had done little of what I considered to be "direct teaching." Unlike student-researchers in the study reported by Brice-Heath, who became involved in ethnographic inquiries after a semester of learning about research from reading and hearing what others had done, students in this project spent very little time preparing for research. Rather, they became engaged in actually doing research at the outset. By our fourth

session at the beginning of October, students like Kim and
Njeri had already conducted and written up their first
interviews. They became involved immediately both because
Marcy was afraid students would lose interest if they had
to wait too long to begin gathering data, and because I
became interested in testing the power of activity-based
learning. We have gained from the power of ethnography
to inform as our work together has evolved; it has made
us aware of students' responsiveness to instructional
procedures and thereby allowed us to fine-tune these on
an ongoing basis.

It is instructive that through her involvement in this
project, Marcy's interest in research has intensified, as
she acknowledged with pride during informal chats as well
as public presentations. She says she finds herself "talking
research" with her friends during casual exchanges,
something she never did before. She has also indicated
that since this project began, she has recorded more
systematically what her students say and do—whether in
her log or on sheets of paper, whichever is handy at the
time. Moreover, she has observed her 17-year-old son doing
the same, a development that she considers "truly amazing,"
one of her favorite phrases.

Learning from Students and Teachers

As Marcy and I have assumed different roles as
teachers, students, and researchers, we have discovered
a great deal about the realities of students' lives and their
perceptions of schooling, and also about what it means
to be a teacher in an "inner city" school today. I have also
had the opportunity to reflect upon the relationship between
practice and theory.

Students have articulated a perception of schooling
that, while disturbing, is certainly not surprising, as I had
found in my doctoral research (Mercado, 1988). Both
Rebecca and Shannon maintained that other teachers "put
work on the board and we do it." This was brought out
in early January when, in preparing for our first
presentation, I asked students to tell me what was so
different about our work together, as they had been

insisting. Rebecca explained that Marcy and I give students "the idea and let (them) find out the information and how (they) feel." In other words, we allowed them to "discover" for themselves, a word she also used, and we respected their views.

Students' perceptions of schooling are disconcerting. Equally disconcerting was hearing sixth graders describe the conditions of their lives. "I'm from a block where people be dealing drugs and things like that" (Juan, 10/10/89). "It (drugs) was a thing I saw everyday in my community, around my block and everywhere" (Miguel, 01/05/90). Not only are students surrounded by these social problems, but in many cases these hit closer to home, as many have candidly admitted.

Coping with these realities and attendant pressures poses a formidable challenge to youngsters at an impressionable age. However, I have grown to appreciate the value of this project, which, by legitimizing analyses of issues of such personal significance to students with informed and caring adults, may be an important means of helping them deal with the conditions of their lives. I have also been impressed with students' compassion for others and their drive to do something about the problems that surround them. As John expressed it, "We have so many problems, we want to get away from it, but then you think you want to help other people" (03/02/90).

Similarly, I have gained a deeper regard and respect for teachers like Marcy, who deal with situations unimaginable to me as a teacher on a daily basis. It is remarkable that Marcy's enthusiasm and commitment to what she does remain constant. But, it would be misleading to suggest that assistance has been unidirectional as students and teacher have also helped me to cope with personal matters as well as professional responsibilities. Yes, we have "helped each other out," as students express it.

I have also learned about the power of practice to modify and inform theory. Although I had organized activities to be consistent with Vygotsky's theory so that students learned through verbalization and collaboration with peers, there is much that I am discovering about this process, particularly the influence that social relations between and among students have on collaboration and learning. Unfortunately, the absence of recording equipment precluded the possibility of capturing the details of interactions during small group activities. I expect to address this concern during a follow-up study currently in the planning.

Using School/Community Resources more Effectively

There are many special programs in "inner city" schools that provide speakers who are considered authorities on such topics as teen pregnancy and substance abuse. All too often, these programs "are thrown at the kids," in a helter-skelter fashion as one of the family case workers told me as we were preparing for the Christmas party. However, through Marcy's initiatives, these programs have become an integral part of the research activities of her class. Students have interviewed these authorities or requested information specifically related to their concerns during class presentations. Marcy has also enlisted the assistance of individuals and institutions outside of school. Recently, she took a group of girls to North Central Hospital after school, where they were able to meet with a hospital worker who gave them information on babies with AIDS.

Some Level of Funding is Essential

Hindsight has increased my understanding of the need to have college recognition for this type of activity, with or without special funding, particularly for junior faculty in programs/schools of education. While being part of the Adopt-a-Class Program has brought some recognition and a common bond with our Dean, who also has an adopted class, what I find I need most is time to develop research guides and other instructional materials and to document our activities. At this time, however, I have been told that release time is forthcoming for the Fall semester, in time for initiating the second phase of this study.

Marcy is similarly overextended, and while she is a willing participant in this endeavor, we often lack the reflection time we need during the school day. Although the school administration is aware of the project, no special efforts have been made as yet to provide uninterrupted planning time on the day we get together. Gordon Wells may be correct in saying that time for teacher collaboration in research should be part of teachers' contractual agreements, if this is to work as it should (during an Exchange with Teacher-Researchers presenting at the Boston Conference on Language, in October 1988).

Conclusions

This project has initiated Puerto Rican and other minority students in an intermediate school in the South Bronx into the world of educational research. It is impressive to see that within a relatively short period of time, these "at-risk" sixth graders have learned a great deal about research—working like researchers, talking like researchers, and making presentations like researchers. More importantly, they have learned that they are capable of doing more advanced work than they are usually given at this level and some have begun to explore career opportunities that had not been considered previously. These findings suggest the successes that are possible under ordinary circumstances and with relatively little money.

This is an ongoing process, therefore new concerns always surface. Greater practice is needed in reasoning like researchers: detecting patterns and positing explanations of patterns across data sets. As students at this age/grade display strong opinions, particularly on issues such as teen pregnancy and drug abuse, calling attention to inferences that may be appropriately drawn from data derived through systematic inquiry has been difficult. In fairness to the students, little specific attention has been given to this aspect, as other concerns required initial consideration. Attention will also be given to co-authoring a research report that captures the voices of all participants more completely than has been possible in this document. There is always something new to look forward to as we work and learn together in this collaborative manner.

REFERENCES

Board of Education of the City of New York (n.d.). Informative leaflet on the Latino Adopt-a-Class Program. New York: Author.

Brice-Heath, S. (1985). Literacy or literate skills? Consideration for ESL/EFL learners. In P. Larson, E.L. Judd, & L. Messerschmidt (Eds.), *On TESOL 84: A brave new world for TESOL.* Washington, DC: TESOL.

Brown, J.S., Collins, A., & Duguid, P. (1989). Situated cognition and the culture of learning. *Educational Researcher, 18*(1), 32–42.

Cole, M., & Griffin, P. (Eds.) (1987). *Contextual factors in education. Improving mathematics and science instruction for minorities and women.* Madison: Wisconsin Center for Education Research, School of Education, University of Wisconsin-Madison.

Ellsworth, E. (1989). Why doesn't this feel empowering? Working through the repressive myths of critical pedagogy. *Harvard Educational Review, 59*(3), 297–324.

Farrell, E., Peguero, G., Lindsey, R., & White, R. (1988). Giving voice to high school students: Pressure and boredom, ya know what I'm saying? *American Educational Research Journal, 25*(4), 489–502.

McDermott, R. (1977). The ethnography of speaking and reading. In R.W. Shuy (Ed.), *Linguistic theory: What can it say about reading?* (pp. 153–185). Newark, DE: International Reading Association.

Mercado, C.I. (1988). An ethnographic study of classroom help with language minority students. Unpublished doctoral dissertation, Fordham University.

Moll, L.C., Vélez-Ibañez, C., & Greenberg, J. (1989). Year one progress report—Community knowledge and classroom practice: Combining resources for literacy instruction. (IARP Subcontract No. L-10). Washington, DC: Development Associates.

Pearson, P.D., & Dole, J.A. (1987). Explicit comprehension instruction: A review of research and a new conceptualization. *The Elementary School Journal, 88*(2), 151–185.

Roth, K.J. (1989). Science education: It's not enough to 'do' or 'relate.' *American Educator, 13*(4), 16–22, 46–48.

Vygotsky, L.S. (1978). *Mind in society: The development of higher psychological processes.* Cambridge, MA: Harvard University Press.

CHAPTER 8

On to College: Dropout Prevention is Possible

Andrés Rodríguez, Jr.

Introduction

Students who drop out of school before they have attained the abilities to work productively in a competitive, technological work place face difficult lives economically and socially. Puerto Rican students on the U.S. mainland have a very high dropout rate. This chapter addresses the dropout problem among Puerto Rican students and discusses possible solutions. It reviews a number of programs and initiatives that have been successful in providing the incentives that keep Puerto Rican and other minority students in school. Even more important, these programs encourage students to achieve the skills and to attain the knowledge level that will make them competitive in the job market and productive, capable members of families and society.

First, the Problem

Students dropping out of school before they receive a high school diploma is a national problem in the United States. Over 750,000 high school students drop out of U.S. public schools annually, and an average of 4,250 drop out daily over a total of 180 school days (National Center for Educational Statistics, 1989; Weis, Farrar, & Petrie, 1989). While the problem is acute for every category of youth, the dropout rates for Hispanics, African-Americans, and Native-Americans may be two to four times the number of white non-Hispanic youth. Nationally, over 39% of Hispanic youth are not enrolled in any school, public or private, and never graduate from high school, compared to 13% for white non-Hispanic students (Gingras & Carreaga, 1989). Among students of Hispanic origin, Puerto Ricans have a higher than average dropout rate. Of the Puerto Rican adults in U.S. cities, almost 55% never graduated from high school (U.S. Bureau of the Census, 1989).

Without the educational background needed in today's job market, Puerto Ricans face a difficult future. More than 45% of Puerto Rican adults on the U.S. mainland are unemployed and on public assistance programs. And 49% of Puerto Rican children under age 18 continue to live below the poverty level (De La Rosa & Maw, 1990; U.S. Bureau of the Census, 1989). The high poverty rate will probably continue. Generally, poverty rates are higher among single-parent families headed by females, and it is currently estimated that 60% of Puerto Rican households are female-headed (Marín, 1989). To further compound matters, over 16% of Puerto Rican female high school dropouts become pregnant by the tenth grade at around 14 to 16 years of age. It appears from the statistics that a cycle of poverty has enclosed Puerto Rican youth.

There is no doubt that the Puerto Rican dropout rate is alarming (New York Times, 1988). In cities like New York, close to 70% of Puerto Rican youth drop out of high school before reaching the tenth grade, and from 45 to 65% is the dropout rate in other major cities (Fernández & Vélez, 1989). The problem may be even more serious when it is considered that the count of Puerto Rican high school dropouts has been too general and underestimated within the aggregate type data in which Puerto Ricans are included in a broader Hispanic category (Aspira, 1989). To understand the predicament of Puerto Rican students, it is necessary to look at many aspects of what is really a complex, multifaceted situation. Data are difficult to interpret because the definition of dropout differs among researchers.

What is a Dropout?

Definitions of dropouts are varied. The U.S. Bureau of the Census (1989) states that a dropout is "any person who is not enrolled in school or is not a high school graduate, or the equivalent." Others define the dropout as a "pupil who leaves school for any reason except death, before graduation, or completion of a program of studies without transferring to another school" (Gingras & Carreaga, 1989).

An important issue, however, that is not frequently addressed is that of students who remain in school, but who do not develop the skills needed for their working, personal, and social adult lives (Weis, Farrar, & Petrie, 1989). In other words, can a student be physically present and still have dropped out? A student who is in school, but failing to acquire skills is termed a student at risk (Slavin & Madden, 1989).

Another issue arises with transfer students. As Hahn & Danzberger (1987) point out, political pressure on urban school communities may affect the reporting of transfer students to or from other schools who are in the dropout category, just to keep the school-leaving rate down. Schools may report student transfers when actually the students have dropped out. Some schools may report only those 16 years of age or older who leave school, while the younger ones go unreported.

Thus it becomes difficult to sort out, monitor, and count the actual cases of students who drop out. It is even more difficult to monitor and categorize students who are push-outs (undesirables), disaffected (students no longer wishing to remain), educational mortalities (those who fail), capable dropouts (those who do not fit into the normed school demands), and stop-outs (those who leave and return within the same school year) (Hahn & Danzberger, 1989; Weis, Farrar, & Petrie, 1989).

New Research Emphasis

In past research on minority dropouts, emphasis was placed on identification of student characteristics which defined a dropout or a student who was academically at risk of dropping out of school. At-risk students appeared to share some characteristics with dropouts, such as high levels of truancy, low academic achievement, low socioeconomic status (SES), and specific linguistic/cultural traits which could be identified throughout a student's schooling (Hahn & Danzberger, 1989). Socioeconomic, linguistic, cultural, and home variables were looked at as contributors to dropping out of school (Steinberg, Blinde, & Chan, 1984). A shift in the research paradigm has occurred which has permitted the identification of other variables in addition to those related to person or home.

The critical issues that underlie a student's decision to leave school are seen not in the students themselves, but in the contextual and systemic level of public schooling, that is, in school leadership and governance, teaching practices, overcrowding, and other conditions (Educational Priorities Panel, 1989). Current research focuses on the systemic and school-based causes of high school leaving. Students' interaction with the school and community, class size, educational equity in programmatic and fiscal resources, issues of school choice and school reform, and a plethora of other school and community variables have a definite impact on the lives of at-risk or dropout minority youth. Of crucial importance are the roles of teaching practices, school organization, parental involvement, and business-school partnerships in affecting student dropout (Lehman College, 1989). It is now felt that if high school dropout causes lie in the schools, community, and society, remedies must be found there too (Lehman College, 1989). Yet few public school reform movements seem to be directed to ethnic minority students (Gingras & Carreaga, 1989; Pérez-Miller, 1989).

What frequently characterizes ethnic minority students, such as Hispanics, from mainstream students are their linguistic/cultural differences. Such differences were perceived as deficiencies. Language other than English usage and cultural differences were linked to early academic failure, especially when low SES was combined with the first two factors. Steinberg, Blinde, and Chan (1984) concluded that youngsters who were Hispanic and economically disadvantaged were most likely to leave school. It has recently been noted, however, that although academic failure is one of the major reasons for language minority (LM) school leaving (Fernández, Henn-Reinke, & Petrovich, 1989), academic failure in turn can result from poor teaching practices, negative interactions with school staff, tracking and ability grouping, inflexible and/or irrelevant curricula, biased assessment practices, and special education overreferrals (Boston Public Schools 1989a; Weis, Farrar & Petrie, 1989). These factors reinforce student disengagement and are more powerfully related to Puerto Rican school desertion than SES or ethnic/linguistic background (Firestone, 1989).

Looking at Puerto Rican students is a complex matter for another reason: Puerto Ricans as U.S. citizens are free to come and go between mainland and island. Researchers need to take into account the relation of factors such as place of origin, migration, and acculturation to dropping out of school. The language factor appears to be especially pertinent. A number of studies offer information that helps to understand the Puerto Rican dropout. The next section reviews those studies and tries to identify the characteristics of Puerto Rican dropouts and at-risk students.

Characteristics of Puerto Rican Dropouts and At-Risk Students

A study conducted by Fernández, Henn-Reinke, & Petrovich (1989), under the sponsorship of Aspira—an organization committed to improving the educational opportunities of Puerto Rican students—has helped identify the characteristics of Puerto Rican dropouts. The study consisted of a longitudinal, multi-method investigation based on archival (student records), primary (interview), and one year follow-up data sources. Puerto Rican at-risk and dropout students numbered 161 (27%) within a total sample of 597 Hispanic students (309 Mexican Americans, 63 Cuban, and 64 Central American). Selected schools were located in Chicago, Miami, San Antonio, Milwaukee, and Newark. The study sought answers to two basic questions: Why do Hispanic students drop out of school? and Why do Hispanic students stay in school?

The investigators used a questionnaire to gather information on demographics, school attendance, ethnicity, student activities, and perceptions about attitudes of friends and classmates. Other information collected included parental characteristics, language usage, school environment, school issues, homework and studying, academic concerns, and work. Characteristics of the Puerto Rican youth interviewed emerged as follows:

- 97.7% reported their background as Puerto Rican.
- 54.1% were female.
- 65.9% were born in one of the 50 states.
- 54.7% never lived outside the United States.
- 30.4% arrived on the mainland at one-to-three years old.
- 30.4% arrived on the mainland at 10-to-12 years old.
- 65.6% did not complete any grades outside of the U.S.
- 18.7% attended school in a state other than the one in which they live.
- 100% listed sports as the activity they do most, with dancing ranking second, and reading third.
- 51.7% reported receiving awards or recognitions in the last three years.
- Participation in a committee was preferred community leadership activity for past three years.
- 23.4% had been questioned by the police in the last three years.
- 6.9% had been arrested and booked by the police in the past three years.

- 50% had friends or relatives who left school due to pregnancy or child.
- 48.9% reported that none of their close friends used drugs.
- 60.9% reported that some of their close friends are absent from school.
- 54.1% reported that some of their best friends get into fights.
- 88.5% reported a mother or stepmother living at home.
- 50.3% reported a father or stepfather living at home.
- 96.1% planned to be in school next year.
- 84.4% planned to return to the same school.

All students sampled reported that they liked school and recognized that good study habits were important for school success, but admitted that friends and peers may be an impediment to success in school. All students reported that they wanted to hold professional positions (i.e., lawyer, physician, engineer) when they were older.

In another study, Marín (1989) examined the South Bronx Puerto Rican high school dropout and at-risk student population in alternative public school programs. Among the youth examined were 56 graduates, 58 high school equivalency (GED) students, and 50 dropouts. The researcher focused on self-concept; life events; environmental, personal, familial, and social factors; and academic achievement history. The youth came from low socioeconomic status and Spanish-speaking home backgrounds. They were either of limited English proficiency or behind grade level. Face to face discussions, interviews, student record data, and observations of student academic work/interaction in the school setting were held with individuals and small groups.

Results of the study indicated that Puerto Rican youngsters who came to the mainland as adolescents drop out of high school at twice the rate of students born on the mainland. At-risk and dropout students exhibited low self-concept, were of limited English proficiency, experienced academic failure, had parents with little schooling and from low socioeconomic backgrounds. Furthermore, their educational attainment was in the eighth-grade median grade level, and over 60% lived in single parent households. Dropout rates were higher for males than females. Dropouts tended to have a higher rate of crime, substance abuse, unemployment, grade retention, poor socialization, discipline and school-related problems, poor adjustment to mainstream U.S. cultural values and norms, and low expectations for educational attainment. Dropouts were more dependent on grandmothers, older sisters, mothers, or aunts than graduates or at-risk students. For female dropouts, goal setting usually involved getting married and keeping house and caring for their own child—if pregnancy occurred—or siblings.

In a three-year study of New York City's at-risk and dropout students in the middle grades, a dropout prevention program (DPP) initiative was evaluated in 29 schools (Grannis & Riehl, 1989). The program is a goal-driven initiative on early prevention strategies for middle school students. The study focused on school-based facilitation or implementation of DPP, attendance outreach, guidance and counseling services, health services, school level linkages with high schools and businesses, and alternative education programs. Hispanic students who participated in the study were divided into limited English proficient (LEP) and non-LEP groups. Results indicated that the Hispanic LEP students were at a higher risk of dropping out when not provided with an appropriate bilingual education program. The authors concluded that the availability of a bilingual education program for LEP students enables them to achieve higher academically when compared to the English proficient students participating in the DPP initiative.

Other research studies on Puerto Rican at-risk students and dropouts (New York State Education Department, 1988) highlight the need for support and guidance services in the native language; the need for bilingual personnel trained in support and guidance services; and the need to do away with inequity in programs and services for language minority students, who continue to be tracked and denied equal access to advanced placement, preventive, and bilingual enrichment programs.

Some general factors must be considered in any attempt to develop and implement dropout prevention programs. The programs must consider age; gender; life experiences; academic, cultural, linguistic, individual, and family backgrounds; community factors; and the situational contexts of the school, community, and home (Gingras & Carreaga, 1989). A wide range of comprehensive and integrated approaches to the dropout problem exist that are preventive, remedial, vocational, or academic. They may focus on school staff, the family, student, or school organization (Payne, 1989). The variety of strategies reflect the multiple issues affecting the at-risk and dropout Puerto Rican student. Successful approaches and program-types implemented for dropout prevention are presented below. In general, it has been the broader and better integrated programs, approaches, and strategies that have been found to be more effective with Puerto Rican students.

Building Effective Schools

Consumer-driven schools. A consumer-driven (bottom-up) organization is perhaps the most important recent school innovation. In effective schools, teachers, administrators, students, parents, and community members plan and develop teaching and learning practices based on the individual learner's needs and aspirations (Darling-Hammond, 1987). Control is exercised at the school site by its constituents and consumers (Cooper, 1989). In addition, the physical quality of schools—being clean and repaired—not only affects the school climate, but transmits positive or negative messages to students, staff, and the community on the worth or value of public education (Educational Priorities Panel, 1989; Firestone, 1989). Another important feature of consumer-driven schools is to establish the proper match between the culture of the school and the culture of the home. Building this sense of community—still missing in most of today's urban public schools—is thought to be the major reason why parochial schools have been more successful with African-American and Hispanic students than either the public schools or other private schools (Wehlage, 1989).

Value-driven schools. One of the best examples of value-driven schools are Catholic parochial schools. Whether their motivation is moral or economic—or a combination of the two—Catholic schools seem to produce functional communities (Wehlage, 1989). First of all, there is value consistency among the parents of children who attend Catholic schools. Secondly, this value consistency is generated and sustained through functional social interaction among parents, school staff, and children (Weis, Farrar, & Petrie, 1989). The culture and ethos of Catholicism translates into education. According to Wehlage (1989), because caring for others is an important virtue, teachers monitor student behavior more closely and assume more responsibility for the success of youngsters. Teachers care about character development as much as a student's knowledge. These factors have been proven to be important. The Aspira study (1989) found that Puerto Rican youngsters depend on support and guidance from parents, the extended family, neighbors, and friends in the community environment for academic success. Among the reasons for absenteeism given by students in the study, "feeling out of place" was one of them. Moreover, the students ranked discipline and the reputation of their schools in the community as poor or fair. Thus, school membership requires that students establish a social bond between themselves, the adults in the schools, the home and the community, and the norms governing the institution (Comer, 1988; Wehlage, 1989). Value-driven schools, such as Catholic schools, appear to facilitate and stimulate those important bonds.

Schools with strong parental components. The economic commitment and high involvement of Puerto Rican parents in Catholic schools brings under serious scrutiny past research findings attributing school desertion to family or SES factors (Gutiérrez & Montalvo, 1984; Steinberg, Blinde, & Chan, 1984). The Aspira (1989) study found that Puerto Rican parents expect their children to finish high school, to get a better education and better jobs than they themselves attained, to get a college degree, and to marry after they complete their studies. The study also found that parents set important home rules regarding school grades, homework, weekend curfews, bedtime, dating, movies, telephone usage, TV viewing, and church attendance. These rules do not differ markedly from the rules set by white non-Hispanic parents. In addition, the study found that 61.9% of the parents visited schools on a continuous basis. Thus, the view held by some critics that Puerto Rican parents do not value education is unfounded. As Suro (1990) points out, the high Puerto Rican student dropout rate can no longer be blamed on the youth and their families. To find the underlying causes of school leaving, we must look at the educational system.

To sum up, current dropout rates are not generated exclusively by personal or family characteristics. Rather, they result from many factors interacting with one another. By the same token, solutions need not be solely a family responsibility, but need to be shared among families, school, communities, and the private sector. As long as all of these factors continue to function in isolation, they will fail to tap the abundance of human, financial, and community resources available.

Student-Centered Strategies

English as a second language (ESL) instruction. LEP students should be provided with ESL instruction or sheltered English learning opportunities (Watson, Northcutt, & Rydell, 1989). This approach employs principles of second language acquisition in teaching the content areas to make lessons comprehensible and facilitate learning. An example of this approach is New York City schools' Project Great, a dropout prevention program which functions in conjunction with the Bilingual Education Program, mentor, linkage systems and other auxiliary services to high schools and to individual students.

Counseling. Peer and parent counseling are effective ways to work with Puerto Rican youth. In this approach teachers assume the role of student advisors for academic and other problems not related to school. This is especially important if the school is large. Outside professional counseling services from local mental health agencies may provide the school with a student hotline to deal with situational emotional difficulties (Gingras & Carreaga, 1989). Counseling rap sessions can be implemented in the schools, as well as group therapy, to promote students' self-esteem and sense of responsibility and self-worth.

Tutorials. Socialization within the school setting and developing motivation to achieve in school are the most frequently espoused strategies for Puerto Rican dropout prevention in recent research studies (Aspira, 1989; Intercultural Development Research Association, 1986).

Texas-based Intercultural Development Research Association (1986) has begun to identify and help Hispanic youth (including Puerto Ricans) at the third grade of school in large inner cities. In this program at-risk middle and secondary school students tutor elementary children and receive minimal wages. The program focuses on role modeling, parental involvement, training the student-tutors, field trips, and school work experiences.

Incentive programs. Incentives are offered for school attendance, achievement, and for taking the opportunity to assume leadership roles. The potential school leavers assume the responsibility of monitoring their own academic progress and systematically setting goals. There are other aspects of successful incentive programs. In incentive programs school personnel institute cooperative learning approaches which are considered culturally relevant to Puerto Rican youth and help build a sense of commitment to other students and the school. A variety of technological computer-based programs, career education courses, field experiences, and peer and intergenerational (senior citizens, community adult leaders) social support groups may also be used in this approach.

In New York City, three programs following an incentive approach are: (a) the "Stay-in-School" Partnership Program developed between Lehman College and DeWitt Clinton High School; (b) the collaborative effort among Hostos Community College (CUNY), Boricua College, and John Jay College—who have designed on-site GED, bilingual, vocational, and academic training degree programs for Puerto Rican dropouts; and (c) the "I Have

A Dream Foundation" program offering college opportunities for youngsters who make the commitment to stay in school until graduation. Initially an informal challenge from a millionaire to a largely Puerto Rican graduating class in a Spanish Harlem public school, "I Have A Dream" now has the partnership of the city schools and serves as a model to other business-school partnerships for motivating students to have college as a goal.

Alternative School Centered Programs

Career and vocational education programs. Economic necessity and family problems have been cited in the research as propelling school desertion by Puerto Rican youth (Aspira, 1989; Gutiérrez & Montalvo, 1984). Career and vocational development are essential services needed by potential school leavers. Career education programs could be introduced in the elementary school and expanded in the junior high school to provide exploratory career training and to provide job placement and follow-up counseling at the high school. Parents and family members are involved in the program and provide approval and encouragement for career plans (Gingras & Carreaga, 1989). Although some high school programs serving Puerto Rican at risk and dropout youth have not been specifically developed to meet the individual needs of LEP Puerto Rican students, they do provide more intensive individualized and small group instructional and support services, such as health clinics and social services, in addition to vocational and career training.

López-Valadez (1989) studied the impact of vocational education on Hispanic student populations across the country. She found that although the Carl Perkins Vocational Education Act of 1984 makes specific provisions for Hispanic student access to quality vocational programs, the research shows that for both English proficient and LEP Hispanic students, public schools are still not providing access to their quality vocational training programs. On the other hand, vocational education programs are still serving as dumping grounds for underachievers and minority students. However, model vocational programs serving the needs of Hispanic students are emerging in some parts of the country.

Business-Community-School Partnerships/Collaboration. The private sector sponsors and supplies resources for potential school leavers by assisting in implementing programs and activities. Expertise and future employment initiatives are provided to the at-risk student. The Boston Compact is an example of such a program (Boston Public Schools, 1989b). In this collaborative effort, universities, the private sector, community-based organizations, and school alliances not only train Puerto Rican youth in employable skills, but motivate students to go on to college. The "2 + 2 Program" also provides community college linkages to high schools with ethnic minority at-risk students.

The New York-based Macy Foundation program is another example of a collaborative effort. The program is focused on providing a "safety net" to ensure that Hispanic, African-American and Native-American students can not only succeed in high school, but go on to college. Operating in 39 high schools in New York City, Alabama, Connecticut, and Arizona, the program includes a demanding curriculum, with four years of English, math, science, and social studies; a continuing four-year emphasis on reading, writing, and speaking skills; and two years of a foreign language. Class sizes are smaller in the ninth and tenth grades. It has an extended school day program including before- and after-school tutorial and guidance support. A special summer school program is also used in partnership with local universities to help out with curriculum development and teaching strategies. The program has now been operating for almost a decade and participating minority students have been scoring at the 60th percentile or above on standardized tests and are receiving higher grades in math and science courses, although these are the most difficult in content. About 90% of the graduates are attending four-year colleges, pointing to the remarkable success of the program ("Safety Nets," 1990).

Education Reform Movements in Public Education

The Educational Reform movement has also had an impact on dropout prevention, mostly by revising the relation between students and schools. In the public schools educational reform has focused on three phases: The first phase calls for increased standards for student learning; the second phase fosters the professionalization of teachers; and the third phase demands changes in the structure and management of the schools (Kirst, 1989). The school reform movement supports the decentralization of power, control, management, policy-making, instruction, curriculum, and fiscal matters in the hands of local school leaders, parents, community members, and those interested individuals from the private sector or local business community. However, an aging population and declining school enrollments make it difficult for the mainstream consumer and educator to vote on taxes to support public school reforms, and, as a result, the political base of supporters for the public schools has been eroded (Carroll, 1990).

In spite of dwindling fiscal and human resources at the national, state, and city levels, local leaders have worked with Puerto Rican communities across the nation to follow and adapt the course of mainstream education initiatives and find solutions to the appropriate provision of instructional and supportive services for at-risk and dropout students. While problems do exist, there have been efforts to work with Puerto Rican students and to develop successful programs and approaches that will enhance their chances of staying in school.

Recommendations

The following are recommendations for effective dropout prevention programs:

1. *Access to quality programs.* Schools need to provide Puerto Ricans access to quality programs. Systemic school changes—which include school-wide improvement

initiatives, changing institutional practices, and, in general, establishing an environment contributing to students' decision to stay in school—are necessary. Quality programs must take into consideration Puerto Rican students' linguistic, cultural, and academic needs. In addition, average class size is to be reduced, and individualized and personalized instructional practices are to be tailored to the individual needs and abilities of students.

2. *Develop a sense of community.* Parents, staff, community members, as well as students, must be allowed to feel that they belong in the schools. All constituencies should be encouraged to show greater commitment through participation in team-building approaches and setting goals with common principles and beliefs.

3. *Use of available resources.* The schools, in collaboration with the community, can use the available resources, such as community colleges, universities, other community facilities, and private enterprise, to develop dropout prevention programs.

4. *Identification of potential school leavers.* The schools should develop procedures to identify potential dropouts considering not only the linguistic, cultural, family, life experiences, and SES of Puerto Rican students. Such characteristics should be considered in the context of the school, since school characteristics may be contributing to Puerto Rican students' academic dysfunction. Elementary and middle schools should be the starting points. When it comes to dropout prevention, the earlier the intervention is in place, the greater the chance of its having an impact.

5. *Development of strong English language programs.* The dropout potential increases dramatically in LEP Puerto Rican students. Programs with strong ESL and/or bilingual components are needed to keep these students in school.

6. *Development of counseling programs.* Students should be given the opportunity to discuss complex issues relevant to their lives. This includes not only personal problems, but also environmental, sex, and health matters, as well as work interests, training, and jobs.

7. *Initiate research efforts to evaluate effective programs.* Future research must examine the variables and factors in the school culture that create school persisters.

There is not enough known about the positive deviants, those students that against all odds do manage to graduate from high school and to proceed to college. This information could be used to create effective dropout prevention programs.

8. *Strengthening dissemination efforts.* Dropout prevention is a major challenge to educators nationwide and to individual school systems. A myriad of programs are being tried and implemented, but there is a need to increase dissemination efforts so that individual districts can learn from one another. Thus, dissemination should be made a priority in all efforts aimed at dropout prevention.

Conclusion

Although Puerto Rican school leaving is influenced by SES, English language proficiency, culture, family background, and life experiences or events, researchers are finding that the decision to drop out is strongly affected by the school environment, teaching practices, and educational policies.

School-related factors which affect Puerto Rican students' school achievement and motivation to either stay or leave school are dependent on educators. These factors are determined by the design of effective programs to meet the individual linguistic, cultural, and academic needs of the students. Comprehensive and integrative instructional and counseling services which include the effective and efficient learning approaches identified by research are required to prevent Puerto Rican students from leaving school. Across the country informed, sensitive educators are offering such services or initiating programs to provide such services. The cycle of school failure-poverty-school failure is gradually being altered.

Jaime Escalante, a persistent teacher-hero portrayed in the movie *Stand and Deliver*, has spoken of his success with at-risk Hispanic youth (Meek, 1989). Escalante believes that all teaching efforts should be aimed toward motivating students to learn, inspiring in them the desire, the *ganas*,

212   PUERTO RICAN CHILDREN ON THE MAINLAND

to do something; above all, convincing them they can learn. By awakening *ganas*, the minds of students are captured so they can create images: the image of school, the image of college, a belief that they can be somebody.

REFERENCES

Aspira, Inc. (1989). *Aspira's research on dropouts.* Washington, DC: Aspira National Office.
Boston Public Schools (1989a). *Hispanic dropout prevention program.* Boston: Latino Parents Association.
Boston Public Schools (1989b). *Programa para la prevención de deserción escolar de hispanos.* Boston: Boston School Committee.
Carroll, J.M. (1990). The Copernican plan restructuring the American high school. *Phi Delta Kappan, 71,* 358–365.
Comer, J.P. (1988). Educating poor minority children. *Scientific American, 259,* 5, 4.
Cooper, B.S. (1989). Bottom-up authority in school organization: Implications for the school administrator. *Education and Urban Society, 21*(4), 380–392.
Darling-Hammond, L. (1987). Accountability for professional practice. Paper commissioned by the American Federation of Teachers.
De La Rosa, D., & Maw, C.E. (1990). *Hispanic education: A statistical portrait 1990.* Washington, DC: National Council of La Raza.
Educational Priorities Panel (1989). *Building schools for student success.* New York: Author.
Fernández, R.R., Henn-Reinke, K., & Petrovich, J. (1989). *Five cities high school dropout study: Characteristics of Hispanic high school students.* Washington, DC: Aspira.
Fernández, R.R., & Vélez, W. (1989). *Who stays, who leaves?: Findings from the Aspira five cities high school dropout study.* Working Paper No. 89-1. Washington, DC: Aspira Institute for Policy Research.
Firestone, W.A. (1989). Beyond order and expectations in high schools serving at-risk youth. *Educational Leadership, 46*(5), 41–45.

Gingras, R.C., & Carreaga, R.C. (1989). Limited English proficient students at-risk: Issues and prevention strategies. *New Focus*. National Clearinghouse for Bilingual Education Occasional Papers. Silver Spring, MD: National Clearinghouse for Bilingual Education.

Grannis, J., & Riehl, C. (1989). *Evaluation of the New York City dropout prevention initiative—Final report on the middle schools for year three: 1987–88*. New York: Institute for Urban and Minority Education, Teachers College, Columbia University.

Gutiérrez, M., & Montalvo, B. (1984). *Dropping out and delinquency among Puerto Rican youths: A longitudinal study*. Philadelphia: Aspira of Pennsylvania.

Hahn, A., & Danzberger, J. (1987). *Dropouts in America: Enough is known for action*. Washington, DC: Institute for Educational Leadership.

Intercultural Development Research Assocation (1986). *Valued youth partnerships. Programs in caring: Cross-age tutoring dropout prevention strategies*. San Antonio, TX: Center for the Prevention and Recovery of Dropouts.

Kirst, M.W. (1989). Recent state education reform in the U.S.: Looking backward and forward. *Educational Administrators Quarterly, 24*, 319–328.

Larson, K.A. (1989). Task-related and interpersonal problem-solving training for increasing school success in high-risk young adolescents. *RASE, 10*(6), 32–52.

Lehman College, City University of New York (1989). *School dropouts and school completion: Urban perspectives*. A conference presented in association with the Office of the Bronx Borough President, the Division of Postsecondary Equity and Access Programs of the New York State Education Department and the High School Division of the New York City Public Schools.

López-Valadez, J. (1989). Training limited English proficient students for the workplace: Trends in vocational education. *The National Clearinghouse for Bilingual Education: Occasional Papers in Bilingual Education, 11*, 1–11.

Marín, P.V. (1989). Factors contributing to high school graduation among Hispanics. Unpublished doctoral dissertation, Yeshiva University.

Meek, A. (1989). On creating ganas: A conversation with Jaime Escalante. *Educational Leadership, 46*(5), 46–47.

National Center for Educational Statistics (1989). *Dropout rates in the U.S.: 1988*. Washington, DC: U.S. Department of Education.

New York State Education Department (May 23–24, 1988). The language minority dropout: A call for action. Conference Proceedings. Long Island, NY: Multifunctional Resource Center.

New York Times (1988). Editorial: Counting dropouts—keeping students, July 7, p. 15.

Payne, C. (1989). Urban teachers and dropout-prone students: The uneasy partners. In L. Weis, E. Farrar, & H.G. Petrie (Eds.), *Dropouts from school: Issues, dilemmas, and solutions* (pp. 113–128). New York: State University of New York.

Pérez-Miller, A. (1989). Student characteristics and the persistence/dropout behavior of Hispanic students. In I.M. Lakebrink (Ed.), *Children at risk* (pp. 119–139). Springfield, IL: Thomas.

Safety nets for the schools (1990). *Washington Post,* November 11, p. 8.

Slavin, R., & Madden, N. (1989). What works for students at risk: A research synthesis. *Educational Leadership, 46*(5), 4–13.

Steinberg, L., Blinde, P.L., & Chan, R.S. (1984). Dropping out among language minority youth. *Review of Educational Research, 54*(1), 113–131.

Suro, R. (1990). Hispanic criticism of Education chief Cavazos is disputed: Claim that parents are to be blamed for high school dropout rate. *New York Times,* April 15, p. 13.

U.S. Bureau of the Census (1989). *The Hispanic population in the U.S.: March 1988.* Advanced Report, Series P-20, No. 431. Washington, DC: Author.

Watson, D.L., Northcut, L., & Rydell, L. (1989) Teaching bilingual students successfully. *Educational Leadership, 46*(5), 59–61.

Wehlage, G.G. (1989). Dropping out: Can schools be expected to prevent it? In L. Weis, E. Farrar, & H.G. Petrie (Eds.), *Dropouts from school: Issues, dilemmas, and solutions* (pp. 1–23). New York: State University of New York.

Weis, L., Farrar, E., & Petrie, H.G. (Eds.) (1989). *Dropouts from school: Issues, dilemmas, and solutions.* New York: State University of New York.

Wolman, C., Bruininks, R., & Thurlow, M.L. (1989). Dropouts and dropout programs: Indications for special education. *RASE, 10*(5), 6–20.

PART IV

Health and Healing

CHAPTER 9

The Legacy of Health Care for Puerto Rican Children

Sandra Estepa

When the Arawak Indians first settled in Puerto Rico, they brought with them their own beliefs about health and healing. Like other ancient peoples, they believed that good health is achieved only when there is a balance between body, mind, and spirit. Imbalance creates illness or disease.

The Arawak's healing practices involved a mix of natural medicine and religion. The *bohite*, or priest, invoked the gods and goddesses through religious ceremonies and healing rituals. Natural herbs and medicinal plants were used to heal afflictions (Figueroa, 1971).

The legacy left to current day Puerto Ricans by the Arawaks and those who followed them were fundamental beliefs about health: that health is a gift which must be valued, that it must be practiced regularly, and that a blend of natural and supernatural forces facilitate the healing process. Modern medicine has moved away from these fundamental beliefs. The task is to reawaken them and adapt them to present day reality.

In this chapter, I will describe the most salient health challenges confronting Puerto Rican children in the U.S. and the major barriers to health care utilization for the Puerto Rican community. This will be followed by a description of five program models that have managed to overcome both institutional and client-centered constraints to offer quality health care services to Puerto Rican clients. The chapter concludes with some recommendations for improving health service delivery for Puerto Ricans and other minority groups.

Current Health Situation for Puerto Rican Children in the U.S.

The current system of health care delivery is not effectively meeting the needs of Puerto Rican children and their families on the United States mainland. For many Puerto Ricans quality health care is out of reach. The following data, taken from *Avance*, newsletter of the Association of Hispanic Mental Health Professionals (1990) and the Children's Defense Fund (1990), illustrate some aspects of the current health situation. Data refer to Hispanics in general, and where available, to Puerto Ricans in particular.

- In 1986, 21.7% of Hispanics lacked any type of public or private health insurance, compared with 10.1% of African-Americans and 7.7% of whites.
- In 1987, 13% of Hispanic mothers had late or no prenatal care compared to 12% of non-Hispanic black mothers and 4% of non-Hispanic white mothers.
- In 1987, 9.3% of Puerto Rican infants had a low birth weight as compared to 5.6% white non-Latino infants.
- While Hispanics constitute 8% of the U.S. population, as of February 1989 they accounted for 15% of all AIDS cases. Of children aged 0–12 with AIDS, 23% are Hispanic.
- Almost 4 in 10 Hispanic youth live in poverty. The poverty rate among Hispanic 9 to 17 year old children is 35.2%, compared to 13.5% among whites.

While health data are not usually broken down by ethnicity, the alarming statistics of the two U.S. cities with the heaviest concentration of Puerto Rican residents, New

York City and Chicago, suggest that the health status of Puerto Rican and other minority children is precarious.

The Situation in New York City

The health situation for minority children in New York City can best be appreciated by looking at the leading causes of hospitalization among infants and children. Of the 35,840 cases reported in 1985 (N.Y.C. Department of Health, 1989), the leading causes of hospitalization in infants 0 to 12 months were for respiratory diseases, including acute respiratory infections, asthma, and pneumonia. For preschool children (ages 1 to 4 years), there were very high rates of hospital admissions due to asthma; followed by injuries; lead poisoning; digestive diseases; and sense organ diseases, including ear infections. Considering the population make-up of New York City, where in 1980 36% of children ages 0 to 19 were white, 31% were African-American, and 28% were Latino (N.Y.C. Department of Health, 1989), it can be inferred that a large portion of hospitalization cases came from children in minority families.

Another unfortunate ailment for the minority community and for the Puerto Rican community in particular has been the spread of AIDS. Out of 120,000 fully diagnosed AIDS cases, 15% are Puerto Rican (Barrón, 1990). In 1987, pediatric AIDS was the leading cause of death for children 1 to 4 years, followed by congenital abnormalities and accidents. Data through 1988 counted 391 children under 13 years of age as diagnosed with AIDS. Of these, 60% have died. Ninety-one percent of these children were African-American or Latino (N.Y.C. Department of Health, 1989).

An additional compounding factor is poverty. Regardless of whether Puerto Rican families are headed by women, men, or by couples, they exhibit the highest poverty rates in New York City (Rodríguez, 1989). In 1985–86, 39% of all children in New York City lived in families with incomes below 100% of the federal poverty level. An additional 21% of children lived in families below 200% of the federal poverty level (N.Y.C. Department of Health,

1989). Poverty in itself has detrimental health consequences, given its impact on housing, environmental sanitary conditions, malnutrition, and other poverty-related factors associated with high risk of illness.

The Situation in Chicago

A recent study by the Hispanic Health Alliance (Giachello & Aponte, 1989) shows findings on children and adolescents in Chicago that are similar to those for New York City. Giachello and Aponte's study was based on a survey of 1,716 people from 502 households, including 1,680 Hispanics and 36 non-Hispanics married to Hispanics. The survey sample was made up of 57% Mexicans and 25% Puerto Ricans, and the remaining 18% were Guatemalans, Cubans, Hondurans, and Ecuadorans. Some 32% of the sample represented children age 12 years and under, and approximately 13% were adolescents between the ages of 13 and 19 years.

An analysis of selected symptoms and health conditions by particular age categories and by Hispanic national origin indicated that symptoms of cold, ear infection, and cough affected more children under age 5 than those between ages 5 to 17. The symptoms of ear infection and cough were highest among Puerto Ricans under the age of 6 (25%). In addition, Puerto Ricans, regardless of age, were most affected by chronic conditions, such as asthma and bronchitis (Giachello & Aponte, 1989).

Health status is closely related to socioeconomic factors. Puerto Rican families have the highest poverty rates and tend to have poorer health than other ethnic minority groups. Further, the types of illnesses that Puerto Rican children have indicate that what is needed is primary, or basic, health care. The fact that Puerto Rican children are disproportionately affected by chronic diseases which can be prevented bespeaks a health care and social service system that has not met their basic needs. Primary health care is essential in order to maintain good health and reduce the risk of more serious medical problems.

The next sections identify some of the barriers that inhibit access to the health care system for Puerto Rican clients, and describe five exemplary programs that are helping to remedy the situation.

Barriers to Health Care Utilization

A number of barriers inhibit Puerto Ricans' access to the health care system. Some barriers are systemic in nature and result from incompatibilities between the system and its clientele. Other barriers stem from the clients themselves.

Institutional Barriers

Lack of primary health care providers. One major barrier to health care delivery is the lack of sufficient primary care providers. Building on technology advances over the years, increased emphasis has been placed on specialty care. While these advances are necessary, the practice of general medicine must also be maintained.

Primary health care presumes that the physician is the point of first contact for medical treatment. Primary care physicians may be generalists, family practitioners, or internists. They are concerned about the physical aspects of illness, but also about the psychological and socio-emotional aspects. Health care is provided on a continuing basis with hospital services used as back up. The patients are usually ambulatory and able to function at home (Rogers, 1977).

Lack of flexibility in service delivery. Medical services in the U.S. are organized in a way that creates cultural barriers to health care for Puerto Ricans. Medical institutions, particularly hospitals, operate in an overly structured, often rigid style. A patient is seen only by appointment, and a hierarchy of medical service providers are involved in the patient's care, which may lead to frequent visits and fragmentation of services. This is in direct contrast to the Puerto Rican family's view of health care, which tends to be more informal in style: less structured, addressing medical problems at the moment, and more holistic in its approach. In fact, this could be one of the reasons why Puerto Rican families overuse hospital emergency rooms, even when obtaining services in a medical clinic would be more appropriate.

Cultural and linguistic insensitivity. Cultural and linguistic insensitivity creates obstacles to health care delivery. The health care system treats everyone the same. Yet, its lack of sensitivity to Puerto Ricans' interactional style and to their linguistic needs results in a breakdown of communication and reduces the effectiveness of the interaction between physicians and patients.

Client-Centered Barriers

Poverty and SES. Puerto Ricans lack financial access to health care. Due to poverty, many Puerto Ricans require Medicaid to pay for health services. Because of delays in reimbursement, however, many physicians and hospitals do not accept patients with Medicaid. For Puerto Ricans who are "near poor," i.e., working but at low-level, marginal jobs, health insurance often does not provide comprehensive benefits nor cover dependents (NYC Department of Health, 1989). In addition, as Giachello and Aponte (1989) indicate, paid time must often be lost to go or take a child to the doctor, which adds to the overall expense and to the opportunity costs.

Reliance on the extended family. Many Puerto Ricans address problems, including health problems, in a reserved way. They rely heavily on the family, particularly the extended family, as a source of support and advice. They are likely to consult a family member before considering any medical resource for help. In addition, medical anthropologists (see Guarnaccia's article in this book) refer to the concept of "family health culture" as the knowledge and resources on how to treat illness that are passed on from generation to generation, and on which families rely in times of need. As Guarnaccia points out, some insights may come from previous experiences with health care providers; others may have been developed by individual families based on their own experience with a specific ailment.

Reliance on endogenous healers. In addition to traditional Western medicine, many Puerto Ricans also practice "espiritismo," a folk healing system based on the belief that spirits are capable of causing and/or healing illness, emotional upsets, interpersonal conflicts, and other manners of misfortune. A spirit is contacted through an "espiritista," or a medium who conveys information and advice on how to correct the illness. Healing remedies include prayers and invocations, candle lighting, baths, herbal teas, ablutions, and various other rituals. In a study of Puerto Rican children and families living in Spanish Harlem, Alvarez (1983) found that 11% of families had taken their children to consult with a spiritist. Most of the instances for which spiritists were consulted dealt with problems—such as sleeplessness, nightmares, nervousness, or hyperactivity—that appeared to be psychiatric and/or psychological in nature.

Cultural incompatibilities. The quality of the patient-provider relationship may also shape the Puerto Rican patient's behavior regarding health care. For example, the concept of "respeto" is important for Puerto Rican families (Fitzpatrick, 1987). Puerto Ricans are taught to treat physicians and others with respect (defined as dignity, propriety, courtesy) and expect others to show the same respect in return. One of the most common complaints Puerto Ricans have about health care professionals is that they often show "una falta de respeto," i.e., disrespect, in their manner and approach. What is meant is that their behavior or attitude is discourteous, gruff, or condescending. The current general feeling is that health services and providers are out of touch with patients from minority communities.

Bridging Two Worlds: Health Care Models that Work

Despite the obstacles alluded to above, there are program models that work. There are also cultural strengths in Puerto Rican families to build upon. The key is to find the right blend of both to create quality health care services which are both appropriate and accessible to Puerto Rican children and families.

Case Study One: Primary Health Care Center

Betances Health Unit, Inc., in New York City's Lower East Side, is an example of a program model that works in providing health care services to Puerto Rican children and families. Named after the Puerto Rican physician and abolitionist, Ramón Emeterio Betances (1827–1898), Betances Health Unit was established in 1970 by a group of Lower East Side residents concerned with the area's lack of affordable and available health care. Today, the center identifies itself as a community-based primary health care program, with approximately 5,300 patients and 25,000 patient visits per year. Over 65% of the patients served are Latinos, primarily Puerto Ricans, who are living at or below 200% of the federal poverty level.

Betances' philosophy is to provide direct patient care and tailored health education for its clients. The Center's brochure mentions that it treats the whole person, not just the illness. It further states that the Center encourages the patient's participation by asking questions, discussing treatment, telling staff how they can serve patients better, and maintaining follow-up visits, which are as important as their first visit. More recently, Betances has introduced more innovative approaches to health care, such as homeopathic medicine, massage therapy, nutrition counseling, and food supplements. A mobile van travels to shelters for the homeless and provides diagnostic screening, treatment, and health education.

Betances' strengths lie in several areas. The center provides primary health services which are sorely needed and accessible to the community. Staff, who are bilingual and bicultural, provide care to the entire family, first targeting the mothers and children. In addition to medical care, health education and disease prevention are emphasized. Finally, the center adapts its programs to the changing needs of the community, with sensitivity to populations with special needs.

An analysis of patient visits conducted by the center in 1988 (Betances Health Unit, n.d.) indicates that the majority of visits were made by mothers with small children. These women were unemployed, collecting unemployment insurance benefits, or parts of families whose head was employed, but with inadequate or no health insurance coverage. The majority of small children were treated for upper respiratory infections; update of immunizations; nutrition deficiencies; and childhood diseases such as measles, mumps, and chicken pox.

In a concise survey of the patient population served by Betances, nearly one-third of 65 patients who were questioned described their health status as fair or poor, yet only two patients said that they had a regular provider of health care. Few had made a physician visit in the recent past. The patients did not use preventive services, although their health assessment examinations revealed serious health problems.

Over the years, Betances' services have changed to meet the community's changing needs. Today, the center services a more impoverished population, which is, in turn, confronted with problems of homelessness, hunger, substance abuse, and AIDS. The types of illnesses and ailments showing up in adult patients are now being presented by children as well: anemia, diabetes, and hypertension.

The Director of Betances Health Unit, Paul Ramos (personal communication, May 14, 1990), states that their work is a constant struggle. "Our patients represent a microcosm of a small poor community. They present with— and die from—stresses and illnesses that mainstream society has, for the most part, already tackled and overcome." Yet, Mr. Ramos remains committed and confident, "We have to keep trying. That's why we're here."

Case Study Two: School-Based Health Clinic

The East Harlem community of New York City, often referred to as Spanish Harlem or El Barrio, is comprised of 65% Latinos, primarily Puerto Ricans, and 32% African-Americans. El Barrio is beset by economic and social ills, including high unemployment; substandard housing; and elevated levels of poverty, crime, and substance abuse.

Concerned about the poor health status of children in East Harlem, the Department of Pediatrics at Mt. Sinai Medical Center decided to take action by establishing in 1989 a school-based health project in three community schools in the district, two elementary and one junior high school. The objectives of the project are, (a) to increase access to primary care and health screening services in order to enhance school performance and overall health; (b) to conduct appropriate health education strategies to promote healthy behavior; and (c) to facilitate coordination of community resources to improve the efficiency of health and social service delivery in East Harlem (Mt. Sinai School-Based Health Clinic, n.d.).

There are three clinics which operate on-site in each of the schools. The staff consists of a pediatrician, who serves as project director and medical supervisor, along with a pediatric nurse practitioner, a health educator, a medical assistant, and a social worker. The medical team provides primary health care, physical exams, vision screenings, basic laboratory work, and health education to the nearly 2,000 students in the network. A computer at each site links the hospital center's database in order to obtain additional medical information. Services at the school-based health clinic are provided free of charge to the children and are billable under Medicaid or other third party insurance.

The values of the school-based health clinic for Puerto Rican children and families are several. Services are easily accessible to students. In fact, teachers sometimes use the school-based clinic as a resource and take their classes there to learn about parts of the body, nutrition, AIDS, and other topics. Good health fosters good school performance and reduces absenteeism among students. For the family, services at the school-based health clinic reduce the need for acute care visits to the hospital and improper use of the emergency room.

One unique feature of this school-based health clinic is that it targets young children in elementary and junior high schools. This was planned deliberately to address medical problems in children at an early age. Dr. Gary Butts (personal communication, September 27, 1990), medical director of the project, indicated that "many of these children have not seen a physician since receiving their immunizations as infants." He added that "these children never even reach the hospital. We offer preventive and direct medical care on-site while they're in school."

Case Study Three: Coordinated Hospital and Community Services

Montefiore Medical Center is a voluntary hospital located in the Central Bronx, New York City. Increasingly, Montefiore serves as the main tertiary care center of the Department of Pediatrics of the Albert Einstein College of Medicine. The population served by the hospital is 65% Latinos, including Puerto Ricans, Mexicans, and South Americans; 33% African Americans; and 2% other racial and ethnic groups (Montefiore, n.d.). A significant portion of this population is poor and lacks Medicaid or other third party health insurance.

Children with chronic illness, such as asthma, vascular disease, sickle cell disease, chronic renal failure, and diabetes mellitus require services from many different segments of the health care and social service systems. Many Latino and other minority families are unaware of the resources in the community that are available to help. Generally, the coordination of care and the provision of support services have been minimally provided. Chronically ill children now sustain unnecessarily long hospital stays due to the absence of a coordinated program that can manage care outside the hospital.

In 1988, with initial funding from the United Hospital Fund and The New York Community Trust, Montefiore established the LINKS (Linking Individual Needs with Services) project to provide comprehensive health planning, coordination, and referrals for children with chronic illness. The project conducts comprehensive assessments, develops individual care plans, coordinates care, and provides referrals for medical subspecialty services. Other aspects include financial assistance, respite care, early intervention programs, and mental health services. The program staff work as a team, usually consisting of a pediatrician, a nurse practitioner, a social worker, and an office assistant.

In addition to these services, parents are trained to become advocates and to assist with information and referrals for other families with children who have chronic illness. This component enables minority families to acquire the skills they need to help manage their child's illness.

The leadership role that this medical institution is providing through this project is unusual and commendable. It provides a model for other medical institutions for coordinated service delivery and a means to empower families in obtaining access to necessary services for their chronically ill children.

Case Study Four: Harnessing Community and Cultural Resources

In Hartford, Connecticut, the Hispanic Health Council is an example of a project which makes effective use of cultural strengths and community resources. According to Schensul and Borrero (1982), the Council was established as an outgrowth of the Puerto Rican Health Task Force, formed in response to an incident in 1972 in which an eight-month-old baby died from dehydration after being taken to two hospital emergency rooms on continguous days. The baby's mother was Puerto Rican and spoke only Spanish. The incident set off a heated confrontation between the Puerto Rican and the medical communities of Hartford. The Task Force provided a forum for Puerto Rican residents and hospital administrators to meet and to devise strategies for corrective action in the future. As the Task Force's work ended, Puerto Rican leaders decided to pursue issues in other areas. In collaboration with medical anthropologists at the University of Connecticut, they created the Hispanic Health Council in 1978 (Schensul & Borrero, 1982).

Since then, the Hispanic Health Council has served as a research, training, and advocacy organization directed to the improvement of health in the Puerto Rican community of Hartford (Schensul & Borrero, 1982). Comprised of medical anthropologists, faculty from the

University of Connecticut, and leaders from Puerto Rican agencies, the Hispanic Health Council has conducted studies on demography, health behavior, and health resources. And it has served as a clearinghouse for health-related data on Puerto Ricans on issues such as sterilization, otitis media, asthma, crisis intervention, family health, and minority recruitment into the health fields. This, in turn, has led to action research and policy development (Schensul & Borrero, 1982).

In all its work, the Hispanic Health Council has made good use of interagency networks to facilitate community organization and empowerment. It has organized networks to address communication gaps, to conduct cultural sensitivity training, and to improve service coordination (Borrero, Schensul, & García, 1982).

The Hispanic Health Council has found that having a bilingual staff is a definite plus, but more important than language is an understanding of cultural mores. Staff training has been particularly useful in sensitizing health care professionals around Puerto Rican cultural beliefs and behaviors. Technical assistance and follow-up support are also necessary to assure effective patient/provider interaction. According to Borrero, Schensul, and García (1982), change can occur, but only if a commitment to a long-term effort is made on the part of the medical institution.

Another important, yet often neglected, aspect is the need to inculcate health, illness, and healing information from a community standpoint and to offer culturally appropriate health services. The Hispanic Health Council best articulates this approach to health care for Puerto Ricans (Schensul & Borrero, 1982). In addition, Singer (1988) speaks of the need to "take seriously the cultural side of illness and the consequent need for a culturally sensitive approach to treatment" (p. 59). He identifies five different components of health programs: (a) linguistic and cultural accessibility; (b) availability, meaning flexible hours and appointments; (c) cost appropriateness; (d) generalized service delivery and broad-scoped consultations; and (e) incorporation of folk ideology (Singer, 1988, p. 57).

For instance, anthropologists who have studied the role of "espiritismo" in health care delivery for Puerto Ricans on the mainland (Garrison, 1977; Harwood, 1977, 1981; Singer & García, n.d.) view "espiritismo" as a cultural strength and not as a deterrent to health care services. In a project of the Hispanic Health Council, spiritists were seen as a helping resource. While they continued to provide Puerto Rican families with spiritual help, they were also trained on how to refer families for professional health and mental health services through local agencies. Agency staff also called upon the spiritists for help with particular patients (Borrero, Schensul, & García, 1982).

Case Study Five: Community Health Planning

In order to deliver appropriate child health care, it is important to plan and develop services which reflect the community's priorities. Dr. Philip J. Porter, a pediatrician in Brookline, Massachusetts, has designed a national program model, the Healthy Children Program. The project, funded by the Robert Wood Johnson Foundation, stimulates and assists communities to develop health care services for children. Rather than providing funding for programs, existing resources are redirected and reorganized to provide services. The model uses a two-pronged approach: (a) an assessment phase that helps a community determine the gaps in health care services for children, and (b) direct technical assistance for those communities most committed (Robert Wood Johnson Foundation, 1989).

The Healthy Children Program has worked with community networks interested in organizing special programs for children in need in redirecting financial resources to children's services, and in shaping public health policies which affect children. To date, 78 communities nationwide have received technical assistance and 43 communities have initiated new health programs for children, teenage pregnancy programs, comprehensive primary care for mothers and children, and school-based health clinics (Robert Wood Johnson Foundation, 1989).

The Healthy Children program has identified six key elements essential to a community's success: (a) strong leadership; (b) a well-defined program; (c) resources; (d) an institutional home; (e) a specific plan of action; and (f) a political strategy (Robert Wood Johnson Foundation, 1989). A network of community leaders and interested parties should drive the health planning effort. Borrero, Schensul, & García (1982) have also pointed to the need to include advocates and sympathetic sectors, defined as "influential individuals or staff of a particular program or department with a track record of community matters." (p. 131). These would refer to public health personnel, police, school representatives, local business managers, and so forth.

The Healthy Children Program offers a fine example of a project which has many applications. For Puerto Ricans, it offers both an opportunity and a challenge to help shape the health services for their children.

Conclusion and Recommendations

Puerto Rican families face many challenges in trying to obtain quality health care for themselves and their children. The crisis of AIDS, for example, underscores the strain on the already overburdened health, education, and social service systems and highlights the need to break down barriers and to identify innovative ways of working together.

In each of the case studies presented, there are lessons for both the Puerto Rican community and for health care service providers. In each case the services resulted from a call to action, triggered by community dissatisfaction or resulting from concerns by health care providers. In either case, the important message is that cultural strengths, effective health models, and community resources do exist. The task is to bridge these elements to create one comprehensive system of care. Some guiding principles to follow in planning health care services for children are:

- Quality health care should be ensured for all disadvantaged children.

- Those communities with poor health status should be targeted.
- Community-based health models should be emphasized.
- A full range of primary care services should be provided, including health, mental health, social services, prevention, and education.
- Options should be offered to assure that health services are accessible to poor families who are medically uninsured or under insured.
- Health services should be delivered with cultural and linguistic sensitivity.
- Interagency coalitions should be used to develop a comprehensive network of community-based health and social services.

In order to achieve good health, a great deal of healing must take place for Puerto Rican children and their families. Puerto Rican families in the U.S. experience high rates of poverty and are burdened with numerous problems.

Many argue that more funding is needed for more services. However, in this time of shrinking financial resources, reorganization of existing services may be more feasible. Developing public-private funding partnerships, building networks of community agencies, and replicating program models that work are some ways by which to build a more effective health care system. Mechanisms for evaluation should also be included to measure program progress, help implement mid-course corrections, and assure accountability.

As Puerto Ricans become better versed in the use of community resources, they will make better use of hospitals and other health care facilities. Similarly, they should make their voices heard by participating in agency advisory boards, planning councils, and coalitions which shape services and policy.

Providing quality health care to Puerto Rican children and families requires a bridging of two separate worlds, each with its own culture, norms, and values: that of health care institutions and that of the Puerto Rican family. Each has a responsibility to work with the other by improving communication, identifying service gaps, and formulating strategies for more effective health services. What will be the legacy to our children and their children? The groundwork we do today will be the basis for our children tomorrow. Like our people before us, we want the gift to our children to be the best it can be. We want our legacy to them to be one of good health or, at least, the tools to obtain good health. Until the one true path to good health is found, we must work with what we have and continue to seek solutions. We owe it to ourselves. We owe it to our children.

REFERENCES

Alvarez, M.D. (1983). Puerto Ricans and academic achievement: An exploratory study of person, home, and school variables among high risk bilingual first graders. Unpublished doctoral dissertation, New York University.

Barrón, A. (1990). Legislative update: Battling the AIDS epidemic. *National Puerto Rican Coalition (NPRC) Reports, 10*(3), p. 4.

Betances Health Unit (n.d.). Unpublished reports, brochures, and survey findings.

Borrero, M., Schensul, J., & García, R. (1982). Research based training for organizational change. *Urban Anthropology, 11*, 129–153.

Children's Defense Fund (1990). *Latino youth at the crossroads.* (Special Report No. 5, January/March). Washington, DC: Author.

Figueroa, L. (1971). *Breve historia de Puerto Rico.* Rio Piedras: Edil.

Fitzpatrick, J.P. (1987). *Puerto Rican Americans: The meaning of migration to the mainland.* Englewood Cliffs, NJ: Prentice-Hall.

Garrison, V. (1977). Doctor, espiritista, or psychiatrist: Health seeking behavior in a Puerto Rican neighborhood of New York City. *Medical Anthropology, 1*(2), 65–180.

Giachello, A.L., & Aponte, R. (1989). *Health status and access issues of Hispanic children and adolescents in Chicago: Analysis of a 1984 city-wide survey.* Chicago: Hispanic Health Alliance, Monograph No. 3.

Guarnaccia, P. (1991). Asthma, the Puerto Rican child, and the school. In A.N. Ambert & M.D. Alvarez (Eds.), *Puerto Rican children on the mainland: Interdisciplinary perspectives* (pp. 237–271). New York: Garland.

Harwood, A. (1977). *Rx: Spiritist as needed: A study of a Puerto Rican community mental health resources.* New York: Wiley.

Harwood, A. (1981). Mainland Puerto Ricans. In A. Harwood (Ed.), *Ethnicity and medical care* (pp. 397–481). Cambridge: Harvard University Press.

Levin, D. (Ed.) (1989). *Report of the Mayor's Commission on the Future of Child Health in New York City.* New York: New York City Department of Health.

Montefiore Medical Center (n.d.). Unpublished reports on the LINKS Project.

Mount Sinai School-Based Health Clinic (n.d.). Unpublished reports.

NYC Department of Health (1989). Report of the Mayor's Commission on the future of child health in New York City. New York: Author.

Robert Wood Johnson Foundation (1989). *The Health Children Program: A special report,* 2(3). Princeton, NJ: Author.

Rodríguez, C. (1989). *Puerto Ricans born in the U.S.A.* Boston: Unwin Hyman.

Rogers, D.E. (1977). The challenge of primary care. In J.H. Knowles (Ed.), *Doing better and feeling worse: Health in the United States.* New York: Norton.

Schensul, S.L., & Borrero, M. (1982). Introduction: The Hispanic Health Council. *Urban Anthropology, 11,* 1–8.

Singer, M. (1988). Indigenous treatment for alcoholism in the Hispanic community. In M. Singer, L. Davison, & F. Yolin (Eds.), *Alcohol use and abuse among Hispanic adolescents* (pp. 55–59). Hartford, CT: Hispanic Health Council.

Singer, M., & García, R. (n.d.). *Choosing folk treatment: A profile of clients in espiritismo.* (Hispanic Health Council Reports, No. 2.) Hartford, CT: Hispanic Health Council.

CHAPTER 10

Asthma, the Puerto Rican Child, and the School

Peter J. Guarnaccia

Introduction

Asthma is the most common chronic illness among children. It is the leading cause of school absences among all pediatric chronic diseases (Freudenberg, Feldman, et al., 1980). Educating asthmatic children to recognize the symptoms of an asthma attack and to manage it properly can decrease the morbidity and mortality of asthma (Clark, et al., 1980; Freudenberg, Clark, et al., 1980; Howland, Bauchner, & Adair, 1988). Schools can play a central role in asthma education. Yet, there is little focus on the needs of ethnic minority children with asthma, particularly among Puerto Rican children, who experience a high rate of asthma.

This chapter focuses on asthma among Puerto Rican children, with particular attention given to how Puerto Rican families cope with asthma and the impact of asthma on school-age children. After reviewing national-level data on the prevalence of asthma, the chapter will focus on the results of an in-depth community study of how low-income Puerto Rican families coped with childhood asthma in the home and in the community (Guarnaccia, 1984). The chapter will end with some recommendations for managing asthma among school-age Puerto Rican children in both clinical and community settings.

National Data on the Prevalence of Asthma among Different Ethnic Groups

The Department of Health and Human Services (1979) report on the *Health Status of Minorities and Low-Income Groups* indicates that asthma is highly prevalent among minorities and among the poor:

> Both the racial and income differential in the prevalence of asthma is unfavorable to the disadvantaged. The racial differential is 1.18. All other races have a prevalence of 34.9 per thousand compared with a prevalence rate of 29.5 among whites. The income differential is 1.59. Persons with family incomes of less than $3,000 have a prevalence rate of 43.7, compared with 27.4 for those with family incomes of $15,000. (pp. 106–107)

The "racial" differential becomes even more marked if one focuses on children. For children under 6 years, it is 1.30. The prevalence for minorities is 36.4/1000, while for Anglos it is 27.9. It is similar in the 6 to 16-year-old group: 1.28 (39.2/1000 for minorities, 30.7 for Anglos).

The Hispanic Health and Nutrition Examination Survey (HHANES) made available data on the prevalence of asthma among different Hispanic groups. Carter, Gergen, and Lecca (1987) report on results from the HHANES and the second wave of the National Health and Nutrition Examination Survey (NHANES II) for children 6 months to 11 years old:

> Both lifetime prevalence and point prevalence were highest for Puerto Ricans than for any other group. . . . Puerto Ricans had a point prevalence (or percent with active asthma) that was 2–4 times higher than for any other group: 11.2% of the Puerto Ricans had active asthma, compared to 5.9% of non-Hispanic blacks, 5.2% of the Cubans, 3.3% of non-Hispanic whites and 2.7% of Mexicans. (Carter, Gergen, & Lecca, 1987, p. 4).

Using the Hispanic HANES and National HANES II, Angel, Worobey, and Davies (1990) and Angel and Worobey (in press) found that the differences were even more striking when examining factors associated with ever having asthma (lifetime prevalence). They examined prevalence of asthma in children by acculturation, measured by language of interview, and family status, measured by two-parent or female-parent household headship. In reporting whether a child under 12 had ever had asthma, Mexican-Americans reported the lowest rates, followed by Anglo-Americans. Between 3.4 and 5.9% of families reported a child with asthma in these groups. African-American families were intermediate, with 7.6% of two-parent families reporting a child with asthma and 9.3% of female-parent families reporting an asthmatic child. Cuban-Americans reported 9.3% of English-speaking families with a child with asthma; over 10% of the Spanish-speaking Cuban-American children had suffered asthma. For Puerto Ricans, the two-parent households reported about 16% of children with asthma. The female-parent families had strikingly high rates of asthma; approximately 20% of the English-speaking and almost 30% of the Spanish-speaking families had an asthmatic child.

These data confirm what has long been suggested in the clinical literature and was initially demonstrated in an earlier community study in Hartford, Connecticut (Guarnaccia, 1984): Puerto Rican children experience higher rates of asthma than do children of other ethnic groups in the United States, even when compared to groups with similar socio-economic and environmental conditions, such as African-Americans.

Overview of the Community and the Study

The author developed the community study of childhood asthma upon finding in the Mental Health Study of Hartford's Hispanic Health Council that asthma was a widespread illness in the Latino community (Schensul &

Borrero, 1982). In that study, 50% of the sampled households in two low-income Puerto Rican neighborhoods of Hartford reported someone with asthma. These findings confirmed impressionistic statements in the literature and data from various studies indicating that asthma was a serious problem in the Puerto Rican community (Harwood, 1981; Karetzky, 1977; Ríos, 1982; Sifontes & Mayol, 1976). Harwood (1981), in particular, argued for the need to disentangle the asthma picture for minority and low-income groups, especially for Puerto Ricans. He alluded to the importance of social and psychological factors in the genesis of conditions such as asthma and to the need to investigate its etiology and treatment in Puerto Rican families.

The present study investigated asthma among Puerto Ricans living in a low-income housing project in Hartford. The study was carried out during 1981–82 and the final report written in 1984 (Guarnaccia, 1984).

The housing projects of Charter Oak Terrace and Rice Heights are the primary ecological contexts of this study. These housing projects are two economically disadvantaged neighborhoods. Charter Oak Terrace (COT) is a federally owned housing project designed for "low-income" families. It was constructed in 1941 to house workers coming to Hartford to work in defense industries during World War II. Many African-American families came from the southern U.S. to work in these industries during this period and in the next two decades. The Puerto Rican community in Hartford and COT grew rapidly in the 1960's and 1970's. Puerto Ricans first came to Hartford as contract workers for the tobacco farmers of the Connecticut Valley. Families settled in Hartford, finding work in a variety of industries. More recent Puerto Rican families have come to seek new opportunities on the mainland and to escape social and economic problems in Puerto Rico. Many have also come to join family members already in Hartford. With the decline of manufacturing in Hartford, unemployment among minority families has risen.

COT, with its 1,000 dwelling units and an estimated 4,130 people, was the largest housing project in the city at the time of the study. About 55% of the families had incomes below federal poverty lines. The housing project comprised 56% Puerto Rican households, 37% African-American, and 7% Anglo-American.

Rice Heights (RH) was a state-owned housing project for moderate income families. It was administratively separate from COT and separated physically by a major city avenue. Residents of RH and COT shared many social ties, shopped at the same local grocery, and experienced similar problems of isolation from the city. Rice Heights contained 74% Puerto Rican, 21% African-American, and 5% Anglo-American households. It had about 300 units and an estimated population of 1,600. Approximately 9% of the families had incomes below federal poverty guidelines. Thus, RH families had more economic resources than COT families.

Charter Oak Terrace and Rice Heights are separated from the rest of the city of Hartford by a major highway, by the Park River, and by a number of industries. All of these contribute pollutants which may affect health and provoke asthma (Guarnaccia, 1981). The highway is a major source of air pollutants. Traffic is heavy in this section of the roadway during both the morning and evening rush hours. Some mothers commented that in the summer their children had to come inside in the late afternoons, as the pollution made it difficult for them to breathe. There is an industrial park across the street and branches of two major manufacturers nearby. The presence of these industries encourages truck traffic past the housing project, adding to the pollution. The smell from the river is another kind of pollution. People often complained of strong, unpleasant odors emanating from the river, which runs uncovered through COT. Once the river leaves the COT/RH area, it runs through Hartford in a closed watercourse.

Not only do these community-level features affect families' health status, but families are also exposed to unhealthy features in the households which have a direct effect on asthma (Guarnaccia, 1981). Rats and cockroaches are of concern to residents because of the health risks they pose. Cockroaches, in particular, are a potential asthma trigger (Kang, 1976; Kang & Sulit, 1978). Families also expressed concern about the effects on their asthmatic children of insecticide sprayed against cockroaches—a difficult problem, since spraying is an integral part of the Housing Authority's pest control program. Dogs roam the community and live in apartments, often as watchdogs. Exposure to animals is a frequently identified trigger of asthma. Often the neighbors' dogs cause problems when the animal hairs are swept into the hall and then become part of the house dust the child plays in. A number of other environmental issues directly result from the poor condition of housing in the community. Rotting floors and walls allow pests easy access and are the source of molds, another asthma trigger. Drafty doors and windows increase the risk of respiratory infections. Crowded living conditions also contribute to the spread of lung infections and make environmental management in the home difficult. Exposure of the child with asthma to cigarette smoke can also serve as an irritant for sensitive lungs. Smoking was quite frequent among families in the community.

The physical conditions which isolate the community not only affect families' health, but also create problems of access to health services. Many families do not own cars, especially in COT. Bus service to these communities comes once an hour and the trips to other areas of the city are long. A bus ride to the closest hospital takes 15 to 25 minutes, to downtown shopping, 30 to 45 minutes, and to a Catholic hospital, an hour. Transportation is not the only problem of access. While many families have some form of medical assistance to help pay for care, only the health centers and hospitals will accept medical cards readily. Thus, COT/RH families' access to medical care was severely limited until residents organized their own neighborhood health center in March of 1979. The Asthma Project worked closely with the health center in all aspects of its work.

Method

The first step in the Asthma Project was to identify households where someone had asthma. From this population, a sample of households was selected to explore families' health cultures and coping strategies for dealing with childhood asthma. The author developed a short questionnaire, in both English and Spanish, based on the work of Lelah, Harris, Avery, and Brook (1976) and the Medical Research Council (1976). This questionnaire contained the following questions:

1. Does anyone in your family (household) have asthma? If yes, who has asthma? If no, has anyone in your family ever had asthma?
2. During the past year, has anyone in your family had an episode of wheezing with cough at night, chest tightness or congestion, shortness of breath, difficulty breathing?
3. Were you (or a member of your family) told you had asthma by a doctor or a nurse? When?

An answer of "yes" to any of the questions identified someone with asthma. The names, ages, and relationship to the person being interviewed were collected for all individuals identified as having asthma.

A "symptom definition" approach to asthma was the most practical way to carry out the study, as it focused on illness rather than the disease. Medical anthropologists (Kleinman, 1980) distinguish between disease and illness: "*Disease* refers to a malfunctioning of biological and/or psychological processes, while the term *illness* refers to the psychosocial experience and meaning of perceived disease." (p. 72).

In studying families' coping repertoires for asthma from a community perspective, relevant cases became those that were defined as asthma from the perspective of the family. It was important to understand how families who perceived their children as suffering from this illness managed asthma at home and used health care resources. Thus, both the pragmatics of case definition and a theoretical approach to illness led to the selection of the symptom questionnaire.

Once case definition was completed, a random sample of 140 families was selected for interviews. The process resulted in a sample of 94 families: 61 Puerto Rican, 25

African-American, and 8 Anglo-American. This chapter will focus on Puerto Rican families.

Families were administered 90-minute interviews concerning their understanding of, and strategies for, coping with asthma. The interview consisted of four parts: (a) families' understanding of asthma and lung illness using an explanatory framework (Kleinman, 1980); (b) course of the child's asthma, severity of asthma, and family history of asthma; (c) health practices related to asthma, home treatments, use of health care institutions, and hypothetical situations exploring parental decision-making; and (d) basic socio-demographic information and social contact data.

One of the first goals of the study was to establish the distribution of asthma among households. A short screening survey was developed, and 1,079 of the 1,300 units in the community were surveyed. The results are presented in Table 1.

Table 1

Results of Asthma Survey

Ethnic Group	Child Only	Child & Adult	Adult Only	None
Puerto Rican (N=615; 55%)	99 (16%)	31 (5%)	103 (17%)	382 (62%)
African-American (N=422; 38%)	37 (9%)	15 (4%)	35 (8%)	335 (79%)
Anglo-American (N=79; 7%)	6 (8%)	3 (4%)	6 (8%)	64 (80%)
Totals (N=1116)	142 (13%)	49 (4%)	144 (13%)	781 (70%)

The striking feature of these results is that 38% of the Puerto Rican households report at least one person with asthma, in contrast to 20% of the non-Puerto Rican households. This is consistent with the national figures cited earlier.

Findings and Discussion

The Child's Experience with Asthma

The child's experience includes his/her history of the development of asthma, the causes the family has identified as precipitating attacks, and the family's estimates of the severity of the child's asthma. Families use this information as a guide on how to act in both preventing and treating asthma. Families' perceptions of severity affect when and where they seek help for coping with attacks. The child's experience with asthma affects the development of family management strategies for the illness.

Sex differences in asthma. Both the sex of the child and the age of first attack affect the development and severity of childhood asthma. Boys are more likely to develop asthma. Their asthma persists into adulthood more often than girls' asthma. The sex ratio in this group of children was heavily skewed towards males, as has been reported in much of the epidemiologic literature on childhood asthma. Fifty-nine (63%) of the children with asthma from the family interviews were male and 35 (37%) were female. These figures reflect the sex distribution of asthma in the complete community sample, as well. Forty (43%) children experienced their first asthma attack during their first year of life; by age 3, 70 (76%) children had had their first attack. After the first three years, children's first attacks became widely scattered from 4 to 12 years of age.

Causes of asthma. The most common causes of asthma attacks in young children are respiratory infections and food allergies. Mothers were asked the question: "Why do you think it [asthma] started when it did?" to see if this pattern existed in this community. Twenty-one (42%) Puerto Rican mothers reported that they did not know why the asthma started when it did. Table 2 lists the reported causes of asthma. Puerto Rican mothers gave considerable weight to living conditions; they also mentioned heredity, allergy, and respiratory infection as causative factors.

Table 2

Reported Causes of Asthma
(N=61)

Living Conditions	6
Born with asthma	5
Change in weather	4
Respiratory infections	3
Other illnesses	4
Allergy	2
Heredity	2
Don't know	21
No response	14

Because of the importance of living conditions as a precipitant of asthma, the relationship between the first asthma episode and where the family lived at the time was explored. For almost half the sample (47%), asthma started in COT/RH. Another 35% lived in Hartford, but not in COT/RH, at the time of the first attack. The majority of Puerto Rican children developed their asthma upon coming to urban areas of the mainland, where they encountered new living conditions and climate.

The respondents who lived outside COT/RH when asthma started were then asked about changes in the child's asthma upon moving to the community. For Puerto Rican children, 11 (32%) of the children's asthma worsened, 9 (26%) stayed the same, and 14 (41%) improved. Many of the children whose asthma improved had lived in very poor private housing in Hartford, where lack of heat and drafty conditions were common. Moving to COT/RH, in spite of the many problems, was an improvement in housing conditions. However, other children encountered a new set of asthma triggers in the housing project which worsened their asthma.

Knowing the triggers of a child's asthma is important both for predicting the prognosis and for identifying interventions to remove asthma triggers. Children whose asthma is allergic tend to have a worse prognosis, particularly when asthma is complicated by eczema.

Mothers were questioned about what they perceived as the major triggers of their children's asthma attacks; their responses appear in Table 3.

Table 3
Major Reported Triggers of Asthma
(N=61)

Cold weather	22	(28%)
Respiratory infection	11	(14)
House pets and pests	11	(14)
Dusts	9	(11)
Pollens	9	(11)
Dry heat	3	(4)
Dampness	3	(4)
Change in weather/temperature	2	(3)
Exercise	2	(3)
Don't know	7	(9)
No response	4	

Respiratory infections (especially bronchitis and pneumonia) and allergies (especially hay fever and eczema) affect the development of childhood asthma. Approximately 35% of Puerto Rican children had had bronchitis and 30% pneumonia, usually prior to the development of asthma; they had low rates of hay fever (12%), but more significant histories of eczema (36%). Thus, a common pattern in the development of childhood asthma includes a serious respiratory illness (bronchitis or pneumonia) in the first year of life, followed by the appearance of wheezing and asthma. Usually, the children continue to experience wheezing with colds or other viral respiratory infections. Another common pattern is the development of allergic illness (especially eczema) at an early age, which then becomes complicated by asthma. These children are more responsive to allergic triggers of asthma such as dusts. A smaller third group of children develop asthma as a result of multiple complicating illnesses; these children are responsive to both infectious and allergic triggers.

Parental Experience with Asthma and Allergy

Asthma impacts the entire family. It is a chronic illness with erratic, acute episodes, and it frequently interrupts the life of the child and those around her/him. The history of the family's experience with asthma affects the family's response to individual episodes and the development of long-term strategies for coping with the illness. Many families have experienced asthma for several generations, a pattern seen in this community as well. Family history is a predisposer to developing asthma. Family patterns, however, appear to result as much from shared migration history and home environment as from genetic predisposition.

Family history. Since family history is a key issue in the development of asthma and since mothers are the primary care-takers of children, understanding of the mothers' history of asthma and allergy is important. Some 63% of the children had a parental history of asthma or allergy, and 52% children had one parent with asthma or allergy. Both parents of 10 children (12%) had asthma or allergy, and 30 (36%) children had no immediate family history. Thus, there is considerable family history of asthma and allergy in this community. However, this strong family pattern does not imply genetic transmission of the asthma or allergy. This finding may be the result of an interaction between a predisposition to develop allergy and living in an unhealthy environment. Many of the mothers developed their asthma upon arrival in the community in response to the same "asthma load" as their children.

Twenty-two of 59 (37%) Puerto Rican mothers suffered from asthma; 16 of 57 (28%) experienced an allergic illness as well. If one examines the length of time with asthma or allergy by ethnicity, one finds that Puerto Rican mothers exhibit a bimodal distribution, with 11 of 30 (37%) having had their illness since childhood and 16 (53%) having developed their illness in the last five years. One potential explanation for these findings comes from studies of the effects of migration on asthma/allergy. Mothers who developed their asthma/allergy in childhood developed their illness in response to conditions in Puerto Rico, where asthma and allergy are also common. Mothers who developed their illness within the last five years are experiencing the stresses and new exposures of migration along with their children. Puerto Rican mothers suffer greatly from the cold weather they encounter upon arriving in Hartford, as well as from the exposure to new allergens and respiratory infections. These patterns of the development of asthma in the mothers highlight concerns similar to those of the child's experience with asthma, and reflect on factors affecting the severity of asthma.

Asthma Severity

A variety of criteria was used to explore the severity of the child's asthma, including the frequency and persistence of symptoms and the extent of interference of these symptoms with the child's normal activities. Specific coping behaviors reflect recent experiences with attacks and their consequences. The work of Lelah, Harris, Avery, and Brook (1976) provides a tested set of questions for assessing the severity of children's asthma. Some responses to these questions follow.

A major concern for children with asthma is the extent to which it affects their normal activities; their ability to play with friends and develop peer relationships, and their ability to regularly attend school. While 24 children had no reported interference with normal activities, 34 experienced interruption of their normal routines several times a year, 15 experienced at least monthly symptoms that prevented normal activities, and 8 had symptoms several times a week that interfered with play and school attendance. During the past year, children missed from 0 to more than 40 days of school as a result of asthma. Up to 31 mothers reported that asthma had affected their children's performance in school. Eight children were held back in grade because of absences due to asthma, and four children were in special school programs, at least in part due to asthma.

Children who had also had pneumonia and/or eczema had more severe asthma. Regardless of the related illness, the more of these four illnesses (bronchitis, pneumonia, hay fever, eczema) a child had, the more severe was the asthma. The development of these illnesses in childhood appears to indicate an increased risk of asthma and strongly relates to having more severe asthma. For Puerto Rican children, emotional involvement as a feature of asthma is related to severity as well. The longer a child had been in Hartford and in COT/RH, the more severe the asthma appeared to be. This was an important finding. While the expectation was that asthma would improve over time, neither current age nor age of first attack correlated with severity for Puerto Rican children. Rather, the environment of Hartford and of COT/RH appeared to cause the children's asthma to worsen over time.

Conceptions of Asthma

Pienso que asma es como una flema que tapa los tubos respiratorios. La persona respira más rápido de lo normal y se puede ver que es asma ya que busca aire para respirar. Se pone cansada y tiene que acostarse en la cama. Y tiene dolores en el pecho.

I think that asthma is like a phlegm that closes the bronchial tubes. The person breathes more rapidly than normal and you can see it is asthma because she is looking for air to breathe. She becomes tired and has to lie down in bed. And she has pains in her chest.

(Mother's comments about a Puerto Rican female, age 12.)

Respira fuerte y sale un pitito. No puede respirar Está casi muerto en mi brazos. Sus labios se ponen azules. Le afecta cuando cambian las estaciones de invierno y verano. Ahora no tiene ataques. Siempre

He breathes hard and a whistle comes out. He is almost dead in my arms. His lips become blue. It affects him when the seasons change to winter or summer summer. He does not have attacks

está con mucho catarro.	now. *He always has*
Es desinquieto cuando	*a cold. He is restless*
juega; le da mucha	*when he plays; he*
tos.	*coughs a lot.*

(Mother's comments about a Puerto Rican male, age 4.)

Important features of family health culture are the definitions and descriptions families use to identify particular illnesses and to assess the severity of illness episodes. Families' ideas about illness also include the impact of that illness on the child who is sick and on the rest of the family. These concepts and assessments affect families' health behaviors. Families' descriptions of asthma highlight the signs and symptoms they use to identify an attack. Families' assessments of the effects of asthma on their children influence how they choose to cope with an attack both at home and in health care institutions.

Table 4 summarizes mothers' responses to the question: "What is asthma?" All responses were open-ended; interviewers recorded the mothers' own words. The largest category of responses was breath-related descriptions of asthma and discussions of the effects of asthma on the lungs. The Spanish terms are included with the symptom category as a reference for other researchers and for providers who want to learn asthma vocabulary.

Table 4

What is Asthma?
(N=61)

Difficulty breathing/shortness of breath	16
(*Falta/corto de respiración, se queda sin respiración*)	
Wheeze or whistle	7
(*Ronquillo, pito*)	
Chest congestion	6
(*Tapan los pulmones, flema en los pulmones*)	
Bronchial problem	5
Suffocation	3
(*Asfixiarse*)	
No response	24

How asthma begins. Asthma is often seen as beginning with a cold. This observation is corroborated by the frequency of listing lung infections and cold weather as major triggers of asthma and of identifying winter as the worst time of the year. Harwood (1981) suggests that this sequence is congruent with and reinforced by notions of disease sequence based on the humoral theory of disease. The humoral theory of disease is based on balances within the body between hot and cold, wet and dry. Physical conditions, foods, and emotions can all upset bodily balances. Three mothers reported that asthma was frightening, created fear, or was an emotional problem. Three mothers mentioned dying from asthma: "can die from it," "seems like he is going to die," and "wants to die."

Describing asthma. While about a quarter of the mothers did not know how to respond to the question: "What is asthma?," they had much to say when asked to describe an asthma attack. Attacks are part of the mothers' personal experiences, whereas a definition of illness comes from an "expert." Again, breath-related descriptions accounted for the largest number of responses. The response categories and their frequencies are listed in Table 5.

Table 5
Descriptions of an Asthma Attack
(N=61)

Hard to breathe	23
(*No puede respirar, dificultad en respirar*)	
Wheeze	20
(*Ronquillo, pito*)	
Short of breath	18
(*Pecho apretado, dolor de pecho*)	
Coughing	10
Suffocates	9
(*Asfixiarse*)	
Rapid breathing	2

(Note: Respondents gave more than one answer)

The list of physical symptoms associated with an asthma attack is much more extensive this time. Symptoms of respiratory infection are particularly prevalent.

The concepts of asthma and fatiga. The other important symptom which appears in this section is fatigue. Eleven of the mothers describe their children as weak, lacking energy, and not able to do anything. An additional three Puerto Rican mothers use the term *fatigada*, which has the double meaning of both worn-out and with *fatiga* (i.e., asthma):

Tos, que le ataca la gargania. Parece que se ahoga. También le ataca el pecho y el estómago. Los ojos lo verá en blanco. El niño se cansa cuando juega; se fatiga y se queda sin ánimo o fuerza. Es una tos sin descanso que le causa la fatiga.	*Asthma is a cough that attacks the throat. It seems like he is drowning. It also attacks his chest and stomach. His eyes look white. He becomes tired when he plays; he becomes "fatigued" and is left without spriti or strength. It is a cough that does does not rest that causes the "fatigue."*

(Mother's comments about a Puerto Rican male, age 13.)

Puerto Rican families had one descriptive term for asthma (*asma*) which is particular to their culture: *fatiga*. Forty (75%) of the Puerto Rican mothers who responded to a question asking the difference between *asma* and *fatiga* answered that they were the same. Those who felt that there was a difference described *fatiga* as breathlessness due to exercise, a lighter illness, one which does not close (*tapar*) the lungs, and one which can be cured in the home. *Asma* was seen as more dangerous, stronger, an illness which blocks the lungs, and which requires a trip to the hospital. Harwood (1980:432) found similar differences in his Health Center Study in New York City, where a majority used the two terms interchangeably. When they were distinguished, *fatiga* was seen as ". . . an acute condition, accompanied by wheezing, a cough and high fever. . . ."*Asma* was ". . . a chronic condition, characterized by shortness of breath and wheezing." This interchange of *asma* and *fatiga* appears particular to Puerto Ricans and is further evidence of the salience of this condition in the Puerto Rican community. Key informants from other Hispanic groups use the term *fatiga* very differently. The key element common to *fatiga* in Hispanic cultures is its association with losing one's breath.

Asthma-related problems. The effects of the physical and emotional symptoms of asthma produced a variety of problems for children and their families in this community. Mothers were asked: "What were the chief problems your child's asthma has caused him/her?" The major problems included: cannot play with other children (22); loses appetite (16), has problems in school (14), and lacks energy (13). Only 12 (21%) of the Puerto Rican mothers said that asthma caused no problems for their children. Mothers were also asked what problems asthma had caused them. The most frequent responses were "worry or nervousness" and "loss of sleep." Twenty seven (47%) mothers reported "worry or nervousness" as their main problem. Many of these emotional symptoms, as well as the physical symptoms, of asthma are dealt with in the home.

Home Care of Asthma

> • Sara wasn't at home; the attack started in school. Her mother went to get her at school and brought her home. Her mother gave Sara her medications at home. The medicines helped Sara for about three hours, then the wheezing began again. Her mother waited for eight hours. During that time she rubbed Sara's chest with Vicks Vapo-rub. After a while, she got substantially better. For the rest of the week Sara felt tired and didn't want to eat. There wasn't any need to take her to the hospital. The attack wasn't a very constant or strong one. (Sara is an eight-year-old Puerto Rican girl.)

- About two months ago, Juan's mother was visiting a friend of hers. Juan began to have an asthma attack at the friend's house. His mother could tell by his chest and breathing. It was not a very bad attack. The children of the woman they were visiting also suffered from asthma. Her friend got some of her children's medicine (Slophyllin) and gave it to Juan. It quickly calmed the attack. God didn't allow Juan to die. (Juan is a two-year-old Puerto Rican boy.)

This section discusses another important aspect of family health culture: knowledge families have about how to cope with asthma at home. Most asthma attacks can be managed at home if the family has sufficient knowledge and resources for intervening in an asthma attack. Some of these home-based interventions are learned from health care providers. Many come from the health culture of this ethnic group. Still other ideas were developed by individual families based on their own experiences with asthma and other illnesses. This cultural information on how to treat illness is often passed from mother to daughter. Some of this information is passed on in the form of statements like "When Juan has an asthma attack, you should . . ." However, much of the information comes from the memories of the mothers, particularly those who had asthma as children.

Identifying the symptoms of an asthma attack. Coping with asthma involves several processes. The first is identifying the symptoms as an asthma attack. Once the symptoms are identified as an attack, various interventions are selected to help the child. Depending on the effectiveness of the intervention, new assessments are made and new treatments tried. These assessments are also based on family health culture—on the criteria families use to identify illness, assess its severity, and select among a variety of coping strategies. The majority of families does something at home when an asthma attack starts, even if later they decide to seek help from health care institutions. Asthma often requires several days, or even weeks, of post-attack treatment at home before the symptoms are gone. This is true whether or not the health care services are used. The home is the key locus of action for asthma.

The first step in the coping process is to recognize the symptoms of an asthma attack. Mothers used a variety of symptoms to tell when their child was going to have an attack. Two common symptoms were changes in breathing, and wheezing. Next in frequency was the detection of a cough. For many of the mothers, a cold was the signal that an asthma attack was imminent. Others said that they predicted an asthma attack if the child complained of tiredness or chest tightness. Another indicator was loss of appetite:

> • José's last attack was in July. When José is about to have an attack, he sits around and looks tired. As soon as his mother sees José is sick, she gives him his medicine. When he has an asthma attack, he coughs, has a fever, vomits and looks purple around the eyes. His mother almost never has to take him to the doctor because she always tries to prevent the attack before it gets severe. Besides giving him his prescribed medicine, his mother keeps the house from being too cold or too hot and gives him liquids. She can judge the severity of José's asthma attacks by the difficulty he has breathing. Only once was his asthma serious enough for him to miss school. The family has a medical card so they don't have to pay for medical visits. They have a car. They need a translator when they go to get help. José's mother always gives him his medicine as soon as he gets a cold. (José is a ten-year-old Puerto Rican boy.)

In all, respondents listed 16 different symptoms which they used for predicting an asthma attack.

Most Puerto Rican mothers expressed considerable confidence in their abilities to identify an asthma attack before it happened. Twenty eight (50%) said that they could tell their child was about to have an asthma attack all of the time; seven (12.5%) said they could never tell when an asthma attack was coming; and another 14 (25%) said that they could tell only sometimes.

Home interventions for an asthma attack. Puerto Rican families reported a large repertoire of behaviors for intervening in an asthma attack at home. Two common home interventions were having the child do breathing exercises and rubbing the child's chest. Having the child do breathing exercises was usually something learned from health care providers. It is important to note that 26 (45%) Puerto Rican mothers reported having their child do these exercises. Rubbing the child's chest serves to calm her/his breathing and aids in general relaxation. This can break the cycle of increasing severity of an asthma attack, as fear and altered breathing patterns increase broncho-constriction, worsening the asthma attack. Fifty-four (93%) mothers reported rubbing their child's chest with either Vicks Vapo-rub or *alcoholado* (alcohol infused with herbs). For Puerto Ricans, the *sobo* or *masaje* (as this rubbing is called) is a key element of health culture.

> A highly important aspect of Puerto Rican home treatment is the use of massage with a variety of balms and compounds. . . . Indeed, giving a rubdown (*dar un sobo*) to an ailing person epitomizes the caring relationship between close kin and undoubtedly serves important psychological functions for not only the sick, but also the caretakers. (Harwood, 1981, pp. 443–444)

Vicks Vapo-rub was overwhelmingly mentioned by mothers, much more than the use of *alcoholado.*

Several families also listed the use of herbal teas as a home remedy. *Yerba buena* (mint) was the most common tea mentioned. A useful home intervention for asthma is to give the child warm liquids. This keeps mucous thinner and alleviates the clogging of the lungs with viscous mucous build-up. Parents in the Asthma Self-Management Project (New York City) reported this as one of the most effective interventions they had learned through the health education project (Columbia University Department of Pediatrics, 1984; Freudenberg, Clark, et al. 1980). Mothers also reported the use of home-made syrups (*jarabes*) to soothe coughing and unclog the lungs. Oils (*aceites*) were another common intervention mentioned by mothers. These oils and syrups are believed to break up the mucous plugs in the lungs, which are a significant part of an asthma attack. Harwood (1981) associates these treatments with the hot/cold theory of disease, as the oils and honey are considered "hot" substances, and asthma and associated respiratory problems "cold" illnesses.

Preventing asthma attacks. Puerto Rican families reported a large repertoire of behaviors they used to prevent asthma attacks. The major interventions were: (a) the use of preventive medicines; (b) use of non-allergic bedding; and (c) doing breathing/relaxation exercises. All of these preventive measures resulted from contact with health care providers, rather than being derived from Puerto Rican health cure.

The more home treatments a family knew, the more successful the family was at coping with asthma. However, success in coping with attacks was negatively related to the use of home remedies. Families who primarily used home remedies and relied less on interventions learned from health care providers appeared less successful in coping with asthma attacks at home. Thus, a combination of interventions from Puerto Rican health culture and from medical professionals appears the most effective strategy for managing asthma at home.

Respondents were given several hypothetical situations concerning childhood asthma to explore their ideas on how to cope with asthma and about what to do in "typical" asthma situations. The following situations elicited these responses to the question: "What would you do?"

The first situation was designed to test mothers' responses to the early symptoms of a mild attack. It also focused on how parents dealt with colds and asthma, as many physicians recommend beginning asthma medications at the first sign of a cold, before asthma symptoms appear.

> Situation 1: It is winter time. José has had a cold for a few days. He is watching TV when he starts to complain of tightness in his chest. He starts to cough a little.

Most mothers responded that they would do something at home. There was an unexpected difference in the effect asthma severity had on decision-making. The mothers of children with more severe asthma said that they would intervene at home; those whose children's asthma was less severe were more likely to seek help in the emergency room or from a doctor. Mothers whose child's asthma was more severe have had more contact with health institutions, have more asthma medications on hand, and are more likely to have had asthma themselves, and thus have had more opportunities to learn how to manage attacks. They are more confident of their ability to deal with asthma at home.

The second situation focused on the parents' relationship with the school system and the extent to which the school was involved in asthma treatment. Most schools discouraged treating the child's asthma there and encouraged the parent to take the child home or to a health service for treatment. There was a feeling among providers that the child's regular source of care was solely responsible for asthma treatment in conjunction with the family. Yet, some of the model school health programs have demonstrated that asthma treatment in school can be both effective in helping the child and in reducing school absences.

> Situation 2: Mrs. Alvarez gets a call from the school nurse that her daughter has just come from class and is wheezing. The school nurse would like Mrs. Alvarez to come get her daughter.

The most common responses were that the parent would get the child and take the child either home or to a medical facility. A small proportion of respondents said that they would bring asthma medications to school so that the child could take them immediately.

Playing and exercise can be a trigger of asthma. Many mothers reported that their children's asthma interfered with their playing with peers. Yet with good home management and awareness of the child's limitations, most children can participate in physical activities. Situation 3 addressed these issues.

Situation 3: María has asthma, which sometimes
bothers her if she plays too hard, but not always.
María's friends are all outside jumping rope and
she decides to join them.

About a third of the parents said they would let María
play, another third suggested that María should play, but
be encouraged to rest when tired, and the final third said
they would forbid María to play. Clients of private doctors
were more apt to "let her play," whereas clients of other
facilities were evenly split between letting and forbidding
the child to play. Clients of private doctors have the most
severe asthma, overall, so severity of asthma is not the
issue here. Rather, it is the kinds of messages parents
receive about exploring the child's abilities and limitations.
As the cases presented at the beginning of this section
and the hypothetical situations indicate, it is the mix of
home treatments with medical interventions which leads
to success. To some extent, Puerto Ricans practice more
of these home treatments as part of their ethnic health
culture. However, a number of these behaviors are learned
from health care providers. A family's health culture is a
mix of concepts and practices derived from ethnic health
culture and learned from health care providers. The broader
the sources of ideas and range of repertoires comprising
the "family health culture," the more successful the family
in coping with asthma. Those mothers who have and know
how to use asthma medications, rub their child's chest,
have their child rest, give their child liquid such as herbal
teas, and help their child do breathing exercises are more
successful at managing an asthma attack at home. While
many of these interventions come from ideas and practices
passed through the family's health culture, others must
be learned and reinforced within health care institutions.

Institutional Treatment Resources

> • Lourdes woke up this morning wheezing, with
> pains in her shoulders and legs, and shortness
> of breath. I gave her her two medicines (Theodur
> and Prednisone), as the doctor said, and they

had positive results. Then I immediately took her to the hospital clinic. At the hospital, a nurse gave Lourdes three injections at 15-minute intervals. They had positive results after about half an hour. The doctor advised me to give Lourdes her medicines as the prescription indicated. Her asthma causes Lourdes to miss school and she can't go to gym class. I worry about her a lot and I'm not calm until she is better. (Lourdes is a 16-year-old Puerto Rican girl.)

• Antonio's attack began at night. I didn't have any medicines. I gave him a massage with Vicks and gave him liquids. It wasn't very serious. I think the Vicks helped him a little to breathe. And it was a little effective. The next day I took Antonio to the clinic. I gave him the medicines they gave me and put him to bed to rest. Antonio misses school a lot. He can't play and doesn't eat. I also suffer from asthma. (Antonio is an 11-year-old Puerto Rican boy.)

• When I awoke, Julián was having an attack, but it was a mild one. I got ready to leave. As I was getting ready, I took Julián to the bathroom and turned on the hot water for him to breathe the steam. Then I took him to the emergency room. I took Julián to the emergency room, where they gave him an injection every half hour. This is the fastest medicine he can have. Then I brought Julián home and kept giving him the Slophyllin. (Julián is an 8-year-old Puerto Rican boy.)

Health care institutions provide important help for families coping with asthma. Most mothers do a number of things at home when an attack begins, such as giving the child asthma medications, using steam from the faucet, and rubbing the child's chest. However, as several of the cases illustrate, these interventions are not always effective in eliminating asthma symptoms. The attack may be a particularly severe one; the interventions may be tried too long after an attack has started; or they may be only partially effective with symptoms persisting. Then the family seeks help from a variety of resources: neighborhood health centers, emergency rooms (ERs), outpatient departments (OPDs), or private doctors.

Choice of Health Resource

The choice of health resource depends on a variety of factors. As part of their family health culture, families have ideas about the best resource to use for various types of asthma episodes. This information is organized as a "cognitive map" of health care institutions, which includes where facilities are located, assessments of the kinds of services available, names of preferred practitioners, and availability of special services, such as translation. Some families seek the resource that is most conveniently located. Others return to the facility where their child was born. Many of the families in this community are limited in their choice by who will accept a medical card or who has Spanish-speaking staff. Some families always return to the same resource each time. Others use a variety of health institutions depending on the family's evaluation of the severity of the attack, on the time of day when the attack occurs, and on the availability of a trusted provider.

Emergency Rooms (ERs). Families may use several health institutions for resolving an asthma crisis. The cases cited earlier indicate some of the reasons families use institutions other than their regular source of care: ERs give fast treatment and are always open; the family's regular provider is not available; their regular care source refers them to an institution with specialized treatment facilities; the family is visiting in another part of town when the attack happens and they go to the closest health resource. No matter what their preferred source of care, families do rely on the hospital both for ER care and for inpatient intensive services. Three quarters of the children made at least one ER visit in the year preceding the study.

Hospitalization. For very severe asthma episodes, children may need hospitalization. These may also occur if the provider feels that the child cannot be stabilized at home and requires an intensive period of monitoring. Families were asked how frequently their children had been hospitalized for asthma in the last five years. Over half the children had experienced at least one hospitalization for asthma within the last five years. Thus, hospital resources are critical for children with asthma, even when they establish contact with a primary care resource.

Asthma information. Families were asked about the kind of information they had received from their regular source of care about asthma, its treatment, and its prevention. Forty-five (48%) mothers responded that they had received no explanation of what asthma was or how it affected their children, 34 (36%) said that they had received an explanation, but could not recount what it was, and 14 (16%) had both received an explanation and could summarize it for the interviewer.

Mothers were also asked if their regular source of care had explained what to do when asthma symptoms appeared. Fifty-eight (62%) said that they had. The instructions mothers received included giving the child asthma medicines (25), helping the child relax (7), using steam or a vaporizer (3), and bringing the child in to the health facility (4).

Thirty-seven (39%) mothers indicated that their regular source of care had given some explanation of how to prevent asthma attacks. It is important to note that 57 (61%) families had received no information on how to prevent asthma attacks. Outpatient departments, in general, did the best job of explaining asthma prevention (42%), followed by ERs (38%), private doctors (33%), and health centers (31%). Specific preventive measures listed included: take asthma medicines (9), clean home frequently and control dust (6), make sure the child rests (4), and avoid pets (3).

Medication. Since medication is the most common help offered by the health institutions, it is important to analyze the medicines used and their effectiveness for asthma treatment. The most frequent first medicines listed were Slophyllin and the group consisting of Theodur, Quibron, and Accubron—bronchodilators in liquid or pill form. Thirty-eight children (43%) had Slophyllin at home and 13 (15%) had one of the Theodur group. Twenty-one families (24%) reported that they had no asthma medications at home. Twenty-five mothers listed a second asthma medication and 11 a third. The most common second medicines listed were the group including Brethine, Alupent, Metaprel and Bricanyl—the aerosol bronchodilators. Of those reporting on the effectiveness of medicines, 47 (69%) said that they were usually effective, 9 (13%) sometimes effective, and 12 (18%) not effective. Families who use the outpatient department or private doctors are better prepared with medications for dealing with an asthma attack at home.

The Role of School

Schools play an important role in childhood asthma. Many children experience asthma symptoms in school. Children may receive some regular or crisis treatment for asthma in school. Asthma affects a child's school attendance and performance. School-based education and treatment for asthma can aid children to better control and understand their illness. Twenty of the 73 school-age children (27%) received some kind of asthma treatment in school, usually help from the school nurse in a crisis. Forty-eight (65%) mothers had talked to the child's teacher about her/his asthma.

Strategies Reported

An important part of the interview was an illness narrative in which the mother recounted the story of the most recent asthma attack. The major strategies used by the families are reported in Table 6. In all, respondents mentioned 16 different strategies in the narrative. The large number of families who resorted to ERs reflected previous reports by mothers that they had had little success in dealing with asthma attacks at home.

Table 6

Strategies Reported in the Asthma Narrative
(N=94)

Strategy	N (%)
Intervening at home; then going to the ER	31 (34%)
Going straight to the ER	23 (26)
Using asthma medications at home	13 (14)
Intervening at home, then going to an Outpatient Department or Health Center	7 (8)
Using a home remedy	4 (4)
No response	16

One factor which strongly affected the choice of care was the severity of the child's asthma. Those families whose children's asthma was more severe tended to use the outpatient departments and private doctors more frequently. Economic factors were also important in the choice of care and limited families' options in choosing their regular care resource. Those families who derived their income from employment were more likely to use an outpatient department or private doctor than families dependent on public assistance. There was a similar relationship to owning a car. Cars appeared more important in access to outpatient departments than to private doctors. Many of the doctors' offices were located near the community, whereas most of the hospital-based resources required a major trip.

In examining reasons for choice of regular care resource, the most frequently mentioned reasons were convenience of location or having the child's records already there. Puerto Ricans who received referrals received them more often from friends or relatives. This finding emphasized the role of the social support network in Puerto Ricans' gaining information on and access to primary care resources. Language appeared as a potent barrier to receiving referrals from within the medical institutions. Language barriers also played a role in whether families received and could understand an explanation of their child's illness. Puerto Rican families much more frequently had not received an explanation of asthma: Thirty-three (56%) Puerto Rican mothers reported receiving no explanation. While interpreters can usually report to the physician what the mother says, it is more difficult for the translator to be a health educator without considerable training and without the commitment of providers to spend the extra time needed for education. Still another area where language was a key issue was in the frequency of asking questions of providers. Families reported that they rarely asked questions of providers. Family and friends were the main source of help when staff were not available. Clearly, the health centers and outpatient departments are the resources which have most effectively organized interpretation services for Spanish-speaking families.

Puerto Rican families frequently used the emergency room in describing the last attack reported in the Illness Narrative. For Puerto Ricans, the most severe attacks went to the ER; the next most severe went to primary care; and the least severe were dealt with at home. Puerto Rican families dealt with mild cases at home; children with severe asthma were brought to the ER for there they have injections, ". . . the fastest medicine he can have" (quote from the mother of Julián, a 15-year-old Puerto Rican boy). Puerto Rican mothers, when they perceived their child's asthma as being severe, also responded with considerable anxiety. Harwood supports this observation in assessing Puerto Ricans' response to lung health problems:

> Upper respiratory infections deserve particular attention in the Puerto Rican population in light of three facts: the higher mortality rates from respiratory disease among Puerto Rican-born children; evidence of a much higher incidence of rheumatic fever in Puerto Rican children than in either black or white children; and the considerable anxiety about respiratory infections observed among Puerto Rican patients in the Health Center Study. (Harwood, 1981, p. 414)

Upper respiratory infections were a major cause of asthma among Puerto Rican children in this community, and there is a relationship between early bouts of pneumonia and more severe asthma.

Families in this community utilize a variety of medical institutions to aid them in coping with asthma. While all families listed a regular source of care, this resource was not always the optimal one to use, from their perspective, for dealing with a particular attack. There were several reasons for this: their regular source of care was not open at the time of attack; the family felt that more extensive equipment was needed than available at their regular care source; or the family decided it was important to get to the closest, most accessible source of care.

Recommendations for Aiding Puerto Rican Children with Asthma

There are many issues raised by this study which have practical implications for families, communities, and health care institutions dealing with asthma:

1. *Improve provision of asthma medications.* There is a need to improve the provision of asthma medications so that families have the medications they need, have a reasonable system for refilling prescriptions, and know how to use their medications. Different health care institutions appear to have different knowledge of, and experience with, a variety of asthma medications. Providers who deal with childhood asthma could meet periodically to discuss medications for asthma management and the various combinations of medicines which appear most effective for different types of childhood asthma. Health education efforts need to be improved in teaching families how to use their medications. Schools could be integrally involved in both the education and treatment process.

2. *Emphasize value of non-medical interventions.* Health care and other providers should pay more attention to the value of non-medicine interventions in asthma and to families' own knowledge and ideas of how to cope with

asthma. Several of the cases and much of the data presented in this chapter show that the families who were best able to cope with asthma were those who combined asthma medications with home remedies and a variety of non-medical interventions. These included rubbing the child's chest, giving the child warm liquids (herbal teas are particularly good here), having the child do breathing/ relaxation exercises, having the child rest, and using a variety of steam treatments. The success of these interventions also depended on the family's ability to recognize the early symptoms of asthma and to intervene rapidly and with confidence. Many of these interventions are already part of Puerto Rican health culture; they need to be recognized and reinforced by health care providers. Others need to be taught by families.

3. *Design and implement effective health education programs.* The time has come for designing and implementing more effective programs of health education in the schools, in health care institutions, and in the community. One approach to increasing parents' confidence and skill in dealing with an asthma attack at home is exemplified by the Asthma Self-Management Project in New York City (Clark, 1980; Columbia University Department of Pediatrics, 1984). This project integrated research, health education, support of community efforts to improve housing conditions, and health professional training. Health education programs and materials were developed both in Spanish and English. The materials and methods developed by the Asthma Self-Management Project are now available from the National Institutes of Health, under the title "Open Airways/Respiro Abierto."

4. *Help families improve their home environment.* Practitioners interested in helping families cope with asthma should provide families with information and training on how to improve their home environment to lessen the exposure of the child to asthma triggers. One aspect of this recommendation is to develop education programs for parents about the kinds of triggers that exist in their homes and how to limit them within the context of their economic resources and environment. Achieving this goal often involves social action as well as home maintenance. The

Asthma Self-Management Project brought in tenant organizers to discuss ways that families can advocate to improve their housing conditions.

5. *Develop school-based asthma education programs.* There is a need to develop school-based programs in asthma education and in aiding children to practice asthma self-management. Asthma has a profound impact on school attendance and performance. Asthma also affects the social development of the school-age child who is stigmatized by asthma and often limited in his/her activities. Schools can play a major role in improving the child's understanding of his/her illness and in aiding other children to be supportive of the child. School nurses and health staff can play an important role in aiding the child to learn effective self-management skills. Schools, through their contact with children, can also be effective settings for developing family education programs about asthma and other health problems.

Summary

Asthma is a serious health problem for Puerto Rican children and has a significant impact on their school performance and social development. This chapter summarizes the findings of a community study of how Puerto Rican families coped with childhood asthma. The chapter begins with an overview of national and community level data which describe the epidemiology of asthma among Puerto Rican and other Latino groups in comparison to African-Americans and Anglo-Americans. A profile is then given of the experiences of Puerto Rican children with asthma. The understandings that Puerto Ricans have of asthma are discussed, as well as the language they use to discuss it, with particular attention to the concept of *fatiga*. Families use a variety of home-based remedies and institutional health care resources to help them manage their children's asthma. The strategies families have developed are analyzed. Recommendations for improving the situation of Puerto Rican children with asthma are specified. These include better provision of asthma medications to families; more attention to families' own knowledge about and remedies for managing asthma episodes; and the development of more effective health education programs in schools, health care institutions, and the community.

REFERENCES

Angel, R.J., and Worobey, J.L. (in press). Intra-group differences in the health of Hispanic children. *Social Science Quarterly.*

Angel, R.J., Worobey, J.L., and Davies, L. (1990). *Mental health and medical care use of children in two-parent and female-headed households.* Paper presented at the meeting of the American Public Health Association, New York, NY.

Carter, O., Gergen, P., and Lecca, P. (1987). *Reported asthma among Puerto Rican, Mexican-American, and Cuban-American children: HHANES, 1982–1984.* Paper presented at the meeting of the American Public Health Association, New Orleans, LA, October.

Clark, N.M., Feldman, C.H., Freudenberg, N., Millman, E.J., Wasilewski, Y., and Valle, I. (1980). Developing education for children with asthma through study of self-management behavior. *Health Education Quarterly, 7,* 278–297.

Columbia University Department of Pediatrics (1984). *Open airways/Respiro abierto.* (NIH Publication No. HRA 84-2365.) Washington, DC: National Heart, Lung, and Blood Institute.

Department of Health and Human Services (1979). *Health status of minorities and low-income groups.* (DHEW Publication No. HRA 79-627.) Washington, DC: Government Printing Office.

Dutton, D. (1978). Explaining the low use of health services by the poor: Costs, attitudes or delivery systems? *American Sociological Review, 43,* 348–368.

Freudenberg, N. (1979). The self-management of childhood bronchial asthma: Implications for health education and child health services. Unpublished doctoral dissertation. Columbia University School of Public Health, New York.

Freudenberg, N., Clark, N.M., Feldman, C.H., Millman, J., Valle, I., and Wasilewski, Y. (1979). The self-management of childhood bronchial asthma: Implications for health education and child services. Paper presented at the meeting of the American Public Health Association, New York, NY.

Freudenberg, N., Feldman, C.H., Clark, N.M., Millman, E.J., Valle, I., and Wasilewski, Y. (1980). The impact of bronchial asthma on school attendance and performance. *The Journal of School Health*, November, 522–526.

Guarnaccia, P.J. (1981). Puerto Ricans, asthma and the health care system. *Medical Anthropology Newsletter*, *12*(2), 9–7.

Guarnaccia, P.J. (1988). Asthma death, too, stalks the poor (Letter to the editor). *The New York Times*, April.

Guarnaccia, P.J., Pelto, P.J., and Schensul, S.L. (1985). Family health culture, ethnicity, and asthma: Coping with illness. *Medical Anthropology*, *9*, 203–224.

Harwood, A. (1981). Mainland Puerto Ricans. In A. Harwood (Ed.), *Ethnicity and medical care* (pp. 397–481). Cambridge, MA: Harvard University Press.

Hogle, J., Pelto, P.J., and Schensul, S. (1982). Ethnicity and health: Puerto Ricans and African-Americans in Hartford. *Medical Anthropology*, *6*, 127–146.

Howland, J., Bauchner, H., and Adair, R. (1988). The impact of pediatric asthma education on morbidity: Assessing the evidence. *Chest*, *94*, 964–969.

Kang, B. (1976). Study on cockroach antigen as a probable causative agent in bronchial asthma. *Journal of Allergy and Clinical Immunology*, *58*, 357–365.

Kang, B., and Sulit, N. (1978). A comparative study of the prevalence of skin hypersensitivity to cockroach and house dust antigens. *Annals of Allergy*, *41*, 333–336.

Karetzky, M.S. (1977). Asthma in the South Bronx: Clinical and epidemologic characteristics. *Journal of Allergy and Clinical Immunology*, *60*, 383–390.

Kleinman, A. (1980). *Patients and healers in the context of culture.* Berkeley: University of California Press.

Lelah, T., Harris, L.J., Avery, C.H., and Brook, R.H. (1976). Asthma in children and adults: Assessing the quality of care using short-term outcome measures. In A.D. Avery, T. Lelah, N.E. Solomon, L.J. Harris, R.H. Brook, S. Greenfield, J.E. Ware, Jr., and C.H. Avery (Eds.), *Quality of medical care using outcome measures: eight disease-specific applications* (pp. 7-95). Santa Monica, CA: The Rand Corporation.

Medical Research Council's Committee on Research into Chronic
    Bronchitis (1976). *Questionnaire on Respiratory Symptoms.*
    London: Medical Research Council.
Ríos, L.E. (1982). Determinants of asthma among Puerto Ricans.
    Journal of Latin Community Health, 1(1), 25–40.
Schensul, S.L., and Borrero, M.G. (Eds.) (1982). Special Issue:
    Action research and health systems change in an inner-
    city Puerto Rican community. *Urban Anthropology, 11*(1).
Sifontes, J.F., and Mayol, P.M. (1976). Bronchial asthma in Puerto
    Rican children. *Boletín de la Asociación Médica de Puerto
    Rico, 68,* 336–339.

PART V

Family Stresses and Support Systems

CHAPTER 11

Migration, Health, and Social Stress Among Puerto Rican Adolescents

Susan Meswick

Introduction

This chapter examines issues of health and migration among Puerto Rican adolescents in Hartford, Connecticut. A public school was the location of an innovative, community-initiated, school-based health screening and treatment program described in more detail in Meswick (1982). The school setting proved to be an excellent site for research into the migration process and its relation to physical health, mental health, education, and social factors.

Most social science and behavioral research on migration focuses on the consequences of migration, that is, what happens to migrants when and after they arrive at a new place (usually the city). Migrants face an array of problems in adjusting to their new environment. Accordingly, researchers have paid particular attention to individual and group successes and failures in adapting or adjusting to new, often multicultural settings. They have also examined the range of social mechanisms affecting such adaptations, the various adaptive strategies and measures developed or employed by migrants. In examining migrant adjustment, most investigators have focused on processes and have generally neglected the stages (i.e., length of time) of adaptation to new environs. Stages of adjustment and adaptation to a new environment are related to the time spent in a new area. Generally speaking, the newest migrants—those at an early migration stage (i.e., less than a year in a new environment)—may be less familiar with the community and its resources than those who have lived in the area for a longer period.

Whatever the mechanisms of adaptation to new environments, time and community responsiveness are important variables in the adjustment to a new area. According to Butterworth & Chance (1981) the length of residence in the city is probably the least understood of all factors, since few studies have tested adequately for the time factor. Even more glaring to these investigators is the total lack of information on generational differences and on how children of migrants organize their social environment.

The past three decades have witnessed an increase in the type and sophistication of studies assessing the adaptation of migrants to their new environs. One particularly promising area is the examination of the effects which migration may have on health. Within the general area of health most researchers have emphasized mental health problems as indicators of adaptational stress (Canino, Earley, & Rogler, 1980; Cohen, 1979; Dressler & Bernal, 1982; Graves & Graves, 1979; Hull, 1979; Johnson, 1986; Kasl & Berkman, 1983; Maltzberg & Lee, 1956; MacKinlay, 1975; Scotch 1963). Few studies have examined the effects of migration on "total" health status as measured by clinical assessment—as opposed to self-assessment—and its relationship to sociocultural variables.

Another important dimension is that studies of the relationships between health, social change, and migration have paid little or no attention to children and adolescents. Investigators often lament this state of affairs. To illustrate, in their review of several major epidemological studies, Michelson, Levine, and Spina (1979) reported that even Leighton's Sterling County Study (1963) devoted little time to children. Likewise, they noted that the important Hollingshead and Redlich (1958) study of the relationship between social class and mental illness in an urban community made no mention of children (p. 10).

This gap in the literature is noteworthy. Slavin (1971) points out that "since migration tends to involve the young disproportionately, the deleterious effect of migration during childhood and adolescence on an individual's subsequent mental health suggests that concentration should be on the problems of children and youth in mobility prone areas" (p. 195). Young people are an important group on which to focus, not only because they may represent a sizeable percentage of the total number of migrants but because they are a particularly vulnerable group in that they are dependent upon those who decided to migrate. They often bear the brunt of the adjustment to new environs without input into decision making. They are thus "epiphenomenol" migrants, those with no choice whether to move. Furthermore, children and adolescents are susceptible to somatic and psychological illnesses related to stresses such as that of migration (Johnson, 1986).

This study of Puerto Rican migrant adolescents attempts to fill some of the gaps in previous research by focusing on: (a) a neglected age group; (b) recency of arrival as a major independent variable; and (c) use of physical and mental health assessment data.

Hartford's Puerto Rican Community

Hispanics in Hartford have shown the most dramatic increase of any minority population during the last twenty years. Census figures from 1960 to 1970 (cited in Backstrand & Schensul, 1982), reveal an increase of 6,236 Puerto Ricans, with the number jumping to 26,677 in 1980. Estimating the Hispanic undercount as anywhere from 15 to 40 percent, community agencies placed the Hispanic population at about 40,000 in 1985. Of these, an estimated 90% are Puerto Rican (J. Schensul, personal communication). Consequently there was a rapid increase in the percentage of Puerto Rican students attending Hartford Public Schools. As reflected in Figure 1, in 1967 the ethnic distribution in the public schools was 45% black,

45% white, and 11% Hispanic. By 1980 the percentage of whites had dropped to 16%, the percentage of blacks remained stable, but Hispanics had grown to 37% of the public school enrollment.

ETHNIC DISTRIBUTION IN HARTFORD PUBLIC SCHOOLS 1967–1981

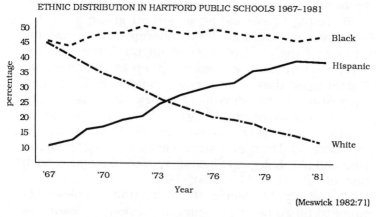

(Meswick 1982:71)

Figure 1

Thus, while the total population of Hartford declined 14% between 1970 and 1980, the proportion of African-Americans and Hispanics increased from 35 to 54% (Health Systems Agency, 1981). Again, due to census undercounts of minority persons this proportion is probably larger.

Although early immigrants to the city were able to find employment niches in spite of their lack of specialized skills, later migrants found a highly competitive job market. Specialized skills and a high school education are often minimal requirements for entry level positions. As a result, unemployment is extremely high for minority persons in Hartford.

One factor which differentiates Hartford from other cities with large Puerto Rican communities is that about 74% of Puerto Ricans in Hartford were born on the island, rather than being second generation Puerto Ricans (Backstrand & Schensul, 1982). Thus Hartford's Puerto Rican community is very different from the more established Puerto Rican communities in New York City, Philadelphia, or New Jersey's urban centers; Hartford does not have a long term multigenerational community of Puerto Ricans. In situations such as these, the task of adapting to a new social and cultural environment is intensified, since there is often a lack of institutional, social, cultural, and familial resources. These resources are usually found in larger cities such as New York. Individuals in small cities like Hartford which lack multigenerational Puerto Rican communities can be expected to experience increased stress related to acculturation (Dressler & Bernal, 1982). The number of problems faced by Puerto Ricans in Hartford is exacerbated by the recency of the migration movement, by the lack of institutional responsiveness to the needs of this ethnic group, and by discrimination.

Method

Purpose of the Study

The study sought to examine health, socioeconomic, and migration data on Puerto Rican adolescents in the context of the school environment. Specifically, it explored the interrelations between and among several sets of social, cultural, health, and migration variables. The questions examined were:

1. What kinds of health—including psychosocial adjustment—problems are found among newly arrived Puerto Rican adolescents?
2. What background factors, e.g., recency of arrival, household structure, mobility within Hartford, are predictive of differences in health status?
3. What groups are under the most stress? What groups exhibit the most health problems, and what types of health problems?
4. What are the patterns of change in physical and psychosocial health as a function of time in Hartford?

Setting and Participants

Hartford's Hale Middle School (a pseudonym) represented an ideal site for applied research on migrant Puerto Rican adolescents. It housed 95% of the city's middle school Hispanic youth, and, due to the ESL and other programs that were being created, it centralized the great majority of Puerto Rican adolescents. In conjunction with local and community action agencies, the author developed a health screening, diagnosis, and treatment program with special Medicaid funding and implemented it at Hale Middle School.

A total of 285 comprehensive physical assessments were performed on students in the bilingual and new arrivals programs at the Hale School Health Program. For various reasons—incomplete records, oversights—only 255 (89%) of the 285 exams were included in the sample. Thus, this study examines data on 255 Puerto Rican adolescents (138 females, 117 males) ranging in age from 11 to 16 years, with a modal age of 13 years, for whom complete data were available.

Procedures and Research Techniques

Data were collected during a period of over two years within the context of a school-based health clinic, which the author was instrumental in establishing. The research strategy included participant observation, interviews (both structured and open ended), and the use of quantitative and qualitative data from school and medical records. Within an ethnographic context, quantitative data regarding health, SES, and migration serve to test specific hypotheses, while qualitative data provide a basic understanding of the social and interpersonal systems and establish the basis for interpreting the numerical data.

Medical records offered a wealth of information. They encompassed thorough medical and family health histories; results of physical exams and of various lab tests; and a detailed household/family/social and migration history elicited from both parents and students. Other qualitative (i.e., descriptive) data were obtained through open-ended and structured interviewing of students, parents, teachers, administrators, counselors, and health care providers; and through participation in various activities in the school setting. Data on mental health status were obtained through psychosocial adjustment ratings by a nurse practitioner with a specialty in adolescent psychology and by a review of school records; this enabled the ranking of students on a scale ranging from 1 (well adjusted) to 3 (severe problems). In addition, school records provided academic data such as results of standardized tests, attendance, and program placement.

Thus, through various data gathering procedures, a series of health, mental health, education, and sociocultural/migration indicators were identified, whose interrelations could be analyzed.

Defining the Stages of Migration

The obtained data enabled identification of the different stages of migration in which students found themselves. Although anthropologists have closely examined adaptive strategies used by migrants to adjust to their new environments, according to Butterworth and Chance (1981), relatively few have closely examined stages of migration. As seen on Table 1, Puerto Rican born students were broken into three groups: (a) New-Arrivals, those in Hartford for one year or less; (b) Recent Migrants, those in Hartford for more than one year, but less than three years; and (c) Resident Migrants, those in Hartford for three years or more.

Table 1

Groups of Puerto Rican Adolescents

Group	Migrant Type	Birthplace	Time in Hartford	N	%
I	New Arrivals	Puerto Rico	1 year or less	87	34.1%
II	Recent Migrant	Puerto Rico	1.1–2.9 yrs.	54	21.2%
III	Resident Migrant	Puerto Rico	> 3 yrs.	63	24.7%
IV	Mainland Migrant	Mainland	a	24	9.4%
V	Non-Migrant	Hartford	Lifetime	27	10.6%

a 21 of the 24 mainland migrants had been in Hartford for 1 year or less.

Mainlanders (i.e., born on the mainland) were split into two groups—those born in Hartford (Non-Migrants) and those born elsewhere on the mainland (Mainland Migrants).

Thus, for the purposes of analysis, the sample of Puerto Rican adolescents was segmented into five subgroups, based on birthplace and length of time in Hartford. These five groups display different characteristics along a range of social and health parameters.

Findings

Migration and Socioeconomic Factors

As length of time in Hartford increases, there is a distinct trend away from "mother-only" households and a movement towards dual-parent households (Table 2). Eighty-five percent of New Arrivals, 72% of Recent Arrivals, 71% of Resident Migrants, 58% of Mainland Migrants, and 56% of Non-Migrants live in single parent households. Thus as migration status moves from New Arrival to Non-Migrant, the likelihood of living with two parents increases dramatically.

Table 2

Migrant Type by Number of Parents in Family[a]

	Single Parent	Dual Parent	N
New Arrival	74	13	87
	85.1%	14.9%	
Recent Migrant	39	15	54
	72.2%	27.8%	
Resident Migrant	45	18	63
	71.4%	28.6%	
Mainland Migrant	14	10	24
	58.3%	41.7%	
Non-Migrant	15	12	27
	55.6%	44.4%	
	187	68	255

Chi square = 13.39; df=4; p=0.009
a Persons in the role of parent, not necessarily biological parents.

Non-Migrants had the most living space, with 48.1% (13) having at least one room for each person in the household. In contrast, less than 20% (17) of the New Arrivals and slightly over 205 (11%) of the Recent Migrants afforded such "affluence" (Table 3).

Table 3

Household Density by Migrant Status
Rooms per Household Member

	< 0.6	0.6–0.9	≥ 1.0	N
New Arrival	26	44	17	87
	29.9%	50.6%	19.5%	
Recent Migrant	15	28	11	54
	27.8%	51.9%	20.4%	
Resident Migrant	11	25	27	63
	17.5%	39.7%	42.9%	

	< 0.6	0.6–0.9	≥ 1.0	N
Mainland Migrant	3	12	9	24
	12.5%	50.0%	37.5%	
Non-Migrant	2	12	13	27
	7.4%	44.4%	48.1%	
	57	121	77	255
		100%		

Chi square = 19.28; df = 8; p = 0.013

As Table 4 shows, as migrant status increases (i.e., from new arrival to non-migrant), there is a marked tendency towards a self pay status, (that is, not eligible for Medicaid), which suggests a somewhat better economic situation for Resident Migrants and for Non-Migrants. One-third of Non-Migrants, 25% of Mainland Migrants, 21% of Resident Migrants, 8% of Recent Migrants, and 4% of New Arrivals are not eligible for Medicaid assistance. Students from Non-Migrant families tend to be the most "well off," at least in terms of economic self-sufficiency. Moreover, it must be noted that only one-third of Non-Migrants and 14% of the entire sample are not eligible for Medicaid. This illustrates the depressed economic profile of Hartford's Puerto Rican community.

Table 4

Medicaid Eligibility by Migrant Status

	Eligible	Not Eligible	N
New Arrival	81	3	84
	96.4%	3.6%	
Recent Migrant	48	4	52
	92.3%	7.7%	
Resident Migrant	50	13	63
	79.4%	20.6%	
Mainland Migrant	18	6	24
	75.0%	25.0%	

	Eligible	Not Eligible	N
Non-Migrant	18	9	27
	66.7%	33.3%	
	215	35	250[a]
		100%	

Chi square = 23.46; df = 4; p = 0.000
[a]Information on Medicaid eligibility unavailable for five students.

Migration and Health

Sources of health care. One of the factors which most dramatically differentiates migrant stages in this study is the source of health care people use. Although about one quarter of the entire sample has no provider of health care, there are consistent variations among the groups. (Table 5 illustrates this point.) Where, for example, only two Non-Migrants stated that they have no provider of health care or use the emergency room for their regular health care, 45.8% of Mainland Migrants and 40.2% of New Arrivals reported no primary health care provider. Some 18.5% of Recent Migrants and 11.1% of Resident Migrants have no source of health care.

Table 5

Sources of Health Care and Migration Status

	None	Hartford Hospital	Other Clinics	N
New Arrival	35	32	20	87
	40.2%	36.8%	23.0%	
Recent Migrant	10	15	29	54
	18.5%	27.8%	53.7%	
Resident Migrant	7	15	41	63
	11.1%	23.8%	65.1%	
Mainland Migrant	11	4	9	24
	45.8%	16.7%	37.5%	
Non-Migrant	2	2	23	27
	7.4%	7.4%	85.2%	
	65	68	122	255

Chi square = 53.06; df = 8; p = 0.00.

　　Similarly, there are variations among the sources of care listed as "primary site of care." Seven sources of health care are noted. A tertiary care center, located in a heavily Puerto Rican neighborhood, is the largest provider of health care to participants, serving 28% (68) of the students. This reliance, however, changes with migrant status. This hospital serves 37.2% of the New Arrivals, 31.3% of Recent Migrants, 24.6% of Resident Migrants, 16.7% of Mainland Migrants, in contrast to 8.3% of Non-Migrants. Thus, for students born in Puerto Rico, there is a strong tendency by the population to use this source heavily in the early year(s) in Hartford and to find other providers as they become more familiar with the city. Non-Migrants overwhelmingly tend to use either the neighborhood health center (38%) or an outpatient clinic run by a Catholic hospital (42%).

　　Physical health problems. Newly arrived students have more physical health problems, including the specific categories of dental, hearing, and skin problems, and parasites. As expected, parasitic problems decrease dramatically as length of time in Hartford increases (Table 6). Many parasitic infections are relatively short lived and can be expected to clear up after the individual has left an endemic area. The only Non-Migrant with a parasitic infection had Giardia lambia, which is also endemic in parts of the U.S. mainland. It is quite possible, however, that some of the parasitic infections were picked up on visits to Puerto Rico, where Giardia is endemic.

Table 6

Number of Parasite Cases by Migrant Status

	None	One or More	N
New Arrival	45 66.2%	23 33.8%	68
Recent Migrant	25 65.8%	13 34.2%	38
Resident Migrant	38 79.2%	10 20.8%	48

	None	One or More	N
Mainland Migrant	14	6	20
	70.0%	30.0%	
Non-Migrant	21	1	22
	95.5%	4.5%	
	143	41	196

Chi Square = 9.24; df = 4; p = .055.

For purposes of statistical analysis, health information
was dichotomized. A child with none or one medical problem
was considered relatively healthy and clustered in one
category; those with two or more medical problems were
put in a second category. As shown in Table 7, as length
of time in Hartford increases the number of relatively
healthy students also increases. This result was expected,
considering the above discussion on health-seeking
behavior. Hence, those with regular health care providers
have fewer medical problems. It must be noted that 21
of the 24 Mainland Migrants are new to Hartford and have
been in the city for less than one year. Their "newness"
and lack of health care providers is reflected in their high
level (70.8%) of two or more medical problems.

Table 7

Number of Medical Problems by Migrant Status

	None or One	Two or More	N
New Arrival	30	57	87
	34.5%	62.5%	
Recent Migrant	27	27	54
	50.0%	50.0%	
Resident Migrant	28	35	63
	44.4%	55.6%	
Mainland Migrant	7	17	24
	29.2%	70.8%	
Non-Migrant	19	8	27
	70.4%	29.6%	
	111	144	255

Chi square = 13.76; df = 4; p = 0.008.

Migration and Mental Health

School records combined with nurse practitioner ratings were used to assess mental health status. A simple additive scale was developed using (a) the psychosocial adjustment rating done by a nurse practitioner with a specialty in adolescent psychology; (b) the number of social and behavioral problems listed by the school; and (c) the presence of a school request for a psychological evaluation of the child. Data for the latter two categories were collected for each child for a one-year period, thus controlling for the greater length of time which non-migrants had in the school system testing. The resultant psychosocial adjustment scale had an alpha of 0.82168, which means this is a reliable scale based on the internal consistency of the items.

As seen in Table 8, the psychosocial adjustment scale frequencies were recoded in three categories, thus enabling contingency table analysis. The group with the lowest percentage of psychosocial problems was Mainland Migrants (62.5% with "no problems"), followed by New Arrivals, with 57.5% on the lowest end of the scale, and 48.1% of Recent Migrants. By contrast, only 27% of Resident Migrants and 22.2% of Non-Migrants were "relatively free" from psychosocial adjustment problems.

Table 8

Psychosocial Adjustment Scale

	Well Adjusted	Some Problems	Severe Problems	N
New Arrival	50	19	18	87
	57.5%	21.8%	20.7%	
Recent Migrant	26	20	8	54
	48.1%	37.0%	14.8%	
Resident Migrant	17	14	32	63
	27.0%	22.2%	50.8%	

	Well Adjusted	Some Problems	Severe Problems	N
Mainland Migrant	15	1	8	24
	62.5%	4.2%	33.3%	
Non-Migrant	6	2	19	27
	22.2%	7.4%	70.4%	
	114	56	85	255

Chi square = 50.75; df = 8; p = 0.000.

Discussion

The Dilemma: Adjustment vs. Well-Being?

As the preceding analysis indicates, second generation Puerto Ricans (i.e., Non-Migrants) are "better off," that is, they live in more adequate, less crowded, dual-parent households. They are less likely than other groups to be eligible for Medicaid and thus a higher SES is inferred. Non-Migrants are more likely to use neighborhood health centers and have fewer physical health problems. However, Non-Migrants have a *higher* incidence of psychosocial health problems.

In contrast, New Arrivals have fewer resources, with most living in crowded, single-parent households, well under the poverty level, with over 90% eligible for Medicaid. Forty percent have no provider of health care, and 65% have two or more medical problems per person, especially parasitic infections. Yet over 57% were considered to be well adjusted.

Recent Migrants tend to have fewer physical health problems than New Arrivals, but 13 (34%) had parasites and 10 (18.5%) lacked a health care provider. They are more likely to live in better housing, with two parents, and with slightly fewer on Medicaid. Nevertheless, their low SES reflects a depressed economic profile. Recent Migrants are more likely than New Arrivals to have psychosocial adjustment problems.

Reflected in the profiles of Resident Migrants is their adjustment to the city in terms of their use of health care facilities, better physical health status, more adequate housing, and more dual parent households. However, only 27% were well adjusted as measured by psychosocial scaling techniques.

Mainland Migrants are distinct from other groups: Although "acculturated" to mainland ways, they are new to the city of Hartford. Mainland Migrants tend to live with two parents and to have a more favorable SES than island-born migrants. Eleven (46%) have no provider of health care, and 17 (71%) have two or more medical problems. Over 62% (15), the highest percentage of any of the five groups, were rated as well adjusted.

Implicit in this study of migrant and non-migrant Puerto Rican adolescents are questions and implications for understanding the processes of social change and acculturation. Migrants are social beings constantly coping with a complex array of environmental, biological, cultural, and social pressures. The hypotheses which guided this research were set within the paradigm of understanding such coping patterns among migrant adolescents. The literature generally portrays a standard pattern of linear adaptation to new environments, with short-term migrants having the most adjustment problems and a steady decrease in problems as time in the new environment increases.

The author had expected youngsters in the New Arrivals groups to experience more health and mental health problems, and to have fewer resources (single parent households, lower SES) to assist in coping with their new environs. Indeed, newly arrived Puerto Rican adolescents did have more dental and medical problems (especially parasitic infections) than other participants. They also tended to live in crowded, single parent, poverty stricken households, had no regular medical care provider, and performed below grade level in school. However, contrary to the author's expectations, New Arrivals were well adjusted, and few experienced psychosocial problems as detected by either the health assessment or the school. These findings corroborate those reported by Cloud (1990) in her study of 35 low SES Puerto Rican youth attending an inner-city intermediate school. Utilizing the Acculturation Questionnaire for Children as well as other measures, Cloud found that the most acculturated group appeared to be the least well-adjusted in the home setting. In addition, the most acculturated group held the most negative views of school and placed least importance on it.

As hypothesized, as length of time in Hartford increases there is a significant positive relationship towards "better" living conditions—including better housing, lower household density, dual parent households, and better economic status. Thus, major social indicators illustrate a definite trend towards a more comfortable lifestyle for long-term migrants and second-generation Puerto Ricans alike. Similarly, there is a definite improvement in physical health the longer the migrant is in Hartford. Non-migrants (second generation) are "healthier" on the average than migrants. Yet, contrary to expectations, the mental health status of long-term Hartford residents is significantly worse than that of more recently arrived migrants. As length of time in Hartford increases, mental health appears to deteriorate, in spite of better social indicators and better physical health status. Unexpectedly, these students have more psychosocial adjustment problems than newly arrived migrants. Similar results were found by Dressler and Bernal (1982) in studying stress among Hartford Puerto Ricans referred to the Visiting Nurse Association. "These persons who have been in the Anglo environment the longest, but who do not have the resources for coping with that environment, have the worse stress outcomes" (p. 10). More recently, reporting on the health status of Latinos in California, Winkler (1990, p. 78) stated, "Indeed, the longer they stay in the United States, the worse off they become."

Exploring and Understanding the Migration Dilemma

Adolescence is a difficult developmental stage for all teens and more so for minority group adolescents. Sociocultural factors—especially status inconsistency—could increase the strain on the individual, causing increased psychosocial problems. Longer term migrants may have more stress because they are more likely to be cognizant of their inferior minority status and lack of opportunities for socioeconomic mobility. Derbyshire (1968, 1970), who studied the adaptation of 89 Mexican-American adolescents to east Los Angeles, found an increase in "role strain" (psychological dysfunction) among U.S. born teens whose parents had been born in Mexico. He demonstrated that this strain was due to the lack of internalizing the parents' dominant Mexican values by the teens.

Adolescent members of minorities not only straddle worlds of childhood and adulthood, but simultaneously must cope with the identity difficulties extended through the knowledge that one's culture is devalued and ignored in the culture in which one finds it necessary to live, play, work, and love. Adolescent crisis under these circumstances is most traumatic. This is significant when the American value system pays lip service to, but belittles, the values, religion, and cohesive family of the Mexican minority's native land (Derbyshire, 1968, pp. 98–99).

In my study of Puerto Rican teens in the Hale School, I observed differences in physical appearance, dress, makeup, jewelry, and "street" orientation among the students. Sometimes recent arrivals from the island could be identified just by their shyness and overall demeanor. On the other hand, non-migrants and long-term Hartford residents were very "tuned into" mainstream American dress, disco music, and street life. Several of the individual cases of severe psychosocial dysfunction were teens who were very much oriented to life in Hartford's inner city mainstream. These teens were experimenting with sex (i.e., asking for birth control, requesting pregnancy tests), drugs, and gangs. Personal observations of extreme cases of generational conflict suggest that students who have lived in Hartford for a longer period of time are more likely to reject their families as primary sources of support in problem situations. Obviously, all teens have difficulties with their parents, but when the adolescents have not internalized their parents' Puerto Rican social and cultural values (respeto a la familia, "modesty" for females, etc.), they are bound to have more difficulties at home with their Puerto Rican born parents.

In his classic work *Childhood and Society*, Erickson (1950) suggests that the mastery of future life experiences for adolescents is dependent upon the success with which they can master their own culture prior to mastering a "new" culture. It seems that long-term and non-migrant students, who are being socialized by their peers and the school into the mainstream, are having problems adjusting as a minority to both the Anglo and the Puerto Rican worlds. They are in some ways "betwixt and between" two worlds; they are less Puerto Rican than newer migrants, yet not Anglos. Long term migrants and non-migrants have adapted to the health care system which is oriented to the medical model (i.e., curing and treating physical problems). However, neither the medical care system nor many long term Puerto Rican residents in Hartford have found effective means of coping with psychological problems.

We need to re-evaluate factors which have traditionally been used as indicators of successful adaptation. The implications of these findings concerning the trajectory of migrant adaptation are that adjustment to new environs does not necessarily occur in a strictly linear fashion, but that the adaptational model is more complex. Longer term migrants may have more economic resources and fewer physical health problems, but they are in an environment in which their minority status "caps" their social and economic mobility. New migrants may face a daily struggle to survive and attain life's basic necessities, but they cling to hopes and dreams of something better. However, after years of discrimination and discouragements, migrants realize they are "trapped" at the bottom of a stagnant economic system which does little for the social or economic advancement of minorities. Thus, the questions raised are "What is adaptation?" and "By what standards (physical comfort or mental peace) do we measure it?"

Recommendations to Educators, Social Scientists, and Health Providers

Parents, teachers, educational administrators, and health care professionals often characterize health care services and public school education as two distinct and separate systems. Yet experience has shown that a comprehensive school based health system can assist in the identification and treatment of health problems which impede learning, as well as improve the overall health status of the child.

Health services in the schools have been shown to contribute to the schools' educational goals by: (a) identifying problems which interfere directly with learning; (b) treating difficulties early, enabling learning to proceed at an optimal rate; and (c) preventing illness, thus reducing absenteeism and facilitating learning. Raising the awareness of parents, educators, and health care providers to the above factors is a crucial step in enlisting their support for school health programs. Health problems have been found to have an effect on academic achievement. In some cases specific health problems such as ear infections have been shown to have a direct negative effect on school achievement.

Beyond the desire to maximize students' capacity to learn, schools also have a strong financial incentive to keep students healthy and in school, since federal and state revenues are generally tied to daily attendance figures. Effective school health programs can reduce the number of absences, therefore improving average daily attendance statistics.

The research described in this chapter goes beyond traditional and academic concerns regarding the relationship between migrant adaptation and social, physical, and mental health. Much of the data upon which this analysis was based was collected in a *service* program, designed and implemented with major assistance from anthropologists, community activists, health care providers, and educators to meet identified needs of the population under study. Due to that effort, the students and, in some cases, their families were able to receive culturally appropriate health care, delivered in a caring fashion. In playing a major role in establishing this health care service program, not only were the author's research needs satisfied, but some of the health needs of the Puerto Rican community were also addressed.

In the process of conducting this research, the author observed radical changes in the lives of some participants. Several students who were inattentive in the classroom, to the degree that teachers asked that they be first on the list for health examinations, were prescribed eyeglasses, a hearing aid, and treated for anemia. Their attention and performance in the classroom improved dramatically (in one instance from D's to A's in one academic year!) Several families had children at home who were mentally retarded and had never been to school. Discussions with the Hale School Health Team made these families aware for the first time that there were educational and other services available for these children.

In discussing community health issues for migrant populations, Slavin (1971) has stated:

> Since the schools . . . are perhaps the most universal of community institutions, linking them to hospitals, medical schools and health centers may provide the quickest material for community diagnosis. . . . Since mobile populations are so heavily constituted by young families, school health agency cooperation, coordination and planning are of primary importance. (p. 199).

In the author's experience this has indeed proven to be true. The synergies obtained by coupling valid academic pursuit (in this case the development of new knowledge about migration, health, and education) and an applied setting clearly can benefit both science and humanity.

Summary

This chapter examined issues of health, education, and migration among Puerto Rican adolescents who attend a middle school in Hartford, Connecticut. This school was the location of an innovative, community-initiated, school-based health screening and treatment program, in which the author played a role in development and implementation. The school setting proved to be an excellent site for research into the migration process and its relation to physical and mental health, education and social variables.

A sample of 255 students was selected from the teens screened by the health program. In addition to the health and mental health status data available, information on recency of arrival, birthplace, household structure, mother's education, homelife, and other migration variables were obtained through interviews with parents and students. School records provided data on attendance, standardized test achievement, program placement, number of moves within the city of Hartford, and social and behavioral problems in school.

Results indicate that new arrivals from the island of Puerto Rico tend to have a depressed socioeconomic profile and a high incidence of physical health problems (especially parasitic disease), lack health care providers, but appear to be well-adjusted and have few psychosocial problems. Conversely, migrants who are longer term residents on the mainland have fewer physical health problems, but a greater number have psychosocial adjustment problems.

REFERENCES

Backstrand, J., & Schensul, S. (1982). Co-evolution in an outlying ethnic community: The Puerto Rican community of Hartford, Connecticut. *Urban Anthropology, 11*(1), 9–37.

Butterworth, D., & Chance, J. (1981). *Latin American urbanization.* New York: Cambridge University Press.

Canino, I., Earley, B., & Rogler, L. (1980). *The Puerto Rican child in New York City: Stress and mental health.* New York: Hispanic Research Center, Fordham University.

Cloud, N. (1990). Measuring level of acculturation in bilingual bicultural children. Paper presented at the annual meeting of the American Educational Research Association, Boston, MA.

Cohen, L. (1979). *Culture, disease and stress among Latino immigrants.* Research Institute on Immigration and Ethnic Studies. Washington: Smithsonian Institute.

Derbyshire, R. (1968). Adolescent identity crisis in urban Mexican-Americans in East Los Angeles. In E. Brody (Ed.), *Minority group adolescents in the United States.* Baltimore: Williams & Williams.

Dressler, W., & Bernal, H. (1982). Acculturation and stress in a low income Puerto Rican community. *Journal of Human Stress, 8*(4), 32–38.

Erickson, E. (1950). *Childhood and society.* New York: Norton.

Graves, N., & Graves, T. (1979). Stress and health: Modernization in a traditional Polynesian society. *Medical Anthropology, 2*(2), 23–59.

Health Systems Agency (1981). Review and analysis of medically underserved areas (MUA) in Hartford. Hartford: Health Systems Agency.

Hollingshead, A.B., & Redlich, F.C. (1958). *Social class and mental illness.* New York: Wiley.

Hull, D. (1979). Migration, adaptation, and illness: A review. *Social Science and Medicine, 13*a, 25–36.

Johnson, J. (1986). *Life events as stressors in childhood and adolescence.* Beverly Hills: Sage.

Kasl, S., & Berkman, L. (1983). Health consequences of the experience of migration. *Annual Review of Public Health, 4,* 69–90.

Leighton, D.C., Harding, J.S., Macklin, D.B., Macmillan, A.M., & Leighton, E.H. (1963). *The character of danger: Psychiatric symptoms in selected communities.* New York: Basic Books.

MacKinlay, J. (1975). Some issues associated with migration, health status and the use of health services. *Journal of Chronic Disease, 28,* 579–92.

Malzberg, B., & Lee, E.S. (1956). *Migration and mental disease: A study of first admissions to hospitals for mental disease, N.Y., 1939–1941.* New York: Social Science Research Council.

Meswick, S.A. (1982). Migration, health, and schooling: A case study of Puerto Rican adolescents in urban Connecticut. Unpublished doctoral dissertation, University of Connecticut.

Michelson, W., Levine, S., & Spina, A.R. (1979). *The child in the city: Changes and challenges.* Toronto: University of Toronto Press.

Scotch, N.A. (1963). Sociocultural factors in the epidemiology of Zulu hypertension. *American Journal of Public Health, 53,* 1205–1213.

Slavin, S. (1971). Migration, residential mobility and community health policy. In J. Eaton (Ed.), *Migration and social welfare.* New York: National Association of Social Workers.

Winkler, K. (1990) Researcher's examination of California's poor Latino population prompts debate over the traditional definitions of the underclass. *Chronicle of Higher Education,* October 10, 15–18.

CHAPTER 12

Puerto Rican Families on the Mainland: Stresses and Support Systems

Clare S. Figler

Introduction

This chapter summarizes a study which compares the stresses and support systems of two groups of mainland-based Puerto Rican families (Figler, 1980). One group of families has handicapped children whose special needs have been identified and range from mild to severe. The children of the second group of families do not have special needs. Utilizing an extensive, semistructured questionnaire format, representative Puerto Rican families living in the Boston urban area were interviewed about their stresses and how they coped with them. The families were asked to discuss their perceived strengths, their problems, and their attempts at solutions.

The Dynamics of In/Out Migration

The establishment of Puerto Ricans on the U.S. mainland is an intriguing feature of which the historical and political base is closely tied to the island's permanent shift from cash sugar/tobacco/coffee-cropping to industrialization (Fitzpatrick, 1987; Lopez, 1973; Mintz, 1975). Beginning in the 1930's, and then propelled by "Operation Bootstrap" of the 1950's, one-third of the population was set in perpetual transit to and from the mainland. Easy access from island to mainland, in addition to U.S. citizenship status, offers Puerto Ricans an opportunity typically not available to other migrants: the option to return home again and again.

Both the island and the mainland populations are ever-changing. The process of in and out migration, perhaps more than anything else, challenges the notion that life on the mainland is better than on the island. Sometimes it is; often it is not. The mainland community offers advantages and disadvantages, stresses and supports. Satisfactions include employment opportunities, learning a new language, more diversified and abundant medical and social services. But these benefits are often achieved at great cost. Highly valued extended family networks are fractured or weakened; children's education is segmented; young and old are affected by the uprooting; life cycles are frequently juxtapositioned; and important family and cultural values are minimized.

On the whole, research with Puerto Rican families in the U.S. has tended to emphasize the stresses and multiple needs of families (Canino & Canino, 1980; Canino, Earley, & Rogler, 1980; Minuchin, Montalvo, Guerney, Rosman, & Schumer, 1967; Rogler, 1965). By contrast, the analysis of more differentiated personal/social dynamics and of the multiple adaptive and coping maneuvers have been the priority of fewer investigators (Garrison, 1978; Nuttall, 1976; 1979; Nuttall, Nuttall, & Pedalino, 1978; Pelto, Román, & Liriano, 1982). The present work is in line with investigations which attempt to document both needs and strengths. By studying families with and without handicapped children, it is also in line with investigations that aim at achieving further differentiation between families.

The migration of Puerto Rican families in and out of the island, and back, is an accepted fact of life. The families interviewed in this study moved to the metropolitan Boston area in response to both internal and external needs. All families in the sample had made a decision to come to the mainland because of a generalized effort "to better their lives." However, the move had a qualitatively different meaning, dependent on whether or not the children had special needs. The group of families without special-needs children wanted to improve the quality of their lives by earning better wages and learning English. These families usually came to the mainland community from a position of strength or at least of anticipated strength. The families of special-needs children, on the other hand, were propelled by a position of weakness or vulnerability, having come to the mainland to seek help for their children.

Framework for Analyzing Family Stresses and Support Systems

The theoretical framework for this investigation was drawn from: (a) the work of Nuttall, Nuttall, and Pedalino (1978), which studied low-income Puerto Rican and Italian families; (b) Bronfenbrenner's (1977) structural ecological systems model; and (c) family process theory as suggested by Kantor and Lehr (1975), Minuchin (1974), and Duhl (1969). A visual representation of the structure and process model of family functioning appears in Figure 1.

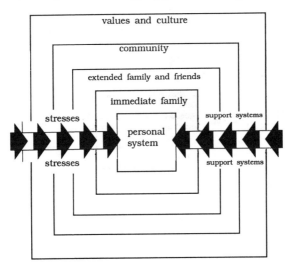

Figure 1

Structure and Process of Family Functioning
(After Figler, 1980)

As seen in Figure 1, the model is conceptualized as an increasing series of concentric squares and depicts the structural components of the family in terms of the following system-related terms: (a) the personal system, (b) the immediate family, (c) the extended family and friends, (d) community agencies, and (e) the cultural values. Under this model, stresses originate at any level of family structure: the personal level, the immediate family level, the extended family level, the community level, and the values/cultural level. Similarly, the support systems which might be drawn in order to cope with stresses also originate from any of these levels. Figure 2 presents the support systems which are available to a family in its efforts to cope with stresses at the personal level, the family level, and the community level.

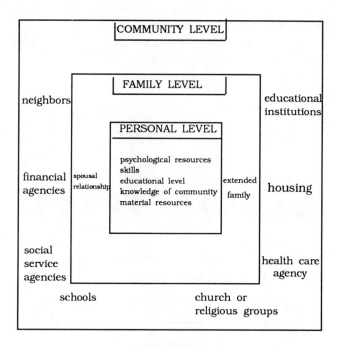

Figure 2
Support Systems of Family Functioning
(After Figler, 1980)

As summarized in Figure 2, the *personal-level support* system includes spousal relationships, parental relationships, extended family relationships. The *community-level support* system consists of neighbors, community agencies which provide financial help, agencies which provide private or public health care, schools, community-based housing or educational agencies, churches or religious groups.

Typically, some families obtain support from one or a few sources; other families involve themselves with many supportive networks. To a great extent, the competence of a family's functioning is related to the effectiveness of its coping strategies, which in turn reduces the levels of stress. The premise of the present study is that there is a direct relation between a particular family stress and the supportive resources called upon to alleviate it.

Purpose of the Study

The major purpose of this study was to investigate the stresses and support systems which exist in the family functioning of two groups: Puerto Rican families with handicapped children and Puerto Rican families with children who have not been identified as having special needs. The following areas were specifically studied:

1. The stresses impinging upon the families. What common stresses are encountered by all Puerto Rican families? What specific stresses are encountered by families of handicapped children in comparison with stresses on families with children not identified as handicapped?
2. The personal-level support system of the families. What are the resources at the personal level used by each type of family?
3. The family-level support system of the families. What are the resources at the family level used by each type of family?
4. The community-level support systems of the families. What are the resources at the community level used by each type of family?

Method

Participants

The sample was composed of 28 low-income Puerto Rican families living in the greater Boston area. Fourteen families had children who had an identified handicap or who were considered to have special educational, behavioral, or physical needs. These children are considered to be "handicapped" or to have "special needs." Their needs range from mild to severe. Fourteen families had children without identified special educational needs. All families were involved in some form of public assistance program such as Medicaid, Aid to Families with Dependent Children, or other programs. Table 1 summarizes the major demographic characteristics of sample families.

Table 1
Demographic Description of Families

	Non-Handicapped Group	Handicapped Group
Mean age of parents	Wife - 36.4 years Husband - 38 years	Wife - 34.7 years Husband - 39.7 years
Mean number of children	2.5	3.7
Mean age of children	12-8 years	12-4 years
Mean education level of parents	Wife - 10.9 years Husband - 9.7 years	Wife - 8.2 years Husband - 7 years
Mean years in mainland	11 years	11.3 years

Procedure and Instrumentation

A semistructured interview schedule developed by the author in collaboration with Ena Vázquez-Nuttall was used, the English version of which appears in Figler (1980). Interviews lasted from two to six hours, with a mean of about two and a half hours. Interviewers were two Hispanic, bilingual-bicultural women with extensive experience interviewing families. At the time of the study, one interviewer was a community worker, well-known in the Hispanic community. The other interviewer was the author, a bilingual school psychologist well-known to the schools and with much personal involvement with special-needs children. Contacts were made through the schools and a community-based housing agency.

Design

The study consisted of an in-depth *ex post facto* survey of 14 Hispanic families with children who have identified handicaps and 14 families with children who have not been identified as having a handicap. Data analysis was both qualitative and quantitative. The quantitative analysis entailed the use of descriptive statistics such as means and percentages; the qualitative analysis consisted of in-depth case studies of representative families.

Findings

Stresses in the Families

Although all families encountered strains at various levels of family structure, as seen in Table 2, each group prioritized these stresses differently. The difficulties encountered by all families included: housing, serious illnesses, finances, schools, emotional problems, spousal relationships, relationships with neighbors, relationships with family members, health care, personal loneliness, and work situations. Families with handicapped children experienced the additional stress brought about by their awareness of a child's deficits, their difficulties with social service or community agencies, their legal and/or institutional problems, and their difficulties with child care.

The types of problems encountered by the two groups of families differed both in quantity and quality. Families from the Handicapped group were stressed more often and more severely. The greatest single source of stress for the Non-Handicapped group was language (speaking, reading, and writing English). In contrast, the major stresses experienced by families with handicapped children stemmed from financial problems, housing difficulties, and problems related to their children's handicaps (diagnosis, follow-up services, schools, illness, awareness and acceptance of child's deficits, and child care). Difficulties with English language learning for the families of handicapped children assumed a less critical focus.

The extensiveness of a child's handicap did not always indicate the level of stress felt by the family. Some families who dealt with severely handicapped youngsters did not feel that they carried a heavier burden than other families. Conversely, some families of children whose handicaps were not considered severe felt that they had a most difficult life. Although more of the families in the group who reared children with identified handicaps reported that they experienced comparatively heavier burdens than were reported by families whose children did not have identified handicaps, there were exceptions. Some families felt less strained than other families, irrespective of the presence of a critical circumstance. Other families felt strain in spite of rearing children whose physical, mental, or educational status was uneventful.

Future Orientation

Families without handicapped children were satisfied with their lives and would not alter much, if this were possible. These families were future-oriented. In contrast, families rearing handicapped children felt that, if offered another chance, they would make different choices in their

Table 2
Areas and Sources of Stresses
Reported by Families

Source of Stress	Stress	Non-Handicapped Group	Handicapped Group
		Number Reported	Number Reported
C	Housing	2	9
P	Serious illness	3	11
P	Finances	2	10
C	Schools	1	8
P	Emotional problems	1	3
P	Spousal relationship	1	1
P	Language	5	5
C	Neighbors	1	3
F	Family (Extended)	1	5
C	Health care	1	4
P	Personal loneliness	1	4
C	Work/Employment	2	9
P	Awareness of child's deficits	—	12
C	Community agencies	—	2
C	Legal problems	—	3
F	Child care	—	9

P = Personal level
F = Family level
C = Community level

lives. The Handicapped group's orientation was one of day-to-day rather than of future.

Why Move?

For families with handicapped children, the decision to migrate to the mainland usually stemmed from the critical incident of having a handicapped child. These families' primary stress reduction was represented by the move, since, it was reasoned, moving itself would eventually offer better support, better medical care, and better educational opportunities for the handicapped offspring.

The timing of the move for families of handicapped children differed from families without special-needs children. The Handicapped group families usually moved to the mainland later in their child-rearing phase of family life. At the time of the move, the children in this group were older. Families of handicapped children typically moved subsequent to facing the agony of having a handicapped child. Relocation on the mainland was the beginning of a process which solidified efforts to obtain needed medical and other specialized interventions for the special-needs youngster.

Contact with Puerto Rico

The extent to which the families visit, call, write, and otherwise maintain contact with kin on the island differentiated the two groups of families. Several of the families from the Non-Handicapped group planned to return to Puerto Rico when the children's education had been completed and when enough money had been saved. In this group, strong ties with island kin in the form of regular mail and telephone communication and regular annual or biennial trips occurred. Having a back-up family network on the island was considered to be a powerful source of strength and support. Much planning was devoted to anticipated visits to island relatives. This was not the case with the Handicapped group.

A possible explanation for the difference between the two groups regarding their involvement with island relatives springs from several factors: (a) the Handicapped group had fewer relatives on the island; (b) generally, the Non-Handicapped group was in the "building" rather than the rearing stage, thus the move to the mainland was one step in their family process, the long-range goal of which was to return to the island. The Handicapped group families, on the other hand, had responded to a critical need—to seek out intervention services for a handicapped child—by migrating. These families did not anticipate their return. If anything, many in the Handicapped group felt that they perhaps *could not return* to Puerto Rico because they were aware that services for handicapped children were insufficient there. In other words, the families in the Non-Handicapped group maintained their island-base family support network; the Handicapped group were isolated from island family networks.

Experiences with Schools

For the group without handicapped children, experiences with schools and school staff were positive. As illustrated in Figure 3, contact with schools was infrequent and socially oriented, such as visits to "open house" or holiday programs. Parents in this group maintained only minimal contact with schools because their children were generally doing well. The reverse was true for parents of handicapped children. Frequent visits to school were perceived as reflecting children's problems, while minimal contact with schools suggested educational progress.

Family Functioning

Families in the Non-Handicapped group reported few encounters with serious illness or accidents. The sibling, spousal and parental relationships were also more positive and stable. Generally, more positive than negative family experiences were reported. The relationship between having a handicapped youngster and experiencing more stress and/or dissatisfactions in life surfaced. Families with children who did not have handicaps seemed to function better.

Rearing Handicapped Children

Families with children having identified handicaps frequently felt overwhelmed, tired, and frustrated. Awareness of their children's deficits was emotionally difficult. The time and effort required to plan for and care for their special needs youngsters left many of the parents physically exhausted. This was particularly true for the mothers. As a result of the intense involvement with their handicapped child over the course of time, the quality of relationships between others in the immediate family—spouses, siblings, parents, non-handicapped children—was strained. Many in this group were resigned to their lot in life as caretakers of their handicapped child.

Disappointment based on feelings that relatives lacked interest or that they did not offer support was more intense than the hurt expressed over community-level inattention. For families in the Handicapped group, help from the family network was desired but, unfortunately, felt to be negligible in most cases. That help in meeting the continuous demands of caring for handicapped children was desperately needed is undisputed. This support was typically not offered by family members. Several of the families stated that if the situation were reversed—if a member of the extended family had a handicapped child and called for help—*they* would certainly offer assistance.

Parents in the Handicapped group talked about their loneliness, their isolation, and the expectation that their status was a permanent one. This group of families was ambivalent about their distant future. Most families were resigned to looking after their special-needs children, and this commitment did not allow for much flexibility in the future.

Education and Employment

All families expressed an unequivocal regret at not having obtained better education before pursuing family life. Better education was perceived as the means to better economic conditions.

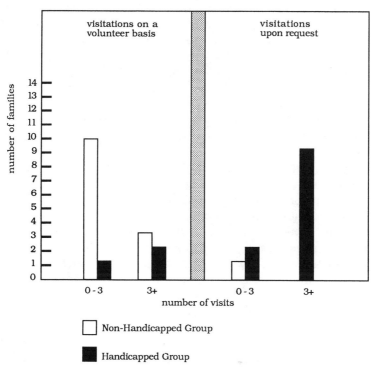

Figure 3

Families' Involvement with Schools

One of the most crucial factors associated with the quality of family life is the work status of the adults in the family. Discussions about work, anticipated training, past work experiences, and related issues were offered spontaneously during the interviews. The most satisfaction with family life was expressed in families where both spouses worked. It was not surprising to find that two-spouse working households came from the group without handicapped children.

The caring for handicapped children defined how the family's time and resources would be used. In most cases, the wife in such a household had to stay at home to care for the child or to be available to accompany the child on the necessary round of appointments with doctors, with school staff, with agency workers. As a result of the mother's "on call" status, she was bound to the home and not easily able to work outside the home. The families in the Handicapped group had less income, less personal satisfaction, and fewer material resources, such as cars.

Happiness with work was most often expressed by the working wife. Most of the respondents denied the existence of dissatisfaction or problems with work. In other words, the family members—particularly wives—who were currently employed were grateful to have a job. Those who had found work planned to remain in their jobs indefinitely.

Housing

Increased income made possible not only better living quarters, but also a better standard of living and easier relationships among family members. Availability of more money for rent by pooling of incomes made quite a difference in the adequacy of the family's dwelling. It is noteworthy that, regardless of income level or involvement with handicapped children, the families who lived in an ethnically oriented and community-controlled housing program had better housing than families who rented privately or families who lived in other—and less preferable—housing complexes.

Many of the families interviewed were in search of better housing. Indeed, preoccupation with housing and the desire to improve such was a repetitive theme. One family had periodically applied for public housing over the last seven years, but was repeatedly told that there were no vacancies. Another family who had been living in substandard housing in a privately owned building was, over a long period of time, unsuccessful in achieving legally required repairs and renovations. It seemed that some families had connected with people who helped them obtain adequate housing; other families were not as successful. More families in the Non-Handicapped group had better housing. However, this is the group which had better personal, family, and extended family resources which were called into play in order to obtain appropriate housing.

There are not sufficient well-maintained apartments for low-income families. Many Puerto Rican families are, and historically have been, short-changed in the housing distribution process. Thus, families in both groups obtained what was available in housing and what was available was often inadequate.

Families reported the following reasons for satisfaction with their housing (rank-ordered): affordable; clean and well-maintained; close to schools, stores, church, medical facilities; near public transportation; spacious; friendly and respectful neighbors; Spanish-speaking neighbors; sense of privacy; a garden.

The dissatisfactions with housing were prioritized as follows: too small; dangerous influences in neighborhood; inadequate access and accommodation for handicapped child; rent too high; utilities and maintenance too expensive; property neglect, rats; insufficient funds for repairs.

Families in both groups reported either positive or neutral relationships with neighbors. Maintenance of harmonious relationships with neighbors was extremely important to most of the families interviewed, even among those who reported dissatisfactions with housing. Negative relationships with people in the neighborhood were reported by two families in the Handicapped group and by one in the Non-Handicapped group. Animosities were not reported by any of the families; the negative reactions related to knowledge about the dangers on the streets, that is, drugs, loitering, rough play, street-corner drinking. Several of the families—mostly in the Handicapped group—reported less-active relationships with neighbors because of the language barrier. Language difficulties were minimal among families who lived in the predominantly Puerto Rican housing complex where access to compatriots and to extended family members was usually but a few doors away.

Several families reported less-active—but generally positive—neighbor relationships. Some of the families felt that personal and family privacy was of the utmost importance. These families sought and obtained their privacy. One family found that involvement with its extensively handicapped child was so time-consuming that little time was left to develop more active give-and-take relationships with neighbors.

Religion

A majority of the families were Catholic and formally involved with their religion. Most families participated in religious services on a regular basis (from once every week to once every month). A respectful stance was maintained by many of the families when they were questioned about their religious participation. Families spoke respectfully about the priest, the Church, and the sanctity of God. However, fervent participation with religion was not inherent in the lives of a majority of the families, whether or not they were Catholic. The one exception was an extremely involved Pentecostal family who participated in church meetings daily, to the exclusion of many secular activities. In this particular family, the husband also served as the church's assistant pastor.

Recreation

A family's participation in and enjoyment of leisure and recreational activities is an important aspect of the quality of its functioning. When material resources were available to the extent that families owned a car, they participated in more recreational activities. In addition, where overall personal resources and knowledge of the community were adequate, the family seemed healthier and stronger. The spousal, parental, sibling systems were satisfying. Because more of the families without handicapped children owned cars, more families in this group went to parks, museums, and other recreational facilities. Overall responses of families from both groups suggest a positive relation to ownership of a car, participation in leisure activities, and more effective family functioning. A worthwhile research project might clarify the significance of these relations. Do families take advantage of leisure time because they have a car? Or, does the ownership of a car facilitate better opportunities for leisure time?

Involvement with Agencies

An important relation exists between the effectiveness of community resources and the extent of their use by the families. A family's involvement with a limited number of community resources does not always suggest less stress or less need for intervention. Use of a limited number of community-level resources most likely reflects that these particular agencies are effective. The agency which serves most of the family's needs is usually a multiservice one.

According to the families interviewed, the staff at community agencies should be courteous, speak Spanish, and express a measure of some personal interest. Accessibility of the agency is an important drawing feature for families, although satisfaction with it was more crucial. If families owned cars, the hardship of reaching the clinic or agency was reduced. However, if the agency had been a supportive intervener in the past, then families continued to use the agency over the years.

Families which relied on a greater number of community-level resources seemed, first of all, to be aware of and knowledgeable about the greater community. Many of these families had been dissatisfied or only partly satisfied with the service of certain community agencies in the past. As a result, they cultivated and increased their repertoire of resources and, through trial-and-error, eventually found the needed support. In certain circumstances, the process of disillusionment and search for needed supportive services was a lengthy one. The most relevant feature about community-level resources seems to be quality, rather than quantity. Although the Boston urban area offers services through many agencies, the Puerto Rican families interviewed participated in a relatively small core of these.

Discussion

Families rearing handicapped children felt less satisfied with their lives. This group experienced many additional stresses in areas of economic status, relationships between spouses, and housing than did families without handicapped children. Families without handicapped children functioned better, had more personal satisfactions, more material resources, more contact with relatives in Puerto Rico, and more consistent participation in the work force. This group was more future-oriented than families with handicapped children. Knowledge of and use of community agencies was found to be more extensive for families who had handicapped children, although this finding generally reflects this group's more extensive need for community-level support.

The following paragraphs summarize the information shared by the two groups of Puerto Rican families living on the U.S. mainland. Tables 3 and 4, at the end of this section, offer a visual summary of the similarities and differences between the two groups of families.

1. The immediate and extended family relationships among most of the families were found to be generally strong and caring. Parenting and maintenance of family were highly valued, as was an emphasis on the traditional sexually defined roles. Membership in a family was considered to be important, and this membership made each person special. The extended family of grandparents, aunts and uncles, coparents, and others was felt to enrich the individual. The value of establishing and maintaining a family was stressed during the childhood years. Roles in which the wife was the mother/homemaker and the husband the breadwinner were perceived as ideal.

The families from both groups drew much of their sense of identity and support from their families: the immediate and the extended family systems. In addition, community involvement and maintenance of goodwill with neighbors was important. Most of the families had a sense of community and participated in neighborhood activities. However, they did not count on the support of outsiders during times of stress. When relatives did not help in times of need, families felt isolated and deprived of an important cultural link. The families' responsibility for helping relatives in need is emphasized by the cultural value system. Isolation from family members was more frequently reported by families in the Handicapped group.

Families in the Handicapped group were more disillusioned with marriage, childrearing, and parenting. For this group, family life seemed less satisfying and more difficult. Strain in the spousal relationship, the parental relationship, and with extended family members occurred more frequently in this group.

2. A difference concerning the number and variety of needs and stresses was found among the two groups. The families having children with identified handicaps reported nearly *five* times as many stresses, stemming from a wider variety of sources, as did families whose children were not identified as handicapped. Most frequently reported as stressful for the Handicapped group were the following (listed in order of frequency): awareness of their children's deficits, serious illness, finances, housing, child care, employment problems, English language problems.

The reported stresses of families without handicapped children were prioritized as follows: lack of English language skills, serious illness, housing, finances, employment.

3. The sources of support which were drawn from the families in the two groups differed. While all the families obtained some degree of help from personal and family systems, the families who had handicapped children drew more of their support from the community resources. Problems presented by the handicap prompted the families to seek more avenues of direct or backup intervention, such as special education programs in the schools or welfare subsidies. Thus, families who had handicapped

children were knowledgeable about and involved with a greater number of community-level resources.

On the other hand, families without handicapped children had far less recourse to community agencies and tended to depend on their own personal or family resources for support. These more direct resources were not as available to families in the Handicapped group because relationships in their immediate and extended family systems were generally less integrated, more strained, and perhaps problematic. The strain of rearing children with handicaps was, in most cases, considerable and ongoing. This stress impacted the family system in a negative way, thus interfering with the quality of family functioning. There were exceptions, however. Some families mustered strength from various levels and functioned commendably in spite of many stresses and burdens. Other families, in spite of a rather strong base of family and personal support, did not function as well.

4. The employment status of the adults in the families was a crucial factor affecting the families' functioning. In families with handicapped children, the wife was unable to work outside the home because of the demands of looking after a handicapped child. On the other hand, many wives in the Non-Handicapped group *did* work. In families where one or both spouses worked regularly, the family functioned better. Because there was more money available, the family could extend their material resources and services. A family's ownership of a car and telephone helped the family cope with many of its stresses. In families where the two parents were working, there was less dependence on welfare subsidies. Welfare subsidies were universally considered as a last-resort measure, whether or not families were involved with them. Employment was felt to be the strategy by which families could terminate welfare subsidies. However, work was not always possible for a variety of reasons, among which were the need to care for young or handicapped children, insufficient education, disabilities, and language barriers.

All families expressed a desire to be better educated. Whether or not husband and/or wife were employed, improvement in education was perceived to be a viable avenue toward better employment. This was not a surprising finding, because a basic reason for the families' move to the mainland had been to improve their economic status.

5. The adequacy of and satisfaction with their housing was a key factor in the families' better negotiation with many of their stresses. Generally, families who lived in well-maintained, affordable, and conveniently located dwellings had a richer and more satisfying lifestyle. In these particular housing situations, children were allowed to play outside, and parents felt that their children were safely away from "street dangers" present in many urban neighborhoods. Families who lived in the more satisfactory housing units were not constantly concerned about the high cost of utilities, the neglect of property, or the lack of space.

Most satisfied were the families who lived in community-controlled government-subsidized units where the neighborhood was predominantly Puerto Rican. A surpising finding concerning the housing status was that a majority of the families of handicapped children had the most inadequate housing and were least satisfied with it. Many in this group were and had been actively seeking more appropriate dwellings, but experienced difficulties finding them.

6. Families from both groups were similar with regard to several personality attributes about which they were questioned. The focal adults in both groups of families rated themselves as hardworking, independent, organized, and ambitious. However, a difference between groups was found regarding future orientation. Families of children who did not have handicaps were more future-oriented. For these families, long-range goals were important. On the other hand, families who were rearing handicapped children found that long-range planning was not meaningful. Many of the families in this group were burdened with managing the present, day-to-day events of their families.

7. Contact with relatives on the island was found to be an important dimension for many of the families. It was found that the families with more extensive and personal ties to Puerto Rico relatives seemed to function better on the mainland. Visits, vacations, letters, and telephone communication with island relatives strengthened the sense of family identity, cultural awareness, and national pride.

Families from the two groups differed in the extent of contact maintained with relatives on the island. Although the average length of time spent on the mainland was similar for families in both groups, the group whose children did not have identified handicaps communicated regularly and kept in close touch with relatives in Puerto Rico. This was not generally the case with families who had handicapped children.

8. Most of the families felt that a minimum amount of contact with their children's schools was best. Frequent visits to the schools suggested the existence of problems with their children. Parents of handicapped children were asked to attend conferences to discuss special education placements and programs for their children. These parents were asked to come to the schools much more frequently than parents whose children did not have identified handicaps or who were in regular education programs. Concerning attitudes toward schools, most of the parents maintained a passive stance. Families trusted schools and school staff implicitly.

Recommendations

Implications for Practice and Public Policy

1. *The strong sense of family among Puerto Ricans should be recognized and appreciated.* Practice and policy geared toward Puerto Rican populations on the mainland should recognize the strong sense of family and the

supportive quality of the family system. With but minimal support, the Puerto Rican family goes a long way.
2. *The nature of the circumstance determines the type of help sought.* Several factors determine the families' involvement with agencies or with community-level support. One factor is the critical nature of the circumstance precipitating the involvement. When the severity of the problem obliges direct resolution, as is the case in a health emergency or debilitating situation, Puerto Rican families will solicit help from available agencies. But personal and family resources are generally exhausted first. Thus, another factor which propels a family to seek help outside of the home is the availability of the family network. Only when personal or family-level support is ineffective, unavailable, or not forthcoming is intervention from the community sought.
3. *Supportive interventions should be practical and free of red tape.* Puerto Rican families would profit from supportive intervention which focuses on flexible personal relationships. Families want to feel that help is available with a minimum of bureaucratic red tape. Counseling support should include practical, systems-related strategies, such as arranging for families to obtain telephones, sharing of accurate information about resource services, facilitating the pursuit of educational and vocational goals. It is crucial that intervening agencies participate with their Puerto Rican clients until the goal is reached because it is not sufficient to diagnose and recommend solutions. Follow-ups should be a part of the total intervention strategy.
4. *Direct personal links between agencies and clients should be built.* Puerto Ricans derive a strong sense of personal worth through direct personal relationships. It behooves service providers to capitalize on this important cultural value. Thus, long-term, rather than short-term, projects should be undertaken. Programs which are funded for short periods of time establish a pattern of disjointed, piecemeal strategies which often terminate when the fiscal year ends. When funds run out, new people are sought, new policies are implemented, and a reshuffling occurs. Funded projects which aim to intervene in certain areas

Table 3

Generalized Summary of Similarities among Two Groups of Families

1.	Strong sense of identity as Hispanic/Puerto Rican
2.	Strong sense of membership in family
3.	Strong "caring" element among nuclear family members
4.	Prefer a personal relationship in community agency involvement
5.	Economic stresses forceful
6.	Desire to be better educated
7.	Prefer infrequent contact with schools
8.	Parenting function of family stressed
9.	Traditional view of sex roles
10.	Resistant to idea of institutionalizing handicapped family members
11.	Overburdened feeling, compared to others
12.	Personality attributes similar concerning industriousness, independence, organization
13.	Length of residency on mainland (11 years)

Table 4
Generalized Summary of Differences
between Two Types of Families

Non-Handicapped Group	Handicapped Group
1. Smaller number of stresses.	1. More stresses.
2. Less varied kinds of stresses.	2. Wider variety of stresses.
3. Housing better; more satisfaction with housing.	3. Housing less adequate; less satisfaction with housing.
4. Less reliance on community-level support: a. less participation in welfare b. infrequent contact with children's schools c. limited knowledge and use of community agencies.	4. More reliance on community-level support: a. more involvement in welfare b. frequent contact with children's schools c. good knowledge and use of community agencies.
5. More reliance on personal- and family-level support.	5. Less reliance on personal- and family-level support.
6. Better immediate- and extended-family relationships.	6. More stressful immediate and extended-family relationships.
7. Regular and frequent contact/communication with Puerto-Rico-based relatives.	7. Minimal contact with Puerto-Rico-based relatives.
8. Plans to return to Puerto Rico.	8. No plans to return to Puerto Rico.

of need for Puerto Rican families must provide for follow-up and continued personal contact.

It would be useful to provide for the training of families so that they can recognize the gradient of problems which they must face regarding their handicapped children. Often a seriously handicapped child is not helped early enough because the parents have little basis on which to judge the seriousness of the problem. Conversely, parents sometimes overreact to maturational and developmental issues about their children. In this case, premature decisions are often made. Information exchanges, follow-up, and consistent contact with Puerto Rican families about the nature of their children's development should be easily available.

5. *Strong links between home and school should be forged.* Our findings indicate that parents strive to maintain a passive, minimally active relationship with their children's schools. Frequent visits and contact with school staff were perceived as indicative of problems with their children. Thus, most of the families adhere to an implicit model with relation to the schools which incorporates the "no news is good news" idea. Schools are generally trusted and held to be infallible. Little overall family involvement with the schools occurs, but this is not only a result of cultural factors. Often the schools make very little effort to encourage Puerto Rican parents' participation in their children's schools.

Even when the language barriers between parent and school are somewhat overcome, it often happens that parents do not respond. This is often the case because messages, notices, or letters from school are cold and impersonal. However, if direct overtures such as telephone calls are made to the family by the school's staff, much reciprocity, cooperation, and goodwill results. When the Puerto Rican parent is positively involved with the schools, it is usually because of a direct and personal relationship with a person from the school. Again, *personal relationship* is important. Community liaisons and school-home workers should be available as intermediaries, messengers, and family advocates.

6. *Families need to be kept abreast of educational programs and options.* Many of the families were not fully aware of the type of programs which the children attended. Most of the families interviewed in the study seemed to believe that their children were involved in a bilingual program, whether or not this was true. Often parents assumed that if Spanish-speaking aides, secretaries, or other personnel worked in the schools, then the children were in a bilingual program. Further, many families were only minimally aware of different possibilities and options concerning bilingual or monolingual school programs. Families often had little basis of comparison for the types of classes available for their children in the schools. Little opportunity or motivation to investigate occurred if their children learned to read, participated with other children, and otherwise developed well.

Parents should be provided with ample opportunities to observe and learn about the options available for their children in the schools. Description of programs, explanation of entry procedures, and information about possible alternatives in education should be clearly communicated to parents in language they can understand. Visits to schools and observation of programs should be facilitated.

7. *Accept and respect return migration.* The unique feature of a Puerto Rican's dream to return to the island must be appreciated. That Puerto Ricans desire to, and often do, return to the island does not diminish the mainland society's responsibility to educate the children and to maintain the sense of dignity of the families. Return migration does not mean disloyalty to the United States. This phenomenon is a built-in socially and economically expedient process for Puerto Ricans that has logical historical and political roots. Island-to-mainland moves are a cyclical process. It happens. It is the *modus operandi* of many Puerto Ricans. It must be respected and accepted for what it is.

However, the findings of this study indicate that Puerto Rican families with handicapped children do not return to the island, even though they harbor a dream to do so. For these families, contact with the island has been severed and this corrosion in their family network system is a source of stress. In contrast, many of the better functioning, less problematic families—those without handicapped children—do return to the island. Interventions geared to mainland-based Puerto Rican families should appreciate that a family's strong ties to the island represents a source of strength and support. Practice and policy should tap the supportive nature of the Puerto Rican family.

REFERENCES

Bronfenbrenner, U. (1977). Towards an experimental ecology of human development. *American Psychologist, 32,* 513–535.

Canino, I.A., & Canino, G. (1980). Impact of stress on the Puerto Rican family: Treatment considerations. *American Journal of Psychiatry, 50,* 535–541.

Canino, I.A., Earley, B.F., & Rogler, L.H. (1980). *The Puerto Rican child in New York City: Stress and mental health.* Bronx, NY: Fordham University, Hispanic Research Center.

Duhl, F.J. (1969). Intervention, therapy, and change. In W. Gray, F.J. Duhl, & N.D. Rizzo (Eds.), *General systems theory and psychiatry,* Boston: Little, Brown.

Figler, C.S. (1980). A comparative study of Puerto Rican families with and without handicapped children. Unpublished doctoral dissertation, University of Massachusetts, Amherst.

Fitzpatrick, J.P. (1987). *Puerto Rican Americans: The meaning of migration to the mainland,* 2nd Ed. Englewood Cliffs, NJ: Prentice-Hall.

Garrison, V. (1978). Support systems of schizophrenic and nonschizophrenic Puerto Rican migrant women in New York City. *Schizophrenic Bulletin, 4,* 561–595.

Kantor, D., & Lehr, W. (1975). *Inside the family.* San Francisco: Jossey-Bass.

López, A. (1973). *The Puerto Rican papers: Notes on the re-emergence of a nation.* Indianapolis: Bobbs-Merrill.

Mintz, S.W. (1975). Puerto Rico: An essay in the definition of a national culture. In F. Cordasco & E. Bucchioni (Eds.), *The*

Puerto Rican experience: A sociological sourcebook (pp. 26–90). Totowa, NJ: Littlefield, Adams.

Minuchin, S. (1974). *Families and family therapy.* Cambridge, MA: Harvard University Press.

Minuchin, S., Montalvo, B., Guerney, J., Rosman, B., & Schumer, F. (1967). *Families of the slums.* New York: Basic Books.

Nuttall, E. (1976). Coping patterns of Puerto Rican mothers heading single family households. *Interamerican Journal of Psychology, 12,* 5–13.

Nuttall, E. (1979). The support systems and coping patterns of the female Puerto Rican single parent. *Journal of Non-White Concerns, 7*(3), 128–137.

Nuttall, E., Nuttall, R., & Pedalino, M. (1978). *Coping with stress: An ecological analysis of Puerto Rican and Italian low-income families.* Report to the National Institute of Mental Health.

Pelto, P.J., Román, M., & Liriano, N. (1982). Family structures in an urban Puerto Rican community. *Urban Anthropology, 11*(1), 39–58.

Rogler, L.H. (1965). *Trapped: Families and schizophrenia.* New York: Krieger.

PART VI

Annotated Bibliography: A Decade of Publications on Puerto Rican Children on the Mainland (1980–1990)

A DECADE OF PUBLICATIONS ON PUERTO RICAN CHILDREN ON THE MAINLAND AN ANNOTATED BIBLIOGRAPHY (1980–1990)

I. History and Immigration

Acosta-Belén, E., & Sjostrum, B.R. (Eds.) (1988). *The Hispanic experience in the United States: Contemporary issues and perspectives.* New York: Praeger.

While this book is devoted to U.S. Hispanics in general, most chapters offer data and/or information on mainland-based Puerto Ricans and provide updated figures on demographic patterns, education, family structure, economic factors, and language, to name a few. At least three chapters deal specifically with various aspects of the Puerto Rican experience, including immigration and identity, culture contact and value orientations, and the concept of latinismo among early Puerto Rican migrants to New York City.

Andreu Iglesias, C. (Ed.) (1980). *Memorias de Bernardo Vega: Una contribución a la historia de la comunidad puertorriqueña en Nueva York.* Río Piedras: Huracán.

A superb account of the life of Bernardo Vega, a Puerto Rican tobacco worker who emigrated to New York in 1916. He tells the story of his own experience and that of many other Puerto Rican immigrants parallel to the historical events ocurring in Puerto Rico. The memoirs are edited with great sensitivity.

Blanco, T. (1973). *Prontuario histórico de Puerto Rico.* San Juan: Instituto de Cultura Puertorriqueña.

This slender volume offers a synthesis of the history of Puerto Rico from Juan Ponce de León's colonization to the U.S. occupation of the island.

Cordasco, F., & Bucchioni, E. (Eds.) (1975). *The Puerto Rican experience: A sociological sourcebook.* Totowa, NJ: Littlefield, Adams.

A collection of essays which provides a political-economic-cultural background on Puerto Rico, followed by an analysis of the migration experience of Puerto Ricans, including a discussion of education on the mainland.

Figueroa, L. (1971). *Breve historia de Puerto Rico.* Río Piedras: Edil.

A comprehensive, yet concise, history of Puerto Rico from precolumbian times to the end of Spanish rule in 1892.

Fitzpatrick, J.P. (1987). *Puerto Rican Americans: The meaning of migration to the mainland,* 2nd. Ed. Englewood Cliffs, NJ: Prentice-Hall.

An exploration of the immigration patterns of Puerto Ricans from the island to the U.S. Gives a historical background of Puerto Rico and the emergence of large-scale immigration, describes the cultural characteristics of Puerto Ricans and the problems they encounter in the United States. Includes chapters on education, religion, family life, and drug abuse.

López, A. (1987). *Doña Licha's island: Modern colonialism in Puerto Rico.* Boston: South End Press.

A history of Puerto Ricans in Puerto Rico and in the U.S. interspersed with the personal stories of people affected by the historical developments.

López, A., & Petras, J. (1974). *Puerto Rico and Puerto Ricans: Studies in history and society.* New York: Wiley.

A collection of articles on Puerto Rican history, social developments and movements, and Puerto Ricans on the mainland.

Maldonado Denis, M. (1973). *Puerto Rico: Mito y realidad.* Barcelona: Ediciones Península.

Discusses the present colonial situation of Puerto Rico and the cultural assimilation of the island. The author also analyzes the myths that have pervaded in discussions of Puerto Rican independence to the effect that Puerto Rico is politically and economically inferior. The author argues that these myths are untrue and intended to perpetuate the colonial situation of Puerto Ricans.

Maldonado Denis, M. (1978) *Puerto Rico y Estados Unidos: Emigración y colonialismo*. México: Siglo Veintiuno.

Discusses the immigration of Puerto Ricans to the U.S. within the context of immigration and exploitation patterns in other parts of the world. The author argues that the situation of the Puerto Rican immigrant in the U.S. is similar to that of the Algerian immigrant in Paris and the West Indian black in London or Manchester.

Nieves Falcón, L. (1975). *El emigrante puertorriqueño*. Río Piedras: Edil.

Based on a research study of Puerto Rican immigrant workers in the U.S., the author explores the history of Puerto Rican immigration, and offers insightful descriptions of immigrant workers and their living and working conditions on U.S. farms. The most valuable contributions of the book are the testimonies of the workers themselves, carefully recorded by the researcher and his team, who recount the squalor of their lives and the grim working conditions they must endure.

Rodríguez, C.E. (1989). *Puerto Ricans born in the U.S.A.* Boston: Unwin Hyman.

Described by the author as a social history of the post-World War II Puerto Rican community, the book focuses mainly on New York City, where the largest concentration of Puerto Ricans living in the U.S. is located. Immigration is examined from a historical perspective, and current statistical data on Puerto Ricans on the mainland are provided and interpreted. Other issues addressed include: race/color, education and special education, housing, and political/economic structure.

Rodríguez, C.E., Sánchez Korrol, V., & Alers, J.O. (Eds.) (1980). *The Puerto Rican struggle: Essays on survival in the U.S.* New York: Puerto Rican Migration Research Consortium.

A compendium of essays containing social commentary and analysis by second-generation Puerto Ricans on their situation in the U.S. Some essays focus on the survival of Puerto Rican culture and touch on issues such as language, history, arts, preferences, religious practices. Other essays address economic and work concerns, politics, the struggle of Puerto Rican women, and issues of color.

Seda Bonilla, E. (1970). *Réquiem por una cultura*. Río Piedras: Edil.

Discusses the social transformation of Puerto Rico after industrialization, the problems of identity, the Puerto Rican immigrant in the United States, and the socialization of Puerto Ricans within a neocolonial context.

Silén, J.A. (1971). *We, the Puerto Rican people: A story of oppression and resistance*. New York: Monthly Review Press.

An analysis of the colonial situation of Puerto Rico which examines issues not commonly discussed in other sources, such as Puerto Ricans in the U.S. military service and the double oppression of Puerto Rican women.

U.S. Commission on Civil Rights (1976). *Puerto Ricans in the continental United States: An uncertain future*. Washington, DC: Author.

An analysis of the situation of Puerto Ricans in the U.S. with data on employment, income, and education.

Wagenheim, K. (1970). *Puerto Rico: A profile*. New York: Praeger.

An overview of Puerto Rico which includes geographical and ecological descriptions, a historical overview, and comprehensive chapters on the economy, government, society, education, culture, and the Puerto Rican diaspora.

II. *Language and Culture*

Alegría, R.E. (1974). *Cuentos folklóricos de Puerto Rico*. San Juan: Colección de Estudios Puertorriqueños.

Compiled and edited by Puerto Rican scholar Dr. Ricardo Alegría, the book includes traditional orally transmitted stories collected from different parts of Puerto Rico. The stories have been adapted and edited for children.

Ball, J. (Ed.) (1979). *Folklore and folklife: Teacher's Manual*. Smithsonian Folklife Program. Washington, DC: Smithsonian Institution.

Geared toward teachers, this basic manual deals with the uses of folklore in the classroom and presents several ways in which it can be incorporated into regular and special classroom activities.

Belaval, E.S. (1977). *Problemas de la cultura puertorriqueña*. Rio Piedras: Editorial Cultural.

The premise of this book is that the most urgent problem of Puerto Ricans today is to draw an outline of a national culture. Because of Puerto Rico's ambivalent position between the two Americas, it is necessary to define the nation's culture, once and for all, in the context of historical, linguistic, and cultural realities.

Beléndez, P. (1980). Repetitions and the acquisition of the Spanish verb system. Unpublished doctoral dissertation, Harvard Graduate School of Education.

A longitudinal study of four Puerto Rican boys living in Boston for a period ranging from three to 20 months to analyze the pattern of acquisition of the Spanish verb system.

Coballes-Vega, C. (1980). A comparison of the form and function of code-switching of Chicano and Puerto Rican children. Unpublished doctoral dissertation, University of Illinois.

The form and function of code-switching among Spanish-dominant and English-dominant children was examined. Results of the study indicate that Spanish-dominant subjects tend to use the language of their peers in interactions.

Colón-Rivas, M.V. (1986). Codeswitching among Puerto Rican kindergarten students in a selected school district in Massachusetts. Unpublished doctoral dissertation, University of Massachusetts.

This study focused on conversational codeswitching among 16 Puerto Rican kindergarten students in the process of learning English. The study sought to determine whether codeswitching is an integral part of the oral language expression of these children.

First-born males showed a high incidence of codeswitching, and Art and Language Arts activities provoked the highest frequency of codeswitching for all children.

The highest degree of codeswitching in the Spanish language was intra-sentential. The noun phrase was the highest category at the one-word switch level. The highest codeswitching in English was inter-sentential.

Dorson, R.M. (1972). *Folklore and folklife.* Chicago: University of Chicago.

A comprehensive introduction, it is designed to teach what folklore is and what folklorists do. "Folklore" and "folklife" are not distinct terms. Both may include verbal culture, material culture, and aspects of social custom. Different sections of the book explore the many fields of folklife studies: oral folklore such as narrative poetry and proverbs, social folk customs such as festivals and games, material culture such as costumes and crafts, music, and dance. The second part of the book describes folklife methodology: how to conduct fieldwork, how to create an archive, how to use artifacts and folk art in a folk museum.

Gili-Gaya, S. (1974). *Estudios de lenguaje infantil.* Barcelona: Vox Bibliograf.

Studied 50 Puerto Rican children between the ages of four and seven years, living in Puerto Rico, to analyze the manner in which they used language as a communication tool. Also analyzed the syntactic structures the children used in expressive language.

Hakuta, K. (1987). Degree of bilingualism and cognitive ability in mainland Puerto Rican children. *Child Development, 58,* 1372–1388.

Assessed the relation between degree of bilingualism and cognitive ability in a longitudinal study of low-income Puerto Rican elementary school children.

Hill, K. (1986). Playing with words: The verbal folklore of Puerto Rican schoolchildren in a mainland setting. *Dissertations Abstracts International, 47,* 02A, 623A. (University Microfilms No. DA8607862.)

Examines the Children's Verbal Folklore (CFV) in Spanish and English of 40 third- and fourth-grade Puerto Rican bilingual program students in New Haven, CT. The study shows the processes of CVF transmission, which includes children's rhymes, sayings, and chants, as used in a variety of contexts. An analysis of CVF itself produced provocative insights regarding Puerto Rican and mainland U.S. culture. The study presents children's folkloric material as valuable for its own charm, wit, and poetry. In addition, it is offered as a relatively untapped resource for improving students' self-esteem and L1 and L2 skills, while laying a foundation for literacy.

Knapp, M., & Knapp, H. (1976). *One potato, two potato . . . The secret education of American children.* New York: Norton.

Dispels the myth that traditional games and rhymes do not play a role in the modern child's life, by documenting and analyzing examples of children's folklore collected in 43 mainland states, the Virgin Islands, the Panama Canal Zone, and U.S. military bases around the world. The Knapps describe the nature, transmission, and operations of children's lore. Among the topics they explore are children's games, rituals, taunts, jokes, sayings, and superstitions.

Marrero, C. (1974). *Antología de décimas populares puertorriqueñas.* San Juan: Editorial Cordillera.

A collection of *décimas*, a popular art form in Puerto Rico, which can be sung or recited. The author gives good background information on the *décima*, including definition, history, structure, linguistic analysis. She then offers the collection in categories such as, love, politics, heroes.

Pacheco (undated). *Rin-ran las canciones de San Juan.* San Juan: Nomar.

A record album which includes children's songs from Puerto Rico. A children's chorus sings the traditional songs on Side A. Side B is instrumental so children can sing to the music.

Palma, M. (1981). *Muestras del folklore puertorriqueño.* San Juan: Edil.

A collection of Puerto Rican folklore through which the author seeks to preserve and promote the island's popular culture. It compiles songs, riddles, lullabies, stories, jokes, proverbs, tongue-twisters and sayings from Puerto Rico and an extensive collection of Puerto Rican children's verbal folklore. Some of the material is illustrated with drawings. The musical notation for the melody lines is provided for some songs. This collection is an authentic and valuable resource.

Strong, L. (1972). Language disability in the Hispano-American child. Paper presented at the 23rd Annual Conference of the Orton Society, Seattle.

Focuses on the problems faced by the Puerto Rican Spanish-speaking dyslexic in an English-speaking school system. The author cites the factors which compound children's basic language problems as inadequate or premature instruction, beginning reading in a second language, frequent migrations between Puerto Rico and the mainland, economic deprivation, malnutrition, inadequate pre- and post-natal care, and inadequate use of the phonics method in reading. She provides recommendations to reduce the degree of dyslexia.

Wyszewianski-Langdon, H. (1983). Assessment and intervention strategies for the bilingual language disordered learner. *Exceptional Children, 50*, 37–46.

Puerto Rican children were included in this study of two groups of 25 Spanish-speaking children, ages 6 to 8. One group was developing normally, the second group was composed of language-disordered youngsters. A series of tests was administered to the children, in Spanish and English, in the areas of word articulation, articulation in connected speech, auditory discrimination, sentence comprehension, sentence repetition, and sentence expression. After an analysis of test results and comparisons between the groups, the author concludes that the language-disordered group made more errors in both Spanish and English than the control group.

III. Schools and Schooling

Abi-Nader, J. (1990). "A house for my mother": Motivating Hispanic high school students. *Anthropology and Education Quarterly, 21*(1), 41–57.

Reports on an ethnographic study of successful Hispanic high school students enrolled in a program which motivated students by creating a vision of the future, redefining the image of self, and building a supportive community. The researcher uses Vygotsky's theory of learning to explain the success of the program.

Athanson, Z.P. (1985). The effects of stress on the performance of an academic task by white, black, and Puerto Rican/ Hispanic fifth grade children. Unpublished doctoral dissertation, University of Connecticut.

Assessed the effects of experimental stress upon the performance of an academic task by fifth grade white, black and Puerto Rican/Hispanic fifth grade children. Results of the study indicate that anxiety appeared to have a facilitating effect upon performance among the three groups. No significant difference was found in the performance of the academic task among the groups.

Baker, J., & Sanson, J. (1990). Interventions with students at risk for dropping out of school. *Journal of Educational Research, 83,* 181–186.

Describes an intervention program employing a case study method for at-risk students, grades 9–12, in an urban high school. The program emphasizes school organization, leadership, and teaching practices which affect student attendance, behavior, and motivation to either stay in school or drop out.

Barrington, B.L., & Hendricks, B. (1989). Differentiating characteristics of high school graduates, dropouts, and non-graduates. *Journal of Educational Research, 82,* 309–319.

Examined the differential achievement and intelligence levels, absence patterns, numbers of failing grades, individual/ family characteristics, and teacher comments on cummulative student records for dropouts, nongraduating students, and graduates in a small midwestern city. Findings confirm that by third grade, potential dropouts can be identified with 66% prediction accuracy; by ninth grade, 90% accuracy prediction exists in differentiating potential dropouts. Recommendations are given for intervention programs at the early and middle grades and for research possibilities in examining the dropout problem in minority students in larger urban areas.

Blosser, B. (1988). Television, reading and oral language development: The case of the Hispanic child. *NABE Journal, 13*(1), 21–42.

A study of the TV viewing habits of 168 Mexican and Puerto Rican children in grades 2, 4, and 7 and their language and reading proficiency. The study took place in the Midwest. Results of the study indicated linguistic differences between the two groups: Mexicans were found to be more proficient in Spanish, while Puerto Ricans were found to have stronger English skills. Positive relations were found between vocabulary scores and morning TV viewing, and reading comprehension and afternoon TV viewing in Puerto Rican children.

Boston Public Schools (1986). *A working document on the dropout problem in Boston.* Boston: Office of Research and Development, Boston Public Schools.

Discusses the school related factors, SES indicators, and student characteristics which precipitate the decision to drop out of school. Examines the opportunities provided by the home, school, and society for the at-risk minority youth and urban students. Also addresses the available nationwide research and data collection on dropouts. The study concludes that both the conditions of the Boston public school system and economic factors are linked to student dropout.

Cordasco, F., & Bucchioni, E. (1982). *The Puerto Rican community and its children on the mainland: A source book for teachers, social workers and other professionals.* Metuchen, NJ: Scarecrow.

Offers a background discussion of the Puerto Rican family, discusses the issues of conflict and acculturation on the mainland, and includes a final section on Puerto Rican children in mainland schools.

Cortez, E.G. (1981). Anglo educators and Puerto Rican children: Understanding across cultures. *English Language Teaching Journal, 35,* 175–177.

Explores the cultural traits of Puerto Rican children and families which need to be understood by Anglo educators. The traits analyzed include group-mindedness, fatalism, respect for education and teachers, time orientation, and absenteeism.

Diaz Soto, L., Gellen, M.I., & Morris, J.D. (1988). The school-related perceptions of Puerto Rican mothers. *Psychological Reports, 62,* 187–192.

Examined the correlations between school-related perceptions of 57 Puerto Rican mothers residing in Pennsylvania and the achievement of their children. Children's achievement was measured by the Iowa Test of Basic Skills. Results of the study indicate a weak correlation between maternal satisfaction and the reading scores, and a strong correlation between maternal satisfaction with teachers and the children's mathematics scores. In addition, 86% of the mothers expressed a preference for English as the language of instruction for their children.

Ervin, M. (1987). Where high school kids learn to think. *The Progressive*, p. 11, June.

Describes a successful Chicago program educating Puerto Rican dropouts.

Hamby, J.V. (1986). How to get an "A" on your dropout prevention report card. *Educational Leadership*, 46(5), 21–28.

Discusses beliefs, philosophy, and values in terms of myths regarding high school dropouts. Eight areas in which schools can make a difference and can establish a commitment to educate all youth and establish accountability measures include: awareness, attendance, achievement, attitude, atmosphere, adaptation, alternatives, and advocacy.

Hornberger, N.H. (1990). Creating successful learning contexts for biliteracy. *Penn Working Papers in Educational Linguistics*, 6(1), 1–21.

Discusses the data collected during a comparative ethnographic study on school community literacy in two languages. Compares and contrasts how two elementary school teachers create successful learning contexts for the biliterate development of Puerto Rican and Cambodian students using non-traditional methods.

Intercultural Development Research Association (1986). *Valued Youth Partnerships. Programs in caring: Cross-age tutoring dropout prevention strategies.* San Antonio: Center for the Prevention and Recovery of Dropouts, IDRA.

Youth tutoring is described as a dropout prevention strategy for middle and high school students working with elementary school pupils. The program revolves around role modeling, parental involvement, classes, training for student-tutors, field trips, and school-work experiences. An evaluation design is outlined, and a review of the research literature and a resource section on peer tutoring models are included.

Intercultural Development Research Association (1989). *The answer: Valuing youth in schools and families: A report on Hispanic dropouts in the Dallas Independent School District.* San Antonio: Center for the Prevention and Recovery of Dropouts, IDRA.

Defines the high school dropout considering time frames, range of grade levels included in calculations, and local accounting procedures keyed to ten research questions. The questions focus on student, family, and community characteristics; and attitudes which are affected by systemic and environmental factors. Recommendations for structured prevention strategies are drawn from students' school history and records, archival data, surveys, and personal characteristics.

Intercultural Development Research Association (1989). *Valued youth anthology: Articles on dropout prevention.* San Antonio: Center for the Recovery and Prevention of Dropouts, IDRA.

A collection of articles regarding the economic loss of dropouts, both to themselves and to society. Describes innovative and effective dropout prevention programs developed by the Valued Youth Partnership Program in collaboration with private corporations. The programs focus on supportive systems for the family, private sector and community-based initiatives, literacy development, and programs for LEP students.

Jackson, B.J., & Cooper, B.S. (1989). Parent choice and empowerment: New roles for parents. *Urban Education, 24,* 263–286.

Examines parental roles in education by discussing the traditional hierarchical roles in conjunction with parents as key choice makers and assuming community network roles. Describes model programs developed in New York City schools with large Puerto Rican populations following individualistic and collectivist perspectives.

Koopmans, M. (1987). The difference between task understanding and reasoning skills in children's syllogistic performance. Paper presented at the meeting of the American Educational Research Association.

Reports on the relation between response time and reasoning task in bilingual student performance. Thirty-nine Puerto Rican students, grades 3 to 6, were asked to solve problems in Spanish and in English. Response times were recorded and students were asked to justify their answers to assess to what extent reasoning led to success in the tasks given. Response times were found to be longer if the justification given reflected reasoning, but it was also found that students needed more time to give an answer in their stronger language than in their weaker language. The study indicates that students have different reasoning strategies at different age levels. Younger students successfully solve problems if they understand what is expected. Older students appear to use a default strategy which often takes more time. The key implication of this research is that a student's strategy, not success in task performance, is a better gauge of learning.

Maldonado-Guzmán, A.A. (in press). Theoretical and methodological issues in the ethnographic study of teachers' differential treatment of children in bilingual bicultural classrooms. In M. Saravia-Shore & S. Arvizu (Eds.), *Ethnographies of communication in multiethnic classrooms.* New York: Garland.

A study including Puerto Rican students and Puerto Rican teachers, which explores the teachers' differential treatment of children in two first-grade bilingual-bicultural classrooms in Chicago.

Martínez, H. (Ed.) (1981). *Special education and the Hispanic child. Proceedings from the second annual colloquium on Hispanic Issues.* New York: ERIC Clearinghouse on Urban Education, Teachers College, Columbia University.

Includes papers on the right of Hispanic children to bilingual special education, the assessment of bilingual Hispanics, teacher training, and Puerto Rican mothers' cultural attitudes toward children's problems.

McLaughlin, M.W., & Shield, P.M. (1987). Involving low-income parents in the schools. *Phi Delta Kappan, 10,* 156–160.

Addresses low-income parent participation in public schools and the differences between rule-based and norm-based policy areas. According to the authors, in the 1990's, social and community-oriented pressures on educators are tied to effective schools and derived from local values, incentives, and cultural norms. Strategies are listed for promoting home-school interaction.

Meléndez, S.E. (1981). Hispanos, desegregation, and bilingual education: A case analysis of the role of "El Comité de Padres" in the court-ordered desegregation of the Boston Public Schools (1974–1975). Unpublished doctoral dissertation, Harvard Graduate School of Education.

Analyzes the role of *El Comité de Padres*, composed mostly of Puerto Rican parents, as plaintiff-intervenor in the Boston desegregation lawsuit Morgan v. Hennigan. The potential for conflict between bilingual education and desegregation is discussed. El Comité is described as a low-income, single-issue group with a few middle-class members. The group, without access to power or decision-makers, was successful in influencing educational policy.

Montero-Sieburth, M., & Pérez, M. (1987). Echar pa'lante,' moving onward: The dilemmas and strategies of a bilingual teacher. *Anthropology and Education Quarterly, 18,* 180–189.

Reports on an ethnographic study of a Puerto Rican bilingual high school teacher which describes her culturally congruent relationship with students, the handling of curricular issues, and definition of her own role.

Nazario, I. (1980). *Intervention in the development of negative attitudes of fourth grade Puerto Rican children toward school.* Unpublished doctoral dissertation, Rutgers University.

Investigated the attitudes of 25 fourth grade Puerto Rican children toward school, education and learning. Results of the study indicate that fourth grade Puerto Rican children did not necessarily like school, that the teacher was not particularly concerned about the children, and that the children did not view school as a happy place to be. The school staff's response to Puerto Rican children was generally found to be non-supportive.

New York State African American Institute of the State University (1986). *Dropping out of school in New York State: The invisible people of color.* New York: State University of New York.

According to this report, the state of emergency in the educational crisis of Hispanic, black, and Native American students stems from legislative, educational, and systemic causes, as well as the historical imposition of Anglocentric culture, tradition, and curriculum on linguistically and culturally different youth. Loss of self-esteem and respect by students and parents toward the mainstream society results in serious problems of racism, discrimination, and equity of services for minority school populations.

Nieto, S., & Sinclair, R. (1980). *Curriculum decision making: The Puerto Rican family and the bilingual child.* Paper presented at the meeting of the American Educational Research Association, Boston, MA.

This study was designed to develop procedures for involving Puerto Rican parents in curriculum decision making. A review of the literature in related areas establishes a rationale for parental involvement and forms the basis for developing the procedures. Two procedures, a questionnaire, and a parent interview were developed for the purpose of obtaining input from Puerto Rican parents as to their perceptions of the responsiveness of school curriculum to the needs of their children. Results of the field testing of the questionnaire are reported and recommendations for future research discussed.

Ochoa, A.M., Hurtado, J., Espinosa, R.W., & Zachman, J. (1987). *The empowerment of all students: A framework for the prevention of school dropouts.* San Diego, CA: Institute for Cultural Pluralism, San Diego State University.

A comprehensive analysis of research on Hispanic dropouts. The authors present a student empowerment model, identification guidelines, school prevention plans, and community, parental and educational areas and roles in meeting the needs of Hispanic students. A step-by-step program process is outlined for dropout prevention, grades K to 6.

Office of Education Research and Improvement (1987). *Dealing with dropouts: The urban superintendents call to action.* Washington, DC: U.S. Department of Education.

Describes collaborative strategies for dropout prevention developed by educators, policy-makers, the private sector, and community agencies. These strategies call for intervention in the early grades, strong school leadership and teaching practices, equity in resources for minority students, accountability, and effective school standards and programs.

Ortiz-Colón, R. (1985). Acculturation, ethnicity, and education: A comparison of Anglo teachers' and Puerto Rican mothers' values regarding behaviors and skills for urban Headstart children. Unpublished doctoral dissertation, Harvard Graduate School of Education.

The sample consisted of 125 Puerto Rican mothers and 35 teachers of their children in New York City. Although mothers and teachers agree on the domain of behaviors for children, discontinuities between them emerge in the importance they assign to a different pattern of behaviors. Teachers considered it more important that children be independent, verbally expressive, and assertive. Mothers placed more importance on obedience and mindfulness of rules. Teachers preferred self-direction and mothers conformity in the preschool activities of the children.

Pallas, A., Natrielo, G., & McDill, E.L. (1989). The changing nature of the disadvantaged population: Current dimensions and future trends. *Educational Researcher, 18*(5), 16–22.

According to the authors, three educational domains—the home, the school, and the community—impact on the experiences of disadvantaged students. They consider five major indicators associated with being disadvantaged: minority racial/ethnic group identity, living in a poverty household, living in a single-parent family, having a poorly educated mother, and having a non-English language background. Projected changes from the years 1984 to 2020 are presented by school age population, racial/ethnic minority status, single-parent family, and poverty level pointing to Hispanic pupils as the most disadvantaged group in the year 2020.

Prewitt-Diaz, J.O. (1984). Migrant students' perceptions of teachers, school, and self. *Perceptual and Motor Skills, 58*, 391–394.

Explored the perceptions of 117 returning migrants and circulating migrant students of teachers, school, and self in Puerto Rico and the U.S. Results of the study indicate that circulating migrant students had more positive attitudes toward teachers, school, and self on the mainland than in Puerto Rico. The returning migrant students expressed a positive feeling toward school, teachers, and self in Puerto Rico.

Rivera Viera, D. (1986). Remediating reading problems in a Hispanic learning disabled child from a psycholinguistic perspective: A case study. *Journal of Reading, Writing, and Learning Disabilities International,* 2(1), 85–97.

Describes a case study of a seven-year-old Puerto Rican child with learning disabilities, who received remedial reading instruction based on the Reading Miscue Inventory (RMI). The RMI was found to be a useful instrument in developing reading strategies, based on a psycholinguistic reading model, for the learning disabled reader. As a result of the reading program, the boy's reading comprehension improved.

Special Issues Analysis Center (1989). *At Risk Students: The Special Case of LEP Students.* Washington, DC: Office of Bilingual Education and Minority Languages Affairs, U. S. Department of Education.

Identifies at-risk factors for dropping out of school in LEP populations from Hispanic backgrounds, including Puerto Ricans. Describes student characteristics, age, achievement levels, and availability and range of services for LEP students. Specific programs directed to at-risk Hispanic LEP students are discussed as are identification guidelines, the need to learn in both L2 and L1, the need to consider the students' culture, counseling, and home/school communication.

San Juan Cafferty, P., & Rivera-Martinez, C. (1981). *The politics of language: The dilemma of bilingual education for Puerto Ricans.* Boulder, CO: Westview.

Analysis of bilingual education policies and programs in the U.S. The authors conclude that these programs do not offer the equal opportunities and social mobility that have been their purpose because the programs do not address the very specific cultural and linguistic needs of Puerto Rican children.

Stern, W.S. (1986). Puerto Rican natural support systems: The feasibility of first mobilizing natural support systems to help Puerto Rican children with school problems prior to referral for special services: A case study of Holyoke, Massachusetts. Unpublished doctoral dissertation, University of Massachusetts.

Fifteen Puerto Rican families were interviewed as well as their human service professionals. Results of the study indicate that a more successful approach for Puerto Rican children with school problems should come first from within the natural support systems rather than imposed from without. The author concludes that many Puerto Rican students are faced with problems that are not academically related but whose side effects show up in deficient performance. By working with the natural support system, schools can focus on such underlying issues before they reach a crisis stage.

Tapia, M.R. (1990). A comparative study of individualistic, cooperative, and competitive motivational orientations in lower socioeconomic class American and Puerto Rican heritage children. Unpublished doctoral dissertation, New York University.

A study of a group of American and Puerto Rican children living in the United States to determine the existence of three motivational orientations: (a) individualistic, (b) cooperative, and (c) competitive. Compares both groups in terms of these motivational orientations. The author discusses the educational implications of the cross-cultural findings and provides recommendations for optimal interpersonal outcome structures to use in school activities.

Torregrosa Díaz, Y. (1986). Biliteracy and its effects on reading achievement among bilingual Puerto Rican and Mexican American students in grades two through four. Unpublished doctoral dissertation, Wayne State University.

Examined the effects of biliteracy among bilingual and non-bilingual elementary school children. The reading scores of 21 bilinguals enrolled in a bilingual program who received initial reading instruction in Spanish prior to reading in English were compared to the reading scores of 18 bilingual students not enrolled in a bilingual program who received reading instruction solely in English. The reading scores of 20 English-speaking Anglo students were also used for comparison. The reading scores of the three groups for grades two, three and four were analyzed. Results of the study corroborated Cummins' Threshold and Developmental Interdependence hypotheses which indicate that the development of L1 among LM children affects the linguistic skills of the children in L2.

Walsh, C.E. (1987). The construction of meaning in a second language: The import of sociocultural knowledge. *NABE Journal, 11*, 141–152.

Investigated the sociocultural and psychological processes involved in the Spanish speaking Puerto Rican child's construction of abstract meaning in the English language and explored the relation between these processes and children's L1 reality. The study also examined the influence of school-based L2 learning on L1 memory processes and lexical/semantic relations at different points in the language acquisition process. Participants were 54 Puerto Rican and 13 Anglo American fourth grade children in an urban area of Massachusetts. Findings indicated that the influence of L1 meaning was strong with regard to culturally meaningful words and occurred regardless of L2 proficiency level. English meaning also affected Spanish words. The author concludes that both social context and culture play a dominant role in language acquisition and semantic organization.

Zanger, V.V. (1987). The social context of second language learning: An examination of barriers to integration in five case studies. Unpublished doctoral dissertation, Boston University.

Presents five case studies of the acculturation experiences of Puerto Rican and Vietnamese adolescents attending transitional bilingual education programs. The author found that the students' isolation from the dominant culture could be attributed to stigmatization, structural isolation, and acculturative patterns. Stigmatization resulted in academic underachievement or in limited L2 development.

Zanger, V.V. (in press). 'Not joined in': Intergroup relations and access to literacy for Hispanic youth. In B. Ferdman & A. Ramírez (Eds.). Albany, NY: SUNY Press.

Analyzes perceptions of predominantly Puerto Rican students about intergroup relations. Concludes that access to conditions that promote literacy development are denied Puerto Rican students in three ways: (a) the failure of the school to incorporate students' language and culture; (b) the racist school climate; and (c) the breakdown in trust between the students and many of their teachers.

IV. Health and Healing

Angel, R.J., & Worobey, J.L. (in press). Intra-group differences in the health of Hispanic children. *Social Science Quarterly*.

Analyzes data from the Hispanic Health and Nutrition Examination Survey (HHANES) on the health status of children among the major Hispanic groups. Data are presented on global health assessments and specific health conditions, broken down for each Hispanic group and by whether the interview was in English or Spanish. Comparing Mexican-Americans, Cuban-Americans, and Puerto Ricans living on the U.S. mainland, the authors found that Puerto Rican children experienced worse health than children from other Hispanic groups.

Carter, O., Gergen, P., & Lecca, P. (1987). *Reported asthma among Puerto Rican, Mexican-American and Cuban-American children: HHANES, 1982–1984.* Paper presented at the meeting of the American Public Health Association, New Orleans, LA, October.

Also using the Hispanic Health and Nutrition Examination Survey (HHANES), examines the prevalence of asthma for Hispanic children, ages 6 months to 11 years old, living on the U.S. mainland compared to non-Hispanic whites and blacks. Also examines social correlates of asthma and use of health care services. The major finding of the paper is that Puerto Rican children experience more asthma than other Hispanics and non-Hispanic whites and blacks.

Clark, N.M., Feldman, C.H., Freudenberg, N., Millman, E.J., Wasilewski, Y., & Valle, I. (1980). Developing education for children with asthma through study of self-management behavior. *Health Education Quarterly, 7,* 278–297.

Describes the development of an Asthma Self-Management Program for inner-city children with asthma. Started with a study of what families were doing to manage childhood asthma as the basis for developing the educational interventions. Focuses not only on transferring information to families, but working with families to develop self-management behaviors for coping with childhood asthma. Resulted in the *Open Airways* curriculum.

Columbia University Department of Pediatrics (1984). *Open Airways/Respiro Abierto.* Washington, DC: National Heart, Lung and Blood Institute (NIH Publication No. 84-2365).

The Open Airways program was developed to assist children with asthma and their families in the management of asthma on a day-to-day basis. A unique feature of the program is that it was designed specifically for inner-city families. Includes a section on advocacy to improve housing conditions, and forms are available in English and Spanish. The package includes full instructions for running different kinds of groups. The package can be purchased from the federal government, and all materials can be reproduced.

Connecticut State Department of Health Services (1988). *AIDS: Knowledge, attitudes, and behavior in an ethnically mixed urban neighborhood.* Hartford: Connecticut State Department of Health Services.

Puerto Ricans and other Hispanics account for a high number of AIDS cases, mainly reported by IV drug users. This survey study conducted through English and Spanish interviews, discusses educational and prevention strategies. Sociodemographic characteristics are noted for Hispanics, blacks, and whites, with data on AIDS-related knowledge, attitudes, and behaviors.

Freudenberg, N., Feldman, C.H., Clark, N.M., Millman, E.J., Valle, I., & Wasilewski, Y. (1980). The impact of bronchial asthma on school attendance and performance. *The Journal of School Health,* November, pp. 522–526.

Reports the results of a study of families having a child with asthma from the ages of 4 to 16. Sixty percent of the families were Hispanic and 36% black. Absence rates for children with asthma were 24% higher than children without asthma living in the same area of New York City. Major findings of the study were: (a) teachers need more information on the management of asthma; (b) parent-teacher communication about how to care for the child with asthma needs to be improved; and (c) Physical Education is problematic for children with asthma. The paper offers specific recommendations to address these problems.

Giachello, A.L., & Aponte, R. (1989). *Health status and access issues of Hispanic children and adolescents in Chicago: Analysis of a 1984 city-wide survey* (Monograph No. 3). Chicago: Hispanic Health Alliance.

Presents findings of a survey conducted in 1984 which examined the health status of Chicago's Mexican, Puerto Rican, Central, and South American children and adolescents. The report also includes references from an extensive literature search on the subject.

Guarnaccia, P.J., Pelto, P.J., & Schensul, S. (1985). Family health culture, ethnicity, and asthma: Coping with illness. *Medical Anthropology*, *9*, 203–224.

Discusses similarities and differences between African-American and Puerto Rican families in coping with childhood asthma. Introduced the concept of "family health culture," which refers to families' beliefs about illness, ideas concerning how to cope with illness, knowledge of various treatment remedies, and ideas of how to prevent illness and maintain health. One of the major findings reported in this paper is that asthma is much more salient in Puerto Rican health culture than in African-American health culture and that Puerto Ricans have more culturally based home interventions for coping with childhood asthma.

Pelto, P.J., & Schensul, J.J. (1987). Toward a framework for policy research in anthropology. In E.M. Eddy & W.L. Partridge (Eds.), *Applied anthropology in America*, 2nd Ed. (pp. 505–527). New York: Columbia University Press.

Though emphasis of this article is on the policy research roles played by practicing anthropologists in a variety of settings where policy is made and implemented, a case study regarding a maternal/child health project in a Puerto Rican community in Hartford serves to illustrate the importance of tying in community needs/research/and policy making.

Schensul, S.L., & Borrero, M.G. (Eds.). (1982). Special Issue: Action research and health systems change in an inner-city Puerto Rican community. *Urban Anthropology*, *11*(1).

This special issue traces the development of the Hispanic Health Council, a research, training, and advisory organization geared to the improvement of health in the Puerto Rican community of Hartford, CT. Research sponsored by the council is reported. Articles deal with a variety of topics: demography, family structure, service utilization patterns, helping resources, fertility control, community/institution interfaces, and training for organizational change.

Singer, M. (1989). *Alcoholism: Impact on the Hispanic child* (Hispanic Health Report No. 5.) Hartford, CT: Hispanic Health Council.

Reviews information regarding the impact of parental alcoholism on the Hispanic child along four general areas: (a) the nature of the Hispanic family; (b) prevalence studies regarding Hispanic alcohol use and abuse; (c) impact of family alcoholism on children; and (d) family factors that appear to protect at risk children from the effects of parental drinking.

Singer, M., Davison, L, & Yalin, F. (Eds.) (1987). *Conference proceedings: Alcohol use and abuse among Hispanic adolescents.* Hartford, CT: Hispanic Health Council.

Discusses the cultural, economic, political, socio-religious, and historical causes of alcohol use and abuse among Puerto Ricans in the U.S. and Puerto Rico. It appears that sex, acculturation, and age are important factors. (For example, older males drink more than other groups.) Machismo still makes denial of alcohol use difficult. The design of prevention and treatment strategies must involve culturally appropriate interventions taking into account spiritual, environmental, and holistic factors and focusing on the individual's relationship to self, family, and society.

Singer, M., Flores, C., & Burke, G. (1989). *Changing patterns of drinking among Hispanic women: Implications for Fetal Alcohol Syndrome.* (Hispanic Health Report No. 6.) Hartford, CT: Hispanic Health Council.

Reviews the literature on alcohol consumption patterns among Hispanic—mostly Mexican-American—women and among Puerto Rican women in particular. Describes a community-based survey of drinking behavior conducted by the Hispanic Health Council among Puerto Rican women and adolescents in Hartford.

Singer, M., & Garcia, R. (1989). *From research to intervention: Substance abuse prevention among Hispanic adolescents.* (Hispanic Health Report No. 3.) Hartford, CT: Hispanic Health Council.

Describes a research/intervention project conducted by the Hispanic Health Council among Puerto Rican adolescent boys and girls in Hartford. The research sought to study drinking behavior among adolescents and to identify family and peer drinking patterns. The Peer Prevention Project, a school-based intervention effort, is described.

Vélez, C.N., & Ungemack, J.A. (1989). Drug use among Puerto

Rican youth: An exploration of generational status differences. *Social Science and Medicine*, 29(6), 779–789.

Examined the drug use involvement of four generational status groups of Puerto Rican adolescents in New York City and in San Juan. Two important relations were found. First, the impact of length of time living in New York varied with the adolescent's gender, with a higher risk of drug involvement observed for female migrants. Second, SES was associated with Puerto Rican drug use involvement in New York City, but not in Puerto Rico.

Wissow, L.S., Gittelsohn, A.M., Szklo, M., Starfield, B., & Mussman, M. (1988). Poverty, race, and hospitalization for childhood asthma. *American Journal of Public Health*, 78, 777–782.

Based on Maryland hospital discharge data for 1979–1982, examines differences between black and white children with asthma. The overall hospital discharge rate for asthma was three times higher among blacks than among whites. Children receiving Medicaid coverage for health care had higher asthma hospitalization rates. Comparing ecologic areas, the discharge rates for the poorest black areas were more than ten times the rates for well-to-do white areas. Discharge rates for well-to-do blacks were similar to those of whites from the same SES group. Some or all of the higher rate of asthma among blacks is accounted for by higher rates of poverty among blacks than among whites.

V. Social Stresses and Support Systems

Canino, I.A., & Canino, G. (1980). Impact of stress on the Puerto Rican family: Treatment considerations. *American Journal of Orthopsychiatry*, 50, 535–541.

The impact of stress due to immigration and poverty on family structure of the low-income Puerto Rican family is discussed. Treatment pitfalls and effective therapeutic techniques are illustrated by a clinical case presentation.

Delgado, M. (1981) Therapy Latino style. In R.H. Dana, (Ed.), *Human services for cultural minorities* (pp. 207–216). Baltimore: University Park Press.

Offers an overview of folk healer traditions and discusses

these traditions in relation to the spiritism belief system among Puerto Ricans. The author recommends the use of folk healers in the provision of mental health services for ethnic minorities.

Delgado, M., & Scott, J.F. (1981). A mental health program for the Hispanic community. In R.H. Dana (Ed.), *Human services for cultural minorities* (pp. 251–264). Baltimore: University Park Press.

Describes mental health programs developed at the Worcester Youth Guidance Center in Worcester, MA, where 92% of the Hispanic population is Puerto Rican. The programs include community education and training; clinical consultation; program consultation and research focusing on Puerto Rican mental health needs, migratory patterns, and effective programs.

García-Preto, N. (1982). Puerto Rican families. In M. McGoldrick, J. Pearce, & J. Giordano (Eds.) *Ethnicity and family therapy* (pp. 164–186). New York: Guilford.

Written with the intent of providing family therapists with a framework for working with low-income Puerto Rican families, the article provides an overview of history/economics, cultural values, family structure, and the effects of immigration on Puerto Rican families. Case studies are used to illustrate certain typical family patterns and therapeutic interventions that are culturally appropriate.

González-Vucci, G. (1985). Puerto Rican mothers' preferences for delivery of mental health services. Unpublished doctoral dissertation, New York University.

Forty Puerto Rican mothers from New York City's Lower East Side were interviewed to determine their preferences for location of mental health services for their children. Mothers were asked to rank order preferred service locations for each of ten vignettes posing children's problems and to rate the importance of staff and approach to treatment variables. Results support the hypothesis of greater preference for school-based services, regardless of a mother's level of acculturation, poverty status, or prior experience with mental health treatment.

Inclán, J.E., & Herron, D.G. (1989). Puerto Rican adolescents. In J.T. Gibbs & L.N. Huang (Eds.), *Children of color: Psychological interventions with minority youth* (pp. 251–277). San Francisco: Jossey-Bass.

Presents issues in the assessment and treatment of Puerto Rican adolescents from an ecological viewpoint. Thus, it focuses on the sociocultural experience of Puerto Ricans living on the U.S. mainland, and discusses demographic, epidemiological, and immigration aspects relevant to this experience. The chapter also deals with clinical concerns in ecologically oriented individual, group, and family therapy with Puerto Rican adolescents.

Ramos-McKay, J.M., Comas-Díaz, L., & Rivera, L.A. (1988). Puerto Ricans. In L. Comas-Díaz & E.E. Griffith (Eds.), *Clinical guidelines in cross-cultural mental health* (pp. 204–232). New York: Wiley.

Reviews a number of sociocultural aspects with implications for clinical practice with Puerto Ricans, such as history and culture, immigration patterns, family values and traditions, religious and folk beliefs including spiritism, and sociopolitical considerations. Also discusses a number of clinical issues including prevalence of various mental disorders, special mental health problems, assessment and diagnosis, use of medication. Several successful therapeutic strategies are presented.

Ruiz, P., & Langrod, J. (1981). The role of folk healers in community mental health services. In R.H. Dana (Ed.), *Human services for cultural minorities* (pp. 217–224). Baltimore: University Park Press.

Based on the authors' work with Puerto Ricans and other Hispanics in the South Bronx, the article discusses the relation between mental health services and the religious beliefs of patients. Mental health practitioners tend to view the Roman Catholicism of their patients as exclusive and to discount Puerto Ricans' strong belief in spiritism. The authors go on to explore the role of folk healers in therapeutic intervention and discuss why folk healers are more effective with the population studied than traditional mental health practitioners.

VI. Behavioral, Psychological, and Emotional Issues

Brenes, C.C., and Westerman, M.A. (1983). *Mothers' contributions to an early intervention program for Hispanic children.* Paper presented at the meeting of the American Psychological Association, Anaheim, CA. (ED No. 237–212.)

Studied the effect of maternal personality characteristics and interaction behavior on interventions with 210 Puerto Rican children and their mothers. Results indicate that the mother's ego development level, self-concept, acceptance of aggression, and trait anxiety were related to the child's relationships with others and to the development of more adaptive personal relations.

Canino, G.J., Bird, H.R., Rubio-Stipec, M., Woodbury, M.A., Ribera, J.C., Huertas, S.E., & Sesman, M.J. (1987). Reliability of child diagnosis in a Hispanic sample. *Journal of the American Academy of Child and Adolescent Psychiatry, 26,* 560–565.

Presents data on the reliability between two Hispanic child psychiatrists in diagnosing a sample of 191 Puerto Rican children between the ages of 4 and 16 years. Results indicated that age or time lapse between interviews did not affect diagnostic reliability, which was found to be high.

Canino, I.A., Earley, B.F., & Rogler, L.H. (1980). *The Puerto Rican child in New York City: Stress and mental health.* New York: Hispanic Research Center, Fordham University.

Brings together data on the mental health of Puerto Rican children collected by major agencies in the New York City area; and reviews the clinical, epidemiological, and sociocultural literature on the mental health of Puerto Rican children. Main hypothesis of the monograph is that Puerto Rican children experience more stresses than do other children and are at higher risk of developing mental health problems.

Cloud, N. (1990). Measuring levels of acculturation in bilingual bicultural children. Paper presented at the meeting of the American Educational Research Association, Boston, MA.

A study of 35 low SES Puerto Rican students, ages 10–14 years, in an inner city middle school. Measures used in studying acculturation and adjustment included Spanish and English versions of the Acculturation Questionnaire for Children, the Student Rating Scales of the Behavior Rating Profile and the Self Observation Scales-Intermediate Level. Results were significant and indicated that the most acculturated group tended to be the least well-adjusted at home and had the most negative views of school.

358   PUERTO RICAN CHILDREN ON THE MAINLAND

Fuentes, E.G. (1983). A primary prevention program for psychological and cultural identity enhancement: Puerto Rican children in semirural northeast United States. Unpublished doctoral dissertation, Boston University.

Evaluated the effectiveness of the Hispanic After School Program (HASP) designed to promote psychocultural enhancement. Participants were Puerto Rican children grades K–6. Results of the intervention program were positive. However, there was a strong relation between what teachers expected academically of students and how these students were subsequently evaluated with respect to classroom behavior. When a teacher considered a child problematic in terms of say aggressiveness or poor behavior, the student would be judged similarly as far as academic expectations.

García Coll, C.T., & Mattei, M.L. (Eds.) (1989). *The psychosocial development of Puerto Rican women.* New York: Praeger.

A volume dedicated to Puerto Rican women. The works are collected around two major topics: childhood and adolescence, and adulthood and aging. By addressing major issues and dilemmas in the lives of Puerto Rican women, many of the articles touch upon the evolving Puerto Rican family on both the island and mainland. Most of the articles are based on either empirical research, thorough literature reviews, and/or on insights gathered from clinical practice.

Guarnaccia, P.J., DeLa Cancela, V., & Carrillo, E. (1989). The multiple meanings of *ataques de nervios* in the Latino community. *Medical Anthropology, 11,* 47–62.

Reviews past psychiatric and anthropological literature on *ataques de nervios* and offers a reinterpretation of the concept by understanding its cultural meaning and the social factors which provoke it. Explores the various symptoms and varieties of experience subsumed under *ataque* and the kinds of life events which may trigger it. Through a series of four case studies (two Puerto Rican, two Central American women), the authors argue that *ataques* are an expression of anger and grief resulting from the disruption of family systems, the process of immigration, and concerns about family members in peoples' countries of origin.

Machabanski, H.S. (1985). Dimensions of behavior problems in Puerto Rican children. Unpublished doctoral dissertation, University of Kentucky.

Participants were 302 Puerto Rican preschoolers attending day care centers in Chicago. Teachers and parents rated children's behaviors. Results indicated, among other things, that Puerto Rican mothers rate their children's behavior somewhat differently than teachers do.

Malgady, R.G., Costantino, G., & Rogler, L.H. (1984). Development of a thematic apperception test (TEMAS) for urban Hispanic children. *Journal of Consulting and Clinical Psychology, 52*, 986–996.

The authors investigated the psychometric properties of TEMAS (Tell Me A Story), a thematic apperception test composed of chromatic pictures of Hispanic characters in urban settings. The test was administered to 210 low SES Puerto Rican children in grades K–6. According to the authors, TEMAS can be used for the personality assessment of Hispanic children who tend to be inarticulate in response to traditional projective tests.

McCollum, P.A. (1980). Attention-getting strategies of Anglo-American and Puerto Rican students: A microethnographic analysis. Unpublished doctoral dissertation, University of Illinois.

Examined the attention-getting strategies of Puerto Rican and Anglo-American children. It was found that Puerto Rican and Anglo children varied in their attention-getting behaviors. Compared to Anglos, Puerto Rican children showed increased bidding for attention, a shorter amount of waiting time between bidding unsuccessfully and rebidding, and a higher number of bids for attention in non-teacher directed activities. Additionally, Puerto Rican children used a higher volume at close speaking distances, used touch as an attention-getting strategy, used extremely long bidding sequences, and did not address teachers by name.

Nine Curt, C.J. (1984). *Non-verbal communication*, 2nd Ed. Fall River, MA: Evaluation, Dissemination, and Assessment Center.

Discusses variations in non-verbal communication patterns between Puerto Ricans and Anglo-Americans. Reports on a study conducted among New York-born Puerto Rican children who retained the ability to understand Puerto Rican gestures even when they did not understand Spanish.

Orsini Navas, B. (1985). Perceptions of deviant child behaviors among Puerto Rican parents. Unpublished doctoral dissertation, Columbia University.

A study exploring parental perceptions of deviant behaviors in children and how these vary as a function of behavior, sex of the vignette character, sex of the perceiver, and social context. The sample consisted of 120 low SES Puerto Rican parents, and a group of 30 non-Puerto Rican teachers. Participants were presented with ten vignettes of hypothetical behaviors of children's characters designated randomly as boys or girls.

Type of behavior was the main determinant in parental perceptions of children's deviant behaviors; it affected the perceived degree of severity, friendliness, fear, sympathy, and control. Externalizing behaviors were seen as more severe and elicited greater fear; internalizing behaviors evoked greater friendliness and sympathy. Boys were found to elicit more sympathy than girls.

Prewitt-Díaz, J.O., & Seilhamer, E.S. (1987). The social psychological adjustment of migrant and non-migrant Puerto Rican adolescents. *Migration World, 15*(2), 7–11.

Discusses patterns of Puerto Rican immigration and explores the relation of these patterns to academic achievement and physical, social, and school adjustment in a sample of 273 migrant, return migrant, circulatory migrant, and non-migrant high school students in seven school districts in Puerto Rico. The researchers found a relation between the students' physical and cultural adjustment: As the level of cultural adjustment increased, physical adjustment also increased. Also found was a relation between social and school adjustment: The higher the social adjustment, the higher the school adjustment.

Trostle, S.L. (1984). An investigation of the effects of child-centered group play therapy upon sociometric, self-control, and play behavior ratings of three- to six-year-old bilingual Puerto Rican children. Unpublished doctoral dissertation, Pennsylvania State University.

Focused upon the effects of 10 sessions of child-centered group play therapy on sociometric, self-control, and free play ratings of 3- to 6-year-old bilingual Puerto Rican children in Pennyslvania. The purpose of the study was to examine the facilitative effects of child-centered group play therapy upon the

48 Puerto Rican children observed. Results indicate that child-centered group play therapy sessions facilitated the children's positive ratings of other peers, self-control ratings, and make-believe and reality play behaviors.

Vélez, C.N., & Ungemack, J.A. (1989). Drug use among Puerto Rican youth: An exploration of generational status differences. *Social Science and Medicine, 29,* 779–789.

Examined the drug use involvement of four generational status groups of Puerto Rican adolescents in New York City and San Juan, Puerto Rico.

Velilla, S. (1980). Self-concept of inner city Puerto Rican elementary school children. Unpublished doctoral dissertation, University of Connecticut.

The study explored whether there are differences between the self-concept of Puerto Rican children ages 9–11 who have lived in the U.S. for three or more years and non-Puerto Rican children attending the same school. The sample consisted of 120 children (60 Puerto Rican, 60 non-Puerto Rican), ages 9–11, of average or above average intelligence. A self-concept scale was administered in Spanish to assess self-concept. Results indicated no significant differences in self-concept scores between Puerto Rican children and children from other ethnic backgrounds attending the same school.

Wu, S.T. (1989). The forty-five hour alternative curriculum: A comparison of reported television and videotape viewing among Puerto Rican, Chinese, and white children. Unpublished doctoral dissertation, Teachers College, Columbia University.

Examined the TV and videotape viewing patterns of 197 children, grades 4 to 6, in three public schools. The researcher used three questionnaires for this purpose. Participants were 77 Puerto Rican, 58 Chinese, and 62 white children. Significant differences in the amount of TV/video viewing were found among the three groups: Puerto Rican children spent about 6.5 hours viewing TV and videotapes per day, white children spent 3.7 hours, and Chinese children spent 2.1 hours. Puerto Rican children who were born in Puerto Rico appeared to spend less time on TV viewing than did Puerto Rican children born on the mainland.

AUTHOR INDEX

Veltman, C.J., 137
Ventriglia, L., 69
Volk, D., 43
Vygotsky, L.S., 180, 188

Wagenheim, K., 18, 19, 122,
  334
Walsh, C.E., 348
Wasilewski, Y., 350, 351
Watson, D.L., 205
Wehlage, G.G., 204
Weinfeld, F.D., 163
Weis, L., 193, 195, 197,
  204
Westerman, M.A., 356
White, R., 191
Willig, A.C., 110
Winkler, K., 291
Wissow, L.S., 353
Withers, C., 69
Wolfe, B.L., 137
Wolman, C., 201
Wood, R., 69
Woodbury, M.A., 357
Worobey, J.L., 239, 348
Wu, S.T., 361
Wyszewianski-Langdon, H.,
  338

Yalin, F., 353
Yates, J.R., 7
York, R.L., 163

Zachman, J., 345
Zahn, L., 111, 112, 116
Zanger, V.V., 137, 348
Zentella, A.C., 43
Zirkel, P.A., 138

SUBJECT INDEX